Harlan T Beverly, PhD
Navigating Your Way to Startup Success

Harlan T Beverly, PhD

Navigating Your Way to Startup Success

___

DE

G

PRESS

ISBN 978-1-5015-1566-8
e-ISBN (PDF) 978-1-5015-0708-3
e-ISBN (EPUB) 978-1-5015-0701-4

Library of Congress Cataloging-in-Publication Data
A CIP catalog record for this book has been applied for at the Library of Congress.

Bibliographic information published by the Deutsche Nationalbibliothek
The Deutsche Nationalbibliothek lists this publication in the Deutsche Nationalbibliografie;
detailed bibliographic data are available on the Internet at http://dnb.dnb.de.

Published by Walter de Gruyter Inc., Boston/Berlin
Cover image: Barisonal/E+/Getty Images
Printing and binding: CPI book GmbH, Leck
♾ Printed on acid-free paper
Printed in Germany

www.degruyter.com

Praise for This Book

Navigating Your Way to Startup Success is a must read especially for first time entrepreneurs.

Harlan understands what investors are looking for: passionate entrepreneurs with authentic progress.

This book offers readers many practical guides to help entrepreneurs find their passion and build momentum.

—Krishna Srinivasan,
Founding General Partner at
LiveOak Venture Partners

Lots of people act like experts in entrepreneurship because they've read the latest theory or are up on the newest startup fad. Harlan takes a different approach by clearly illustrating how to move from concept to execution with practical, real life examples. This book is packed with great concepts illustrated through applicable stories and delivered by a guy who's been there and done the startup thing successfully many times. A must read for anyone pushing the startup envelope.

—Rob Adams,
Director and Founder, Texas Venture Labs,
author of *If You Build It Will They Come?*

Harlan Beverly provides great stories and advice for anyone wanting to start a technology, internet, or software company. Well worth the time to give his ideas serious thought.

—Gary Hoover,
Founder of Hoover's, Inc.,
author of *Retail Handbook 2016*

What Dr. Beverly has written is just brilliant—informative and educational, but also entertaining. Using his personal experiences and academic research, Beverly helps startup founders and corporate innovators alike commercialize new technologies and launch new products. Where most startup authors stop at rhetoric, Beverly adds formulas and analysis tools to help entrepreneurs and intrapreneurs navigate to success, dealing with the unavoidable hazards a startup will face.

—Art Olbert,
Executive with IBM and IT startups

Harlan has accurately captured the path to success for a startup, or really, any organization.

I've built a very successful company helping businesses grow, and many of Harlan's suggestions are core to what we do for our clients. *Navigating Your Way to Startup Success* is the new essential handbook for growth.

—Bill Leake,
CEO of Apogee Results

What excites me about *Navigating Your Way to Startup Success* is Harlan's incredibly precise and succinct advice for startups. This is genuine wisdom that will help any entrepreneur in their quest for success.

—Matthew Pollard,
author of *The Introvert's Edge*,
Executive Director of Small Business Festival

There is so much here, it's difficult to digest it all. Fortunately, Dr. Beverly has organized it all in clever, easy-to-read sections. He has captured the spirit of what it's like to run a high-tech startup and offers sage advice as to the pitfalls to avoid. *Navigating Your Way to Startup Success* is a must-read.

—Bjorn Billhardt,
CEO Abilite,
Founder of Enspire

Harlan has brought to life what it feels like to succeed and fail at startups. The tools and advice contained in *Navigating Your Way to Startup Success* will be immensely helpful to anyone starting a new business or trying to grow one. I even enjoyed Harlan's chapter on sales, and some of the techniques he highlights I agree with in my own books.

—David Masover,
author of *Mastering your Sales Process*

Dedicated to my wife and best friend Elizabeth with whom every success is shared and more filled with meaning.

Acknowledgments

Thank you to all of the startup founders who provided examples throughout this book. This book would not be as helpful or meaningful without your stories in it. A special acknowledgment and thank you to the startup founders who helped me to edit and review the stories of their companies, including in order of their appearance in the book: Andy Shaw, Eric Packer, Naruby Shlenker, Jimena L., Ken Cho, Aseem Ali, Aimy Steadman, James Walsh, Gary Gattis, James Hildebrandt, Tony Howlett, and Robert Reeves.

About the Author

Harlan T Beverly founded and was CEO of Bigfoot Networks, Inc., a gaming hardware company, which was acquired by Qualcomm in 2011. After Bigfoot, Harlan founded and was CEO of Karmaback, Inc., a Social Network Marketing company, acquired in 2013. Harlan then worked for Creeris Ventures as a virtual VP of Marketing for their nine portfolio companies, including Night Owl Games, where he helped attract more than 1,000,000 players to the game Dungeon Overlord. He then became CEO of Key Ingredient, a high-tech food technology startup, which he sold in 2015.

Harlan holds a BS in Electrical and Computer Engineering, an MBA from UT Austin, and a PhD in Business from Oklahoma State University. Harlan teaches entrepreneurship in his class called Lean Startup Essentials at The University of Texas at Austin. He is also the assistant director of the Jon Brumley Texas Venture Labs at UT Austin, the world's first university business accelerator.

Harlan has successfully launched 5 hardware and 15 software products including the Killer NIC, 2007 Network Product of the Year (CPU Magazine). Harlan has also raised over $30MM in venture financing in the challenging intersection of entertainment and technology.

Contents

Chapter 1: Introduction—Why do you want to launch a startup, anyway? —— 1
Bigfoot Networks, Inc. —— 4
The Launching of the Killer NIC —— 5
Common Goals of Entrepreneurs —— 6
Why Goal Setting Is Critical to Startup Success —— 9
The Story of Memory Plush —— 11
Book Organization and Your Own Goals —— 12

Chapter 2: Failing to Start—What's stopping you? —— 15
Failing to Start —— 16
Startup vs. Small Business —— 17
Service, Small Business, Healthcare, Retail, Restaurant, Education,
        Entertainment, and Anything Else —— 20
Failing to Start Reason Number One: You —— 21
Failing to Start Reason Number Two: The Lizard Brain —— 23
Failing to Start Reason Number Three: Where to Begin —— 24
Failing to Start Reason Number Four: The Lawyers —— 27
Failing to Start Reason Number Five: No Money —— 29
The Story of Eric Packer, Inventor —— 30
Conclusion: Failing to Start —— 33

Chapter 3: Your Idea Sucks—How would you know? —— 35
Good Ideas —— 36
Validating Your Idea —— 37
Validating Your Price —— 40
Building a Two Page Website —— 41
Getting Early Visitors to Your New Website —— 43
Quantifying Success: Do Customers Like Your Idea? —— 45
Degrees of Pivots —— 46
The Story of Ordoro —— 48
Conclusion —— 49

Chapter 4: Failing to Ship—Again, what's stopping you? —— 51
The Story of the SmartPrompt Pan —— 51
Minimum Viable Product —— 55
Reason Number One: Being Beholden —— 56
Reason Number Two: Not Good Enough —— 58

Reason Number Three: Not Knowing How —— 61
MVP Requirements —— 63
Types of MVP —— 64
Reason Number Four: Legal, Ethical, and Moral Guidelines —— 67
The Real Reason You Didn't Ship: Fear —— 69
Koffie: Fresh Coffee Delivered —— 70
Three Analytical Tools for Shipping —— 72

Chapter 5: Nobody Cares—What can you do about it? —— 79
How to Know Nobody Cares —— 82
Business to Business: Customers Don't Care —— 83
Business to Consumer: Customers Don't Care —— 85
Which Customer Are You Targeting, Anyway? —— 87
Pivoting on Marketing and Attracting Potential Customers —— 88
Step 1: Proactive Marketing —— 89
Step 2: Begin with the Customer in Mind —— 90
Step 3: Measure, Measure, Measure —— 91
Step 4: Offer Win Win Value —— 92
Step 5: Be Understood in Understanding Customer Needs —— 93
Step 6: Synergize the Message —— 95
Step 7: Sharpen the Marketing Saw through Experimentation —— 96
Marketing when Nobody Cares —— 97
The Big Pivot —— 98
The Story of Spredfast —— 99
Analytical Tool: Dealing with Apathy —— 101

Chapter 6: Somebody Cares—Yippee! Now what? —— 103
The Startup Journey/Phases of the Startup —— 104
How to Know Somebody Cares —— 105
Failing to Scale or Failing at Scaling —— 106
Hitting the Gas —— 110
Test Advertising —— 111
Scaling Facebook Advertising —— 112
Scaling Google Advertising —— 113
Other Advertising —— 115
Non Advertising Growth and Scale —— 117
Watching Out for Roadblocks, Bumps, and Crashes —— 119
The Story of Burpy —— 120

Chapter 7: Oops, We Ran Out of Money—Funding and finance —— 123

Managing Cash —— 124

Building a Financial Plan —— 126

TAM, SAM, and SOM —— 127

Business Models —— 129

Oops, I Failed Again—Denied Funding Based on Business Model —— 131

Bottoms Up Modeling —— 132

How Much Funding —— 137

Types of Funding —— 139

Finding Investors: The "Laser Beam Shotgun" Approach —— 144

The Perfect Ten Slide Presentation Deck —— 147

Term Sheets —— 149

Closing the Deal —— 151

BeatBox Beverages —— 152

Chapter 8: I Got Sued—It can happen to you —— 155

Who Can Sue Whom —— 156

Types of Lawsuits (and Arbitration) —— 157

Avoiding Lawsuits —— 158

Importance and Types of Intellectual Property —— 160

Types of Intellectual Property —— 162

Filing Patents and Trademarks —— 165

Incorporation and the Corporate Veil —— 168

Ways to Get Thrown in Prison —— 169

Insurance for Companies (Liability, D&O, Key Man) —— 170

Lawsuits from Investors/Founders (CEO Power)—Key Ingredient —— 171

When to Sue Someone Else —— 172

The Analytical Approach to Settling (or Not) —— 173

Coming Back from Losing a Lawsuit (Survival) —— 173

Story of Cutting Edge Gamer —— 174

Chapter 9: Help, I'm Sinking—Controlling growth —— 177

Failing at Growth —— 178

Metrics of Growth: Key Performance Indicators (KPIs) —— 179

Sustaining Growth —— 181

Controlling Growth —— 183

Leadership vs. Management —— 186

Company Culture —— 187

Management Span of Control —— 190

Hiring Right — 194
Investing in Growth vs. Investing in Ideas — 196
Agile Development — 197
Power of Profitability — 199
Story of Spacetime Studios — 199

Chapter 10: The Press Hates Me—Bad reviews — 203
Failing at Reviews and Press — 205
Building a Press Plan — 206
When and How to Hire a PR Agency — 209
Customer Reviews (Good and Bad) — 211
Dealing with Forums — 214
Dealing with Social Media — 215
Dealing with Scandal — 216
Product Reboot — 217
Managing Bloggers and Influencers — 218
Dealing with Media Hate — 219
The Story of Psyko Audio Labs — 220

Chapter 11: I'm Bankrupt—Saving costs and finding profits — 223
Going Bankrupt or Insolvent — 225
Taking Action on Potential Insolvency — 227
Cutting Expenses — 227
Cutting Costs: Prototyping vs. Scaling Up — 229
Renegotiating — 231
Raising or Lowering Prices and Calling in Receivables — 231
The Rapid Decline in Price — 232
Raising Additional Funds — 234
Deciding When to Go for Profitability — 235
A Quantitative Contingent Profitability Plan — 236
The Story of IngZ, Inc. — 238

Chapter 12: I Got Fired and I'm the Founder—How? — 241
How to Get Fired and Lose Your Startup — 242
Managing Boards of Directors — 243
Firing and Laying Off Co Founders — 246
Avoiding Getting Fired — 247
To Quit or Not to Quit — 248
When to Sue — 250

Negotiating Your Exit —— 251

What to Expect from the Outside —— 253

The Rest of the Story of Ken Cho, Spredfast, and People Pattern —— 254

Chapter 13: Sold!—Now what? —— 257

Acquisition Exit Analysis —— 258

Earn Outs and New Golden Handcuffs —— 266

Big Company Politics —— 267

Quitting Again —— 270

Investing Your Take —— 271

Mentorship and Advisors —— 272

Teaching —— 273

Starting the New One —— 274

The Story of Phurnace Software —— 276

Index —— 279

Chapter 1
Introduction—Why do you want to launch a startup, anyway?

Have you ever had a great idea that you thought would sell? Maybe you have had an idea for a cool new product, service, or app? Most of us have, and most of us do nothing about it. It might be years later that we see a TV commercial for exactly that idea, right there in front of us. Oh! If only we had pursued that idea, we would be rich now. That little pain of regret that we feel is coming from somewhere inside of us, but from where exactly? Is it really that we wish we were rich? Or is there something else that we wish for? If it had been us on that TV commercial, what about it would make us proud and happy?

In this chapter, we will begin to introduce the overarching concept of this book: that failure is not only the best way to learn, but it is also essential to eventually navigating your way to startup success. When a ship captain navigates the sea, he uses markers in the sky (stars) and may also follow a map and a compass. Despite all these navigation aids however, a ship still almost never sails in a straight line. The currents of the ocean and the direction of the wind determine how straight that ship sails. In order to get from here to there and have a successful voyage, the ship must constantly course correct, sometimes even constantly tacking to make progress upwind. This sailing metaphor is what it means to navigate a startup to success too. Sure, you will have a map (your business plan), and a compass (your bank account), but when you are on the high seas of a startup in motion, learning to tack and course correct is critical to finding your way to success.

Just as a ship will go off course, a startup will have many failures on its path to success. These failures do not mean turn around, run with the wind, and hide. Quitting and giving up is the only true way to fail at a startup. As long as you keep tacking and adjusting to the small failures along the way, you can and will eventually find success. The trick, and the goal of this book, is to show you how to make those failures small, hit them early on, and use those failures to sense the wind and adjust in the right direction. Learning through failure is the technique that thousands of successful startups have used to find their way, and you too will learn this skill.

Before we begin to introduce the process of startup creation and the way to navigate your startup to success, we must first look at what it means to be successful. Stephen R. Covey's famous book, *The 7 Habits of Highly Effective People* focuses its first two habits on exactly this concept: What is success to you? The first habit explains the habit of self actualization, that you can "be proactive"

DOI 10.1515/9781501507083-001

about your life and cause change. The second habit continues with this theme in understanding that to cause change, one must have a goal—one must "begin with the end in mind."

So, what is success to you? Do you believe that you can effect change and make progress towards that goal, yourself?

Let's first look at success. When I started my first company, Bigfoot Networks, Inc., in 2004, I did not understand the difference between a goal and a motivation. I had it in my mind that my goal was to make a billion dollars. Yes, you read that right, one billion dollars. I had even dreamed of how I would spend that money: starting a scholarship fund for my extended family, buying an island, owning a plane, and, of course, never working again. Looking back on it, this goal was perhaps a bit ambitious for a first company, but I truly thought that my idea was big enough to achieve it. What I failed to understand, though, is that in order to achieve such a massive goal, I would need to sacrifice other goals that I didn't yet understand I had. If I evaluated my true motivations a little more deeply, I would understand that maybe that goal wasn't actually what I wanted after all. Was I truly prepared to do what it would take to get that billion dollar check? Was I willing to sacrifice time with my family? Was I ready to put every penny I had into this one endeavor? Was I ready to invest 10, 20, or even 30 years of my life into this goal? The first failure I made as an entrepreneur was not really taking the time to consider if my goal really was what I wanted. What were my true motivations? The best goals should be measurable, achievable, and should reflect what truly makes us happy. We'll explore these themes in this chapter. First, though, I think I should tell you a bit more about myself.

I have a PhD in Business, earned through many years of reading research papers and doing my own primary published business dissertation using complex statistical analysis. The reason this should matter to you is that I do have some understanding of what researchers have come to recognize about entrepreneurship and business. That said, my thirteen years of practical experience, founding three startups, working as a CEO, and being a part of dozens more startups, is much more relevant to this book. If there is a way to fail at a startup, I've done it. I've also overcome it. That's the knowledge I'd like to pass on to you here. I should also mention that I've had startup success; at least, as measured by my own metric of success. This chapter is about finding your metrics of startup success.

In order to understand my own success metrics though, I think it's important to understand a bit more about where I come from—stuff not found on the back cover. I was born in a small town in Ohio called Lima. Lima was an industrial town of about 50,000 residents. It's not small enough to know everyone in town, but it is small enough to know everyone in your neighborhood, and my neighborhood was poor. I grew up poor. Not destitute, but we often relied on welfare checks, government cheese, and food stamps. It's not because my parents were not hard workers—they were and still are. The problem is that unless you've been living under a rock, you know that Lima, like so many industrial towns in this country, died in the 1980s due to industry no longer being economically feasible. We suddenly became an international society, and with that, the industrial revolution left so many towns like Lima with too many people vying for too few jobs. This lifestyle, scraping from paycheck to paycheck, shaped me. I was determined at a young age to break this cycle. I wanted to do more with my life and I was willing to work to get it. I thank my parents for this spirit, because they were always willing to work any side job and do anything to get ahead.

I started my first job at age 10. I was then the youngest paperboy ever in my town. I got the job because my dad vouched for me that he would help me if I needed it, and he did just that. I have always had one job or another since then. I too was and am willing to work any job. I've done sales door to door (more on that in Chapter 5). I've mowed lawns, served food, been a travel planner, and so much more. My favorite job ever was lifeguarding. I enjoyed the independence of the job and the aura of authority it gave me. What I really loved was being the boss (of the pool).

I got lucky—well, my parents created some luck for me. They moved to the nice side of town, right on the edge, the cheapest house they could afford. Because of that move, my sister and I were able to go to the good high school. It was worth it. Shawnee high school had teachers that inspired me. I became fascinated with electricity and, through some grit and hard work, I started getting A grades. My mom filled out all the loan paperwork, and suddenly, I was off to college. I was the first person in my family to go to college. I'm most thankful to my parents for that move to the good side of town.

I finished my degree in electrical and computer engineering in five years. It took me an extra year because I worked all through college, including a year at the Naval Research Labs building space satellites. Some of those satellites were classified, but I can proudly say that at least three satellites are or were in space with some of my hard engineering inside them. My early successes doing electronics for satellites eventually landed me a job at Intel, where I excelled in VHDL/Verilog and ASIC design. What is that? It's complex engineering stuff for making microchips. The pay was great, and I loved Intel. I did not love that I couldn't understand why we were building the things we were, like a 10 Gigabit per second network card (for which I was one of the lead designers). Why were we making this crazy thing? Who wanted it? I sure couldn't afford it, so who could? What's the point?

It was these questions, and my secret desire from my lifeguard days to be the boss, that led me to seek an MBA. My boss at Intel was all for it, and Intel paid for my MBA at the University of Texas at Austin. At first, I thought my MBA classes were boring and useless. The math was insanely easy compared to engineering school, and I felt like I was not getting my money's worth—that is, until my last semester when I took the *New Venture Creation* course. This class brought all the other classes together as a whole, and suddenly, I found entrepreneurship, and my new love: starting companies.

Bigfoot Networks, Inc.

Bigfoot Networks, Inc. was born during my New Venture Creation course at the University of Texas. It was my idea—my crazy idea. I'll explain a bit more about ideation in Chapter 2, but needless to say, I didn't really know at all if Bigfoot was a good idea or not. That didn't stop me from pitching it to the class and recruiting my two co founders, Bob Grim and Michael Cubbage. I chose them because they had marketing experience (Bob from Advanced Micro Devices) and finance experience (Mike from Dell), two skills I did not have at the time.

My pitch, which didn't change even as we were raising our second $8,000,000 round, was simple. I wanted to end all lag in online games, and I knew how to do it. Did I really know how to do it? Yes, sort of. I had become an expert in network technology while working at Intel, and I had a master plan for how to actually end lag. The big idea: a network interface card, the thing your network wire plugs into. What? Yes, a network card for gamers that not only reduced lag in all games, but it could also potentially end all lag in games that were optimized for our network card. How? Simple: Put the server into the card, and ta da! No more lag.

I thought that this was a billion dollar idea and the next big thing. It almost was: This book will tell the rest of the Bigfoot story, as well as the story of more than 12 other startups that I've been involved with in some way.

Even at the start of Bigfoot, I knew that a billion dollars was not needed to make me happy. In fact, money has never been a big motivator for me. In my surveys and interactions with students (mostly millennials), I have found that money is only needed up until a point. We all want to feel safe and secure, not like we are scraping the bottom of our check each month (like my parents did). Beyond that, we often value other things more. Once Bigfoot Networks started shipping products and making money, I started to think deeply about my one billion dollar goal. I was already pretty darn happy, actually. My salary was more than sufficient, my family was happy, and I really did like the people I was working with. I started calculating how much money it would take for me to truly feel safe. For me, it turned out to be two years' salary. That's it. My salary was around $150K at that time, so $300K in my bank account was my number. Why two years? I could not imagine not being able to get a job in two years of looking.

You might fail where I failed with Bigfoot Networks around this time. I knew that a billion dollars was not necessary to make me feel happy. Unfortunately, my goal for Bigfoot Networks was still to make one billion dollars. The failure with the goal of my startup not aligning with what made me happy was that when push came to shove, as you will read in later chapters, I made some bad decisions chasing that billion dollar dream. My other goals—to change the world, to be the boss, to enjoy my co workers—were constantly at risk of being sacrificed. Ultimately, I was unwilling to sacrifice people and my morals just to make a buck, even a billion of them.

How was it a failure to not understand what success looked like? Well, I had already achieved success and didn't know it. In fact, I blew right past it.

The Launching of the Killer NIC

It was a gorgeous San Francisco day in 2006, and the line outside the convention center was already long. People were queued up, their desktop computers sitting at their feet. These people, these gamers, seemed a little crazy to most. They were wearing Call of Duty t shirts, chugging Mountain Dew, and lugging 50 pounds of computer equipment, all for who knows what reason. They were there for LAN-Fest 2K6, one of the largest computer LAN parties of the day, It was set to be a big party, and the top sponsor, Bigfoot Networks, was making their formal launch of the Killer Network Interface Card at the event. To the gamers, being at LANFest 2K6 meant seeing the latest and greatest technologies, discovering a way to get an edge or advantage, and probably getting some free swag too.

A few hours later, and there I was on stage, about to formally announce the Killer NIC, Bigfoot Networks' first product, available at Newegg, the world's largest gaming hardware retailer. My ad agency had put together a great promotional video, we had hired models, and we had swag like no other. We were handing out necklaces made of real metallic heatsinks in the shape of the letter K, for Killer, which we used on the actual product as well. They looked cool as hell, and gamers loved them.

"Ladies and gentlemen, the founder, inventor, and CEO of the Killer NIC, Harlan Beverly!" The intro video ended, and I stepped on the stage.

"Yell if you hate lag!" I screamed at the crowd of about 300 gamers.

The crowd went wild.

"Yell if you love swag!" I said again, gesturing at the models on stage with me to toss out t shirts.

"Well, if you want the edge in games, you had better get the Killer."

The crowd cheered again. *Heck, these gamers like the Killer*, I thought. *Neat.*

"Who wants a Killer NIC right now?" I screamed.

Hands went up, people were screaming, and I gestured for my models to hand out free units to a bunch of the attendees in the front row. It wasn't the first units we had shipped, but it was the first time I'd done it in person, seen the excitement, and felt like a TV star.

It was at that moment that the reality of what I had accomplished in less than two years truly set in: I had done it. I had an idea, I got funding (at that point, it was a little over $4,000,000 invested), and I had actually built and launched the product. I launched. It shipped.

For me, like so many entrepreneurs before me, actually shipping the product and seeing it in the hands of customers was truly a moment of success. It was a major part of my feeling of being a successful entrepreneur. In retrospect, that moment of launch, where I was already making $150K/year, was the moment of my success. Unfortunately, I realized it too late; I ended up sacrificing what truly made me happy by chasing this unrealistic dream of a billion dollars. Needless to say, I am not a billionaire today, so there is more to this story.

Common Goals of Entrepreneurs

Each year at the University of Texas at Austin, I teach entrepreneurship to about 200 young undergraduate students and 100 or so graduate students—that's roughly 300 new entrepreneurs per year. As part of the first class of the semester, I have students share their entrepreneurship motivations with the class. The results of this information collected over the past two years might surprise you as it surprised me (see Table 1.1)!

Table 1.1: Reasons Entrepreneurship Students at UT Want to Start Companies (2 years of data)

Reason	Quantity	Percent
Be their own boss	433	83%
Change the world / Social entrepreneurship	326	63%
Make $100K very quickly (within 1 year)	153	29%

Reason	Quantity	Percent
Make $1MM (within 2 5 years)	244	47%
Make $10MM (within 5 10 years)	87	17%
Make $1B (within 10 30 years)	36	7%

The overarching reason my students wish to pursue entrepreneurship is to be their own boss. This is not the only reason though. Most students are also interested in making money that is above and beyond what they could otherwise make with a normal job. Many students also want to change the world. This should not be surprising, given that "what starts here changes the world" is the University of Texas' slogan. This data, to me, underlies the critical idea of motivation. We start companies for more than just wealth. Sure, we'd all like a billion dollars, some of us would be happy with $100K, but we want other things too. Most of us are not willing to sacrifice our souls, or our other goals, to get the riches we want—we'd also like to change the world.

Financial gain is a very common motivation. The challenge, though, is quantifying that goal. The critical question to ask is: At what point, or at what level of my bank account, will I feel as though my entrepreneurial endeavor was successful? The one billion mark was a high mark for me, not the low mark. In fact, within just one year after launching the Killer NIC at Bigfoot Networks, I had already achieved my success mark of $300K. The lowest amount in your bank account you need to feel successful might be higher or lower, depending on a lot of factors, such as how you grew up, for example. It's very personal. Here is a good formula you might consider using to set the lowest financial goal of your startup success:

Your Goal Bank Account Balance = Monthly Salary * Your Average Time Between Jobs * 2

This formula is good because it gives you a one hundred percent cushion for finding your next job. This is by no means an upper limit—who is going to turn down a billion dollars? Instead, consider it an initial goal. The more realistic the financial goal, the more you can emphasize or trade off against your other goals. Do you know how good it feels to go into work every day being your own boss, doing what you love, and working with people you love? I do. It's worth a lot of money to me.

While we are on the topic of common goals of entrepreneurs, I think it is important to consider that goal of changing the world. Just like a huge, possibly unreasonable financial goal, changing the world may be too large of a goal. If we set a goal this high, it might be a long time before we can feel like we've achieved it. It also sets us up to perhaps make some bad choices along the way. Remember, you don't have to realize every goal of your life, all at once. It is far easier and more practical to achieve goals one at a time, perhaps with a series of startups or business opportunities. Instead of setting such an immeasurable and perhaps overly ambitious change goal, I find it useful to start with a more reasonable goal. Changing the world, after all, can happen even by just showing the world that change is possible. How about quantifying our change goal (as will be a habit throughout this book) into something more actionable? Here is a formula to consider for your change goal:

Change Goal = Shipped * Number of Lives Changed * Dollar Impact of that Change

Breaking this equation down, remember that if you don't ship (launching your product or service), you will never change anyone, except maybe yourself. You must ship; it's binary, one or zero. Now, consider how many lives you've impacted or will impact, and the dollar amount impact of that change. If you can't translate it to dollars, that's okay—instead, translate it to the simple quantity of lives impacted, and it's still a clear goal. The only question remaining is: How many lives do you need to impact in order to feel like you have made a real contribution toward changing the world? Is it 10, 100, or 1,000 or more? If I were able to change the lives of 1,000 people, I'd feel pretty good. Why not set that number as your lower boundary? Sure, you can always impact more, but reaching 1,000 people is something to feel proud about.

There are a lot of other potential goals to consider when first starting out. One goal that entrepreneurs often mention during classroom discussion is having a successful exit for their startup. What does that mean? Trying to use success as criteria for success is like trying to define "happy" with the word "happy" in the definition. When I dig deeper, what most people mean by that is a) their investors got a positive return on their investment (didn't lose money), b) they personally got a small amount of money, c) they actually launched the product/service (shipped), and d) the company was purchased by another company (or liquidated) successfully. They have this goal of a successful exit because it sets them up very nicely for their next startup. See, a successful exit means that current and future investors will have more confidence in them as an entrepreneur. Since the first investors were repaid, it is a proxy for thinking that future investors will as well. It also proves that they can launch a product/service and have a good (if not great) outcome. Many investors prefer to fund entrepreneurs who are on their second or third startup, because by then, the entrepreneur will hopefully have learned how to be successful. In other words, they have learned how to fail in order to succeed—exactly what this book is trying to teach you.

Just shipping, launching, and getting your product or service (or app) into the hands of customers are sometimes goals in and of themselves. It can be incredibly rewarding just to see people using and loving your product or service. Okay, you did that—now on to taking that normal job (if you want). Some people are truly happy just to have done it. I know I was, when standing on that stage announcing the launch of the Killer NIC.

Corporate Innovation

Throughout this book, you will see callouts like this to help innovators who are inside their company understand how the topic may apply to *intrapreneurship*. Intrapreneurship is the creation of something new inside an already existing organization, usually with the intent of doing something innovative for the company.

Corporate innovators may have different goals entirely from those listed here. The exercise is the same though. It is important to understand your own motivations, personally. Write them down and turn your goals into hypotheses as will be described later in this chapter.

One common goal for corporate innovators is to be promoted, perhaps just as the head of the new department or initiative, or maybe to work their way up the corporate ladder. Another corporate innovation goal is change the world (or the organization) for the better in some way. Finally, like many entrepreneurs, a common goal corporate innovators have is to see their own idea come into reality (to ship).

A final goal to consider is one I didn't know I had until much later, after a lot of introspection. I wanted to be respected. It's a kind of fame, not true internet or TV star fame, but more localized people want to know me fame. I wanted to be somebody that people wanted to know. Wanting people to know you as someone who is important to the community is actually a more common goal than you might think. We all have the need to belong, and entrepreneurs in particular often have the need to lead, as well. Remember though, the most common goal of an entrepreneur is not just one goal, but several. The end of this chapter has a helpful checklist to help you consider all the goals you might have and some formulas for setting good goals.

Why Goal Setting Is Critical to Startup Success

Why so much emphasis on goals? The first and obvious answer is that without a clear, measurable goal, how will you know if you are successful? Making it all about money could leave you feeling unhappy and evil, and could lead to some bad decisions. Setting goals that are too high might leave you feeling incomplete and as though you never achieved success. Setting goals too low can demotivate you and your team, and possibly lead to some bad decisions. Nevertheless, having clear goals in mind before you do anything, even if they are too high/low/etc., is still better than having no goals at all. Remember, without a goal, you cannot determine if you have had startup success, and that's what this book is all about!

Speaking of this book, a key concept of this book is the hypothesis. A *hypothesis*, just like any kind of scientific inquiry, is an assertion, a belief, or an assumption about some phenomenon in the universe. Unlike an assumption, however, a hypothesis will have an actual testable value associated with it. In other words, a hypothesis will have a specific target defined (usually a number) above or below which, you can confirm or deny the hypothesis. Scientists like to make sure there is a sufficient sample size and margin of error built into the confirmation (or disconfirmation) of a hypothesis, just to add stronger support to the idea that the hypothesis is true or false. For the purposes of this book, however, we will assume one of two scenarios for the hypotheses we create:

1. That the hypothesis is qualitative or intangible and numbers lend support to how we *feel*, but it's up to us to determine based on feelings if it succeeded or not.

or

2. That we have collected at least 50 samples, and that's good enough for most areas of science, so we use 50 samples as a proxy for the validity of the hypothesis test.

So, for the *goals* of our startup, it's really a hypothesis or a set of hypotheses. In fact, it's a qualitative hypothesis, because although there are numbers involved, they only help to inform us as to how we think we will feel (successful or not). The hypothesis of my success then would be correctly stated as:

> I believe I will feel successful if I have accumulated a bank account with $300K, shipped my product, changed the life of at least 1,000 people, get to enjoy my job, get to work with people I like, and get to be my own boss.

See how this hypothesis includes the assumption "I believe I will feel successful" followed by the measurable items, all of which I believe are essential to my feeling of success? At any point in time, I can test this assumption and examine how I feel, and see how well this assumption is holding up. Conversely, I can see what areas I need to work on in order to feel or maintain the feeling of success. We will use this method of creating a measurable and actionable hypothesis throughout this book. The end of this chapter has a helpful table for you to construct your own successful startup hypothesis.

The Story of Memory Plush

Meet Waffles the Corgi. Waffles the Corgi is the first product from Memory Plush. Memory Plush is a company born in my class at the University of Texas at Austin. Student Andy Shaw and his classmate and partner Sherrill Feng founded it in 2016 to solve the problem of their favorite stuffed animals falling apart during washing or with excessive use. Along the way, they discovered that using a removable memory foam stuffing, they could not only extend the life of their stuffed animals, but they also made for nice pillows for kids and adults alike. Andy started my class with the idea, and after the first week, he was confronted with the question I ask all the entrepreneurs I meet: What's your goal?

"Dr. Beverly was asking an important question, and I really didn't give it as much thought as I should have at the time. I was thinking: I have no idea what my goal is, other than becoming an entrepreneur." —Andy Shaw, 2017

After a lot of discussion, trial, error, and success, Andy's perspective changed to be more specific and to encompass success as more than just money.

"Now that I've had such a successful Kickstarter campaign, more than doubling our initial Kickstarter goal, I think I finally get it. I find meaning in delighting customers, working with my partner, and traveling for business."

Memory Plush started as just an idea to make better stuffed animals. Unsurprisingly, many of Andy's classmates were skeptical of his startup idea. Andy himself was worried when he first started my class at UT as to whether or not his idea was even worthy of being a startup. I quickly corrected him on this notion and explained that often—actually, incredibly often—what many people think is the most obvious and uninteresting idea turns out to be one of the best. In the next chapter, I will discuss ideation and how to tell if your idea is good or not. Needless to say, Andy's idea was not only good, but it also turned out to be great.

Andy did not give up on Memory Plush; he persistently created a minimum viable product (MVP) by hand sewing covers for off the shelf stuffed animals in the shape of his own dog Waffles, an incredibly cute corgi. He went through the process of getting feedback (some of it negative) for his product. He even sold a few of his handmade items, all so that he could fail fast, and learn. One of his goals was to build some for real, not just hand sewn MVPs. Andy and Sherrill worked hard to find a contract manufacturer (CM), negotiate rates, and get a final design. It wasn't enough, and Andy was going to fail; he wasn't going to ship.

Why? He was going to fail because he couldn't afford the minimum order quantity (MOQ) from the CM.

One of the most important attributes of a successful entrepreneur is tenacity or persistence. Andy never gave up on success or his goals of shipping, doing it himself, and actually launching. He would not let the one failure—lack of capital—be the end. He persevered and decided to try crowdfunding to get the needed capital. He set the target amount at the MOQ from the CM, and was blown away by the results. He received more than double his desired amount for his Kickstarter campaign. What's more, Andy was able to donate over $1,300 from the Kickstarter to Queen's Best Stumpy Dog Rescue, a corgi rescue that does amazing work. Memory Plush is now working to come out with even more breeds of their Memory Plush dogs so that all dog owners can get a Waffles that resembles their pet. This is what it means to fail your way to success. I could not be prouder of Andy and Sherrill and their corgi!

Book Organization and Your Own Goals

This book is organized to help you identify the most common failures that founders experience when creating a startup. Each chapter will begin with a true story from my own experiences, the details of my failure, and how I eventually overcame it. The chapter will then introduce a method of quantitatively assessing the failure, your potential exposure to it, and offer techniques for how to either prevent it or overcome it. Finally, each chapter will end with a true story from another entrepreneur I know, how they experienced and overcame the failure, what they learned from it, how you could use the quantitative method outlined in the chapter to assess your own risk (exposure) to the failure, and the amount of learning and progress toward success when you overcome that failure.

Navigating your way toward startup success? Yes. I fundamentally believe that the only way to succeed in a startup is to get out there, launch, and fail as fast as you can so that you can plot a new course and navigate your way eventually to success. Failing fast means learning fast, and learning gives you the navigation aids to help you eventually succeed. Each chapter, you will learn not only what it is like to launch, run, and eventually sell a startup, but also how to take each failure along the way and use it to navigate into what will ultimately yield the success you are looking for.

The question remains, however: What success are you looking for? Don't move on to the next chapter until you have at least thought about this or, better yet, written it down. To help you navigate around this first potential failure (an unclear or imprecise success metric for yourself), the following table is presented for you to recreate and fill in. Don't use this to necessarily estimate how good your idea is—we'll do that in the next chapter. For now, just consider what success as an entrepreneur is to you. What would it look like?

Table 1.2: Define Success as an Entrepreneur for You

Success Item	Value
Financial: Total dollars in your bank account Min = (Monthly Salary * Months to Find a Job) * 2	
Financial: Target monthly salary	
Intangible: Be your own boss (1 or 0)	
Intangible: Shipped product/service (1 or 0)	
Intangible: Enjoy your job (scale 1 to 10)	
Intangible: Have a successful exit (1 or 0)	
Intangible: Enjoy working with your co workers (scale 1 to 10)	
Intangible: Personal Fame (scale 1 to 10)	
Quantifiable: Change the world Min = (Shipped * Number of Lives Changed * Dollar Impact of that Change)	

Chapter 2
Failing to Start—What's stopping you?

It was 1993 and I was in high school. Nirvana, Aerosmith, and Boys II Men were heard constantly on the radio. No, I didn't have big hair—that was the 80s—but I did have a car and it needed gas. I was willing to work just about any job for gas and going out money. I also had a fair amount of old Star Wars toys, Nintendo games, and of course many somewhat valuable baseball cards.

"We could have a garage sale," my friend Richard said, as though it were genius.

"At whose house? Because my parents will want a cut," I replied, knowing my family's long standing garage sale policy. Granted, they usually sat there the entire time and all I did was lay stuff out, but still, I was pretty sure they would want in on the action.

"Mine, I guess," Richard said somewhat dubiously.

"Do you think people even want this junk? I mean, do the people who shop at garage sales even know what these are worth?" I asked, pointing to my baseball cards and Star Wars toys.

"Well, they'll know what these are worth," Richard replied pointing to my Nintendo games.

"Yeah, just about nothing. Everybody has the Super NES now, and nobody wants these old NES games," I said, to my chagrin.

After that, we just sat there drinking our Cokes and thinking how the world hates us, Nirvana blasting from our boombox.

"Dude, let's get on your BBS again," Richard said, referring to the newly launched Gopher system I had shown him last week. I was always "into the computer stuff," as Richard liked to say.

"Why?" I asked.

"I don't know, maybe you could sell your stuff on there," Richard said.

"Hey, that's a pretty good idea," I replied, booting up my trusty Commodore 64. After hearing the lovely sounds of the dial up beeps, we were soon lost in the joys of reading the bulletin board system on Gopher. It was filled with silly discussions on topics such as Nirvana coming out with a new album, or how unrealistic the movie *WarGames* was compared to reality.

After about an hour, I had posted a listing for my baseball collection, explaining that I'd ship it anywhere in the US for a flat fee of $2.

It took exactly ten minutes for me to sell the collection.

"Wow, that was fast!" Richard exclaimed.

DOI 10.1515/9781501507083-002

"Yeah, you know what? My parents are always taking a cut of my garage sale earnings, right?" I said to Richard.

"Yeah, mine too."

"So, hey, what if we sold stuff on here for them, and took a cut of our own?"

"Yeah, that's a good idea, man."

"Dude, I bet we could sell just about anything on here."

"You could offer to sell lots of people's stuff and start a whole new forum for it," he suggested.

"Yeah, if I had a PC, I could even make a graphical page, like the new Gopher has," I said, dreaming. I knew I could never afford a real PC, but maybe I could borrow my other friend's PC for a while.

"We'd make a killing," Richard said.

"We would, but we'd probably get in trouble. I mean, it's probably illegal or something."

Two years later, eBay launched.

Failing to Start

You may not have invented eBay before it existed, but I bet that you probably thought up Uber, Netflix, the iPhone, or Groupon before these companies did. Sometimes the idea is not even that big, it's just a stool for your feet while you poop. Yes, the Squatty Potty was probably in the minds of millions of people before it launched on Shark Tank in 2014.

The fact is: We all have ideas. Ideas for new products and services pop into our brain whenever we see a current product not quite doing the job or we see a problem that needs solving where there is no obvious solution at hand. Ideas usually strike us when we are at our most creative: walking alone on the street, exercising, taking a shower, and even while using the toilet. I already had four ideas just this morning while writing this chapter (not on the toilet). I was thinking about how there should be an eBay for trading stuff, not just selling stuff. I was thinking that there should be wireless power converters for older cable powered devices. I was thinking just now how I wish a robot were mowing my lawn. This last one is a technology that I know exists, but which is just too expensive for me to really consider. I was thinking, maybe I could make that robot lawn mower cheaper using off the shelf parts. That's just this morning's host of ideas.

We quickly discard most of the ideas we have as unrealistic, not viable, or kind of stupid. I have this idea for a smart swing set with sensors on the swings that count how high you get. Yeah, kind of stupid, right? Or is it? We don't have a lack of ideas. We have too many. We worry too much about people stealing our idea, or assume that it must certainly already exist. All too often, a quick Internet search reveals that someone already came out with the idea or is working on it. Even if we can find nothing else like it, we fail to pursue it. We had the idea, but we never even started. This chapter will cover this failure in detail: failing to start. Starting, literally launching something as fast as you can, is the best navigation tip to get you on your voyage to success.

In Chapter 3, we'll discuss how to decide which idea to actually pursue and how to validate that idea as the best idea. In this chapter, though, we'll uncover the five biggest reasons that people don't start companies, even if they are full of ideas. It's pretty easy to fail at entrepreneurship if you never even start.

Some readers may have already begun their startup, and may not think these failures to start apply to them. I encourage you to read this chapter. It may be insightful to learn more about the attributes of the entrepreneur, company formation, and how to deal with risk—all topics that will be covered in this chapter. For those of us who have a great idea, but no knowledge of where to begin or are simply too afraid to get started, this chapter is definitely for you.

Startup vs. Small Business

There are many debates in management science about what kinds of businesses should be considered a startup. Entrepreneurship as a study can cover everything from selling roses in the street to inventing and selling flying cars. Rather than get into the debate about what is and isn't a startup, I encourage you to define it for yourself. This book also uses case studies of businesses I consider to be startups. These case studies serve to illustrate the main ideas qualitatively, but, where possible, this book also offers a quantitative technique for you to assess your own situation. What makes this book unique, I believe, is that it's not just case studies of successes, but it includes case studies about failures too.

Management researchers do a fair job of defining what an entrepreneur is. An entrepreneur, besides the obvious point of someone who starts a company, is someone who has to make many decisions with limited knowledge in order to manage scarce resources.[1] This implies a few important ideas. First, it implies that the person needs to be willing and able to make decisions. These decisions are

---

[1] Casson, M. *The Entrepreneur: An Economic Theory.* Edward Elgar Publishing, Incorporated, 2003, pp. 19–20.

often made in the face of incredible uncertainty. Do you really know if your idea will succeed? Do you know if spending money on this ad is worthwhile? Newness leads to uncertainty. If, for example, you were starting a company such as a car dealership or a tax preparation firm, those businesses are fairly certain in their business models and outcomes. They are established markets that customers understand, need, and know how to navigate. However, if you are building a new kind of car, such as a solar powered car, now that's much more uncertain than a regular car dealership selling Toyotas. Incidentally, there is also a scarcity of resources implied. You are not Amazon or Intel launching a new product; they do not have scarce resources, so their decision making is not as risky. Instead, Intel uses a technique called zero based budgeting (ZBB) to decide which projects to fund and which ones not to fund. ZBB is the simple process of estimating the net present value (NPV) of the investment and accounting for a 12% discount rate. In ZBB, you rank all projects according to their NPV and choose all projects that are positive, in order of returns, until you run out of budgeting. If that all sounds complex to you, don't worry—startups don't use this method. Why not? Startups can't do ZBB because it is uncertain what the returns will be for their new idea. Startups also do not have budgeted dollars just sitting around waiting to be spent. You don't have any budget for a startup (at first) unless you are somehow independently wealthy. Most startups have both scarce resources and scarce knowledge, and thus the entrepreneur must become an expert in making decisions in this climate of uncertainty with limited funds.

Corporate Innovation

If you are working inside a corporation, more than likely they do not think of themselves as a startup. So, if you are doing corporate innovation, are you creating a startup inside an organization? The answer is maybe. More than likely you will have to follow some justification process like ZBB to justify your corporation's investment in your idea. Sometimes your idea gets funded in a way such that a new department or subsidiary gets formed, often called a skunkworks. Sometimes however, your idea gets incorporated into an already existing department or project. Regardless of how your idea gets integrated into your organization, the rest of this chapter, and really this book, still applies. In order to propose and pursue your idea in the first place, you will need to exercise the same entrepreneurial traits, skills, and tasks outlined in this chapter and the remainder of the book. Your challenges, however, may be with your own boss or management team; it's still risky, and it still takes guts.

Now that we know what an entrepreneur is, it is helpful to understand what entrepreneurship is. In other words, what gets counted as a startup and what is simply a small business? As previously mentioned, management scientists don't always agree on this point. In my opinion however, there are a few things that might make a company more like a startup rather than a small business. One aspect of a startup is its newness or the uncertainty of the endeavor.[2] The degree of innovation involved in the endeavor is one of the ways to place a business on the startup scale. The innovation could be in technology, product, service, approach, business model, or market.[3] As already discussed, a car dealership is usually more like a small business because it is not a new kind of business and the product or service is also not new; the returns are likely to be well understood, so the risks are well understood. The other quality of a startup is its potential to scale. The problem with the car dealership is that it is not an easily scalable business. In order to scale it up, you would have to open more dealerships all across the country, each one progressively further away from you and requiring more money to open. While this franchise model could be a scalable model (for some startups, it is), most car dealerships don't open with this model in mind. Unless they have created a new method of selling cars (such as Cars.com), they aren't really being novel. Restaurants are often not considered startups for this reason; they don't scale well, and they also usually lack novelty. Occasionally, a restaurant franchise concept will come along that is novel enough to be considered a startup, but most restaurants are small businesses, and there is nothing wrong with that. Figure 2.1, below, presents one way to think about the differences between startups and small business, but remember that it's a scale, not a binary. If someone has what you believe is a small business, but they are calling it a startup, let them. You should only bother to judge your own business and how startup like it is, rather than argue against someone else's hopes and dreams.

Regardless of where your idea for a company falls, a startup or small business (or right on the line), the reasons you are failing to start it are probably the same. Whether it is a lack of money, fear of lawyers, or just not knowing where to start, there is something holding you back. I've divided these reasons into five categories in the following sections.

---

[2] Kao, Raymond W. Y. "Defining Entrepreneurship: Past, Present And?" *Creativity and Innovation Management*, vol. 2, no. 1, Mar. 1993, pp. 69–70. *Wiley Online Library*, doi:10.1111/j.1467-8691.1993.tb00073.x.

[3] Gartner, William B. "What Are We Talking about When We Talk about Entrepreneurship?" *Journal of Business Venturing*, vol. 5, no. 1, 1990, pp. 15–28.

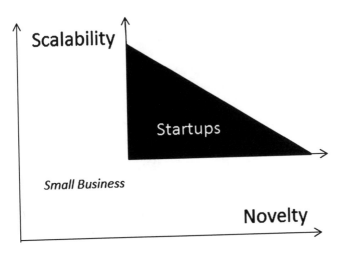

Figure 2.1: Startup vs. Small Business

Service, Small Business, Healthcare, Retail, Restaurant, Education, Entertainment, and Anything Else

No matter where your startup idea lands on the novelty and scalability curve, this book applies to you. Even small businesses such as restaurants and retail outlets need to generate revenues, and this book will help you get there faster. My experience with business has shown that customer discovery, validation, and early sales can help people avoid over investing in bad ideas. In the following chapters, you will learn how to get quantitative evidence that customers will want your product or service, that you will be able to scale up your business to meet your goal, and how to time your big investments in time and money to follow validated ideas rather than make big, uninformed gambles.

The techniques described in this book, including the two page website technique described in Chapter 3, are valid for any type of business. You may have to adjust the offering or technique slightly to accommodate your special situation, but each step of the process is important. Skipping early customer validation is a particularly bad idea. Healthcare, for example, is often confusing because of the complexity of the healthcare ecosystem. Who is your customer anyway? Is it the patient, the doctor, or the insurance agency? In some cases it can be all of the above. You need to validate that the patients have a need for the results (for example, less wait time, more information, better outcomes), and that the medical institution (doctor or hospital) is aware and willing to pay for a better solution.

This means building out two customer types and validating both of them, before you invest too much in developing your solution. Your two page website might be two different websites targeting each audience separately, and the call to action might not be a pre order, but a "sign up to stay notified" instead. It's still validation, especially for healthcare where customers (e.g. patients) often have little say in what is offered.

Similarly, restaurants are hard to get early validation for because you don't have the location yet nor the food available. People don't generally pre order a restaurant experience. Nevertheless, you should still test your restaurant concept with customers before you actually rent that space and invest in your idea. Do your target customers like the food? Hold some parties, maybe invite some investors and the target audience, and see what they think of your food. Do they like the concept? A two page website can tell you that too. Here in Austin, one of the most successful pizza restaurants in the city, Homeslice Pizza, started with a simple pizza concept and then literally held parties in people's homes to drum up support, get feedback, and even collect pre orders and investments in their restaurant. The point is, no matter your idea, you should not skip customer validation. Making sure your idea matches your goals is also important. I believe every chapter of this book is helpful, even if you may need to adjust it slightly to match your specific idea. In fact, it is usually the case that your idea or situation is unique and special compared to other people's ideas. You should figure out how to adjust to achieve your goals instead of skipping any steps.

No progress is made, however, unless you actually get started. Regardless of your business type, regardless of your goals, and regardless of if you agree with all the ideas presented in this book or not, if you don't get started, you will never achieve success. The next five sections will help you get past your fears and get started already!

Failing to Start Reason Number One: You

The biggest reason people don't start a company with their idea is themselves. It's you. You are the one holding back and not doing it. This book is not a "rah rah you can do it" book. That's not what I'm talking about. Lack of self confidence is just one of the personality traits that prevent people from starting companies. This book is more about understanding what those personality traits are that hold people back. From there, it's up to you to decide to work on them or not.

Why bother with understanding what a startup is compared to a small business? Simple, it has to do with you. As it turns out, because of the novelty and scalability, startups are usually more risky than small businesses. It is precisely this risk that holds people back from starting. One of the key traits of an entrepreneur, therefore, is that they are much more risk tolerant than other people. Researchers have identified and called this "lower dispositional prevention focus orientation."[4] This term means that entrepreneurs are not as worried about failing or losing money as much as other people are. This book takes this concept one step further and argues that loss and failure are essential to eventually navigating your way to success. Going into a startup endeavor being aware that you will encounter loss and failure over and over can fundamentally change how you might think about entrepreneurship. It's about minimizing that loss, optimizing what you learn from those failures, and putting that knowledge to work in order to eventually become successful. If you are comfortable with potential failure and loss, then you are more likely to try this whole startup thing. Entrepreneurs don't fear loss as compared to the potential upside of success, and neither should you. That's not an inspirational speech—it's management science.

Speaking of inspiration, as already mentioned, self confidence is very important. This is a separate concept from risk tolerance. You can be able to take risks, and still have low self confidence. It's about your attitude and outlook on life. Entrepreneurs have to believe that they will have some chance of success and that they can do what it takes to try. Academics call this *self efficacy*, which can be defined as the belief that you are capable of doing the tasks needed to pursue the entrepreneurial endeavor.[5] This belief does not mean that you necessarily know how to do the tasks needed, but that you believe you can figure it out. Later in this chapter, we'll look at a few of the tasks related to getting started that you may not know how to do. Seeing what skills will be needed should help give you more self confidence that you can actually do it. The successful entrepreneur simply believes that they can do the necessary tasks, one way or another. I believe in you, just as I do all my students. I try in my classroom to instill self confidence by having the students see that they can do it by actually doing it. This book will try to do the same for you.

Not convinced that you can do it yet? Consider the story of the six year old entrepreneur.[6] Ashwin Gowland invented the washable sticker to solve the

---

[4] Hsu, Dan K. "Who Becomes an Entrepreneur? The Dispositional Regulatory Focus Perspective." *American Journal of Entrepreneurship*, vol. 8, no. 1, 2015, pp. 94–115.

[5] Chen, Chao C., et al. "Does Entrepreneurial Self-Efficacy Distinguish Entrepreneurs from Managers?" *Journal of Business Venturing*, vol. 13, no. 4, July 1998, pp. 295–316. *ScienceDirect*, doi:10.1016/S0883-9026(97)00029-3.

[6] https://gaptoothkid.wordpress.com

problem of stickers not coming off of things, despite ripping, washing, and rubbing. While it may be that his mom helps him with many of the startup tasks, the kid sure has confidence, as you can see if you watch his business pitch on YouTube. He simply believes his mom can help him make it happen. Now that's confidence!

There are many other personality traits that may also contribute to the success of the entrepreneur. This chapter, however, is focused primarily on those traits that get people to start companies, not necessarily succeed with them. In later chapters, we'll discuss how passion and persistence play key roles in ultimately achieving success. Why might that be? As you'll soon see, failure is not true failure for the passionate, persistent entrepreneur—it's only a step along the way. It's learning. If we can persist and stay true to our cause (our goal from Chapter 1), then we can eventually find success. It may just take a while.

Failing to Start Reason Number Two: The Lizard Brain

The "lizard brain" is a term coined by Seth Godin in his popular book *Linchpin: Are You Indispensable?* Essentially, the lizard brain is fear. It's the vestigial part of our psyche that controls our fight or flight response. It's called lizard brain, because even lizards exhibit this fight or flight response in response to threats or even just the unusual. The amygdala is the part of the human brain that generates an emotional response to threats and situations unknown. We all worry, and so do entrepreneurs. The difference is that entrepreneurs have learned to control this emotion and do the things that need to be done, despite the strong impulses to run or hide that might be pulsing in their brains. Fear—of failure, public speaking, asking for the sale, getting rejected, or fear of just about anything—can control you if you let it. Many entrepreneurs, even those who know what to do and are willing to risk it all, don't do so, because fear immobilizes them.

Common fears are failure, success, loss, and stage fright. Fear of failure is obvious, but fear of success? Yes, many people are afraid of success—what it might mean, how they might feel, and whether they even deserve it. Trust me, you do. We all deserve success, as long as we are willing to work to achieve it. Fear of loss is the worry that you'll lose your house, your job, your savings, or something else. I can't relieve your fears very much, other than to say that what was once earned can be earned again. Being an entrepreneur involves being willing to take risks, including that savings, that job, and yourself. This book will hopefully organize the process of startup creation in such a way that you will not take a large risk at the wrong time. It's better to take small risks and fail a lot (and learn) than to take big ones and not be able to try again.

How do you know if you have the lizard brain? An awesome video by Paul Durban and Martin Whitmore on the subject lists five items to check for to see if the lizard brain might be secretly controlling your decision not to start (or not to ship).[7] These five items include:

Procrastinating
Being Overly Critical
Feeling Anxious (whether invented anxiety or not)
Obsessing Over Details
Making Excuses

If you sense yourself doing any of these things, it might be simple fear controlling you. To combat this fear and to overcome the failure to start, Seth Godin suggests a number of actions. First, let it be okay to have a bad idea now and again. Second, stop excessively planning and building in contingencies—you are wasting time. Third, if your fear is telling you to do something, do the opposite but on a smaller scale. Fourth, embrace failure, and make failing a welcome friend that helps you learn and grow. Finally, make no excuses, and just ship it already! These suggestions, also outlined in the video mentioned above, are great ways to start recognizing and overcoming your fears, and ultimately just doing it.

Failing to Start Reason Number Three: Where to Begin

One of the main ways we procrastinate (part of the lizard brain, as mentioned above) is by making the excuse that we don't know where to begin. There actually is an answer to this question, but that's not entirely the point. If you truly have a lot of self efficacy and risk tolerance, then this question should not be holding you back. People with enough self efficacy will simply research it. You'll find reference to this concept throughout this book—just look it up. When confronted with a question or a need to know how to do something, the passionate, self confident entrepreneur will find some way to get it done. Often, a short and simple online search is all that is required. Of course, this book, in my not so humble opinion, is also a great resource to keep on your bookshelf and serve as a reference for when you aren't sure what to do.

---

[7] https://www.youtube.com/watch?v=JAoFPIHBu6U

So, here is an answer to the question of where to begin. Begin with Chapter 1's concept of keeping with the end in mind. Understanding your goals and desires cannot be understated. This may take some personal introspection and time. Don't procrastinate on it. Write down your thoughts (perhaps using the table provided in Chapter 1) and move on. Get a first draft of your goals and then move on to the next step: starting.

What the next step is depends on whether you already have an idea or not. If you do have an idea, great! Your next step is to test your idea and see if anyone likes it. Chapter 3 will walk you through the process of idea and market validation. If you don't have an idea, you are not alone—of the hundreds of entrepreneurship students I teach each year, less than 30% start my class with an idea. For the rest of the students, we follow a simple process, and within one hour, they all have an idea to work on. In the coming paragraphs, I'll share a tool that may help you get an idea, hopefully a good one.

What is this magical ideation process? Well, it's actually an intersection of three key ideas about startups that you need to understand and then optimize in your mind. Why so difficult? Anything that looks like magic is probably really hard work, right? Yeah, it is, but it doesn't have to take long. There are four steps to finding a good idea.

The first step is to identify your passions. What kind of things do you do for fun? What are your hobbies? If money were not an issue, what would you like to do with your time? What is your dream job? These are just a few of the questions you could ask yourself to help you find your passion. I'll use myself as an example to illustrate finding your passions. For fun, I like to play video games, watch movies, swim, and travel. If I had a lot of money, I'd probably travel the world and live in ocean side villas. I'd buy an infinity pool and have a bunch of pool parties; I'd build a drive in movie theater and play games on it while in the pool. My dream job is to be the CEO of a big gaming company such as Valve or Activision Blizzard. These are my passions—to get a great idea for yourself, you should identify yours. By the way, is it any surprise that I made a video game hardware company as my first startup?

The second step is to identify a need. A need is a problem that someone has that is so intense, you just know (or believe) that they would be willing to pay to solve it. In my business pitches, I call this a burning need. The need is so clear that it's burning a hole in their pocket. This need could be a business to consumer (B2C) need—for example, fewer lags in games, or low carb pizza. It could also be a business to business (B2B) need, such as excess inventory buildup or high defect rates. Either way, the key idea is a willingness to pay. A problem is something people can usually live with, while a need is a problem so intense that they are willing to pay to resolve it. If you want to get started on part four, try to think of needs in areas that you are passionate about—this will make it easier to find the optimal idea.

The third step is to think big. Now that you have identified a need, you must think of solutions to that need. Don't limit your thinking to solutions you can do yourself; that's not what beginning a startup is about. The best startups solve the need or problem so completely and elegantly that they become the obvious choice to anyone who might have those problems or needs. Often, entrepreneurs think too small and solve only part of the problem. Worse, they think that their solution needs to be fully thought through and actually built before they can start to pursue it. This is not the case. You should be thinking of a solution to the need that solves it in a way that is not only complete, but also easy for the purchaser of your solution. If you can't think of any solutions, it might make sense to pursue a different need. Don't worry at this stage about whether it is possible to build it. Don't worry that you don't have all the skills necessary to implement the solution. Just focus on coming up with ideas that would truly solve the problem for the people with that need. For example, my low carb pizza problem would be completely solved by a pill I take after I eat normal pizza that destroys the carbs before I digest them. Alternatively, my low carb pizza solution could be a one click app that delivers pizza to my door and tastes like almost any pizza I might want, but uses dough made from almonds or other low carb sources.

The three steps above can be visualized graphically as three overlaid circles (see Figure 2.2). The best starting ideas are those that intersect your passions, a clear burning need, and a solution that is as complete as it can be.

The fourth and final step of ideation is to find as many ideas as possible that are worth pursuing that fit in the intersecting optimal idea section of Figure 2.2. Brainstorming is the process of finding many possible answers to a specific question or problem in order to ultimately discover the best possible solution or answer. Brainstorming should push your limits of creativity and imagination. It is difficult to brainstorm three things at once, so I recommend brainstorming in two steps. First, brainstorm some burning needs for each of your passion areas. Second, brainstorm for solutions to each of those needs. I would not suggest trying to optimize all three of these things at once. Instead, as the final step, simply look at each of the solutions you've come up with and find the one that fits the best at this intersection of completeness, the burning need, and your passion. You are not necessarily looking for the perfect idea, but an idea that you think is worth pursuing. In Chapter 3, we'll discuss how to test this idea and how to adjust it when needed. For now, the answer of where to start is: your idea.

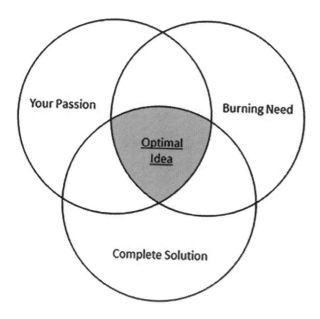

Figure 2.2: Optimal Idea Is at the Intersection of Passion, Need, and Solution

Failing to Start Reason Number Four: The Lawyers

I have nothing against lawyers. Most of the lawyers I know are good people, but that's because they aren't going after me. The ones going after me, I fear, hate, despise, think are wicked, and I think of as evil. They use underhanded tactics, bully, and are truly unjust and greedy. Of course, my own lawyers are none of these things. My own lawyers are defenders of the weak, supporters of the cause, and looking out for my best interest. If this seems kind of silly to you, then you've probably never been sued. I truly hope you never get sued. In Chapter 8, I will discuss what to do if you do get sued, and how it feels to both win and lose. The truth is that lawyers are just people, and most people are not evil—not even the lawyer representing the party that is suing you. They are just doing their job and helping to keep a lawful society. This, however, does not mean that you have to hire one. Remember that running a startup is about managing scarce resources, so don't hire a lawyer unless it is absolutely necessary.

The fear of getting sued is just one of the things that might be holding you back from starting. Remember, failing to start is a sure way to never succeed. You have to get over your fears. Another fear might be the fear of having to pay a lawyer to get you started. In the next section, we'll discuss why you need exactly $0 to start your business, but understand this now: you don't need to pay a lawyer to start a business. I'll say that again: you don't need a lawyer to start a business. *YOU DON'T NEED A LAWYER TO START A BUSINESS.* Why all the emphasis? Am I yelling at you? Yes, sort of. I hear so often, "Do I need a lawyer?" While I'm not a lawyer, and this is not legal advice (I never give that), I can give you very sound business advice. Let's look at the legal things you may think you need.

First, you may think you need a lawyer to incorporate or form a company. You actually don't. You can incorporate by yourself, for a very small state filing fee. Incorporating simply involves some simple paperwork that you need to file either with your home state (which is usually cheaper) or with the state of Delaware (typically costs around $300 including a registered agent).[8] The paperwork for the kind of company you need to form, called a *C Corporation*, involves stating a number of shares (you can just choose 10,000,000 at $0.001 par) and the purpose of your business (state any lawful act or activity). That's it. Sign, include the date, your name, and address, and you are done. Other countries have different processes for incorporation, but generally speaking, you probably won't need a lawyer there either—do some research to find out. If you really, really feel like you need a lawyer, you can hire one online for much cheaper than you might be thinking.[9]

If you are an American citizen, you don't need to incorporate at all to start your business. That's a $0 company formation option. Your social security number allows you to earn money in the United States as a sole proprietor with no additional paperwork. Start your business, earn money, and at the end of the year, simply file your taxes using the long form 1040 and Schedule C (personal business income). That's it. You've got a company. Granted, a sole proprietor company generally can't get a separate bank account, doesn't get a corporate shield, and can't get professional investment. However, when you are first starting (which is what we are discussing), you don't need those things! All you need is an idea and a willingness to get started and to get over your fears.

Finally, there are a lot of other things you don't need a lawyer for when you are first getting started.

1. You don't need a lawyer to incorporate.
2. You don't need a lawyer to launch a product.
3. You don't need a lawyer for business or legal advice.

---

[8] http://corp.delaware.gov/howtoform.shtml
[9] http://legalzoom.com

4. You don't need a lawyer *just in case.*
5. You don't need a lawyer to file a patent (provisionally).
6. You don't need a lawyer to file a trademark.
7. You don't need a lawyer for taxes, customer protection, to understand your risks, or to help you avoid problems.
8. YOU DON'T NEED A LAWYER.

Failing to Start Reason Number Five: No Money

The last major reason that many people fail to start a business is that they have no money. Well, maybe not *none*, but very little, or none that they can reasonably spare. This common concern is worth looking at more closely, because it sets up the next chapter.

Let me try to answer this question of how to start a business with no money with a question of my own. How do you know your idea is any good, anyway? If it is a new idea, as it should be to be a startup, then you have no way of knowing if people will like it or not. If it were not new (which would constitute it as a small business idea), then you probably need money to get started, since the first step of validating the idea of a startup less necessary. You know that people need auto repair mechanics and grocery stores. You don't need to validate a market that already exists. In Chapter 3, however, we'll discuss how you can (with $0) test your new startup idea to see if it's good or not. The critical first step of a startup is to validate your market, but this step doesn't need to cost a thing.

You may be thinking, *Well, I already validated it and now I need money to really get started.* Part of the purpose of this book is to demonstrate that the best validation is sales. You don't think you can sell something you don't have? Try telling that to Michael Dell, the founder of Dell computers, whose entire business model is about taking orders *before* he buys inventory. Try telling that to the thousands of successful Kickstarter campaigns that have successfully taken pre orders without any inventory. Pre orders are a path to startup glory in more ways than you can imagine. After you've validated your market, validate it again with pre orders, as we'll discuss in Chapter 4.

Are you worried that you don't have a prototype and aren't even sure if it will work? These fears are normal, but usually unfounded. Unless you are sending people to the moon (which has been done, by the way), your idea is almost certainly doable. It will take time, money, and effort to actually launch a finished working product, but there are many steps between now (idea) and eventually shipping that you can get started on. The critical concept here is that even if money is required to build prototypes and to launch, you won't get that money without traction. The rest of this book is to help you figure out how to get that traction without money. You need traction, and a lot of it, in order to get money (funding or sales). It takes *traction* to make money, not money to make money.

Here is a final point about lacking initial startup funds. Are you counting on your startup to make you income? Do you need your startup income to pay for your groceries, your rent, or your car payment? If you do, then you are in for a rude awakening. It can take years for a startup to make enough money to pay for a salary (yours). It can take years for a startup to get funded, and thus be able to pay salaries out of investment funds. You are going to need a job, even just an odd job, in order to pay for your living needs up until you are funded or have enough customers to quit your day job. Unless you are independently wealthy, this is how people do it. We don't just quit our job and live off of nothing to start our company. Sure, a few people have enough savings and are able to live off of that for a while. Most of us, though, simply work on our startup on nights and weekends until we have enough paying customers and profits to be able to pay our salary, or until we've secured enough professional investment to pay ourselves to be full time. Chapter 7 will talk about how to secure professional investment in your company. However, without some initial traction (the subject of Chapters 3–6), there is no point in even looking for professional investment yet. You need to get a side job, earn a meager living, and use your spare time to build traction for your startup. You can quit your job later; it's your reward for success, not your driver of success.

The Story of Eric Packer, Inventor

By day, Eric Packer works hard as a client solutions expert at a big high tech company in Austin, Texas. He knows database management systems like you wouldn't believe, and is amazingly helpful to his many customers that he manages when they have problems or need help.

By night, Eric Packer is an inventor. He's invented dozens of amazing gadgets and gizmos to make life easier, such as the electric fly swatter, the automatic lawn mower, and the smart lock for your home.

There's only one problem. Eric Packer has brought none of these ideas to market. In fact, he didn't file a patent, create a website, or discuss these ideas with anyone. As ahead of their time as they were, they were just ideas. Years later, Eric would see his ideas promoted on TV or online. He would see them and be frustrated as hell. Eric had failed to start. He didn't know where to start.

"I absolutely hate the fact that I think of these things and they almost always show up a few years later," Eric said. "It makes me feel like, I don't know, I'm losing at life or something."

"Eric, don't stress about it. Look forward, man—let's talk about your latest ideas," I replied calmly. Having had this very conversation about 100 times before, I knew what to ask next. "Before that, though, what do you want, Eric? What is your goal?"

"I don't know. I mean, I like my job, and it's not like I need more money. I guess I'd like more time to spend with my family," he said dejectedly, while taking a bite of his Taco Cabana taco.

"Right—freedom of time is a big motivator for a lot of us. That's similar to being your own boss," I replied.

"I don't need to be the boss," he said, mouth full of taco.

"Well, if you're not the boss, then someone else will be, and undoubtedly, they'll expect you to work normal or even long hours," I said, taking my own bite of lunch.

Eric and I had just finished Taekwondo nearby. We had been training together for nearly three years before Eric asked me to lunch. Eric knew that I was a startup professor at UT and that I had run many successful startups, but he hadn't asked me about his ideas because he was ashamed that he hadn't done anything with them yet. I was there to try to push him to act on his ideas, or at least that was what I thought.

"Good point," he laughed. Eric is the kind of guy you just like. He's got that trusting smile and eyes, and he is easy to laugh and joke around with.

"So, besides that, anything else? Any other reason you want to do a startup?" I asked. I always ask this question first. Without good reasons, or at least without understanding their reasons, it's hard to give good startup advice.

"Yeah. I mean, it would just be neat to see my idea live, shipped, working, or whatever," he said. "It would be nice to not have to see that someone else created my idea."

"I get it. Shipping is a great reward. How much money do you want to make?" I asked.

"I don't need to be rich. Enough so I can do it full time would be nice."

"Smart. Okay, so, what's your idea?"

"Okay, I'm going to tell you my idea, but you have to promise not to steal it," he said conspiratorially.

"Eric, hold on there. That kind of attitude is not the best way to pitch an idea—it will quickly turn people off. Besides, dude, do you think I *need* to steal your idea? I mean, do you think that little of my own imagination?" I asked.

"Hmm, I never thought of it that way," he said. "Okay, so here goes," he started, with trepidation in his voice. *For a guy who was worried just a second ago about me stealing his idea, now he's worried I won't like it. Something's off here, I* thought.

"So, you know how I love martial arts, right? I mean, I do Taekwondo and Brazilian Jiu Jitsu and all that, like three to five times a week, right?" he asked.

"Yes, go on," I said.

"Right, so, imagine if there was a shopping center filled with different martial arts styles, and other stuff too, like a Taco Cabana, maybe a Jamba Juice, some fitness stores, you know. Like, all in one place."

"Okay..." I said calmly.

"For a monthly fee, you could do all the exercise stuff, and you would get a discount on the shops too. So, if you just want to work out, you can go to the gym right there. If you want cardio, you could go do the spin class. If you want to do some martial arts, do Taekwondo one night, and Jiu Jitsu the next. Get it? It's like a sports center for martial artists."

"Okay, so, what's novel here?" I asked.

"It's all in one place." He replied.

"Hmm..." I said.

"So, you hate it?" He replied.

"Well, no. It doesn't necessarily pass my startup test, but I don't hate the idea. It will take money, though." I said.

"Yeah, I know, I don't have the money to buy or build this. It's just a pipe dream. Just wait—someone will come out with this in a few years and I'll be like, 'I had that idea,'" he said dejectedly.

"I would call this idea more of a small business idea than a startup, but regardless of that, I do think it could meet your goals if you were able to do it. You could be your own boss, make enough money to live on, and spend more time with family. What this is called, though, is real estate investing, specifically commercial real estate investing. It's a pretty well understood business model, and it does take money to get going, but you don't necessarily need money at first. You could get investors for this," I said.

"Really? What do you mean?" he asked excitedly. *Wow, what a rollercoaster of emotions.*

"Well, you can build a website for the idea, and see if you can get dojos or martial arts studios interested in the idea," I started. "Then you could build another website describing the whole package, with the Jamba Juice and everything, set a price, and see how many consumers click the 'learn more' button. You can get a sense for how consumers like the idea."

"I see, but why do all that? That sounds like a lot of work," he replied.

"To test if it's a good idea or not," I said.

"Hmm. Okay, so I have another idea. It's an app..." he said, moving on to his many other ideas.

I guess he doesn't think that idea is worth testing, I thought.

To date, Eric still hasn't started any of his ideas. I'm holding out hope that he will someday start one of them—even the martial arts sports center.

Conclusion: Failing to Start

Failing to start is the most common failure of all. As the case with Eric proves, many people have so many ideas that they don't know which one to pursue. They are in love with the concept of ideas, not the discipline and hard work it's going to take to see them through. Either that or they are afraid of starting, failing, succeeding, or trying. This book will try to show you the methodical steps to navigating your way to startup success. The key, though, is that you must overcome each failure in order to navigate your way to the next step. In order for Eric to overcome the failure to start, he just has to pick one of his many ideas—even one that someone may have already launched—and get past his first failure: his failure to start. Once he gets past this failure, he'll be able to see that his fear of starting was unfounded. He needn't fear failure, as failure is part of the process.

To finish this chapter, I conclude with a quantitative tool to assess and overcome your fear of starting. You may find it helpful to quantify your fears and assess exactly what you are most worried about that's keeping you from starting. Knowledge is the greatest weapon you can use to combat fear. Take a moment to fill out the table below. Assign a score of 0 to 100 for each fear you may have, and then reflect on those fears that are high. Why are they high? What could you do to overcome them? Is there any way you can mitigate those risks? Remember, even the most successful entrepreneurs understand that there are risks to doing startups. We have the same fears you have. We just choose to live a riskier life. No risk means no reward.

Table 2.1: Fear of Starting

% You Fear This (0 100)	Potential Fear
	Failure
	Not knowing what to do
	Losing money
	Not having an idea (or no good idea)
	Being sued
	Needing to incorporate
	Needing to hire a lawyer
	Not having enough money
	Idea not feasible or possible
	Idea will take too much money/time

Chapter 3
Your Idea Sucks—How would you know?

"So, wait, all it does is help you get free beer?" Ryan asked, while staring at me dumbfounded.

"Well, yeah, I mean that's basically it. It's artificial intelligence that helps you find free beer," I replied.

"And that's it, then?"

"Yep. Well, we could do more in the future someday—maybe help people find free food or something," I said.

"That's it?"

"Yep."

We sat there in silence for a long moment. We were eating burgers at one of our favorite meet up spots for lunch in north Austin. Mighty Fine Burgers do in fact have some very fine burgers. I heard the final slurp of Ryan's chocolate shake as he continued to say nothing.

"Well, what do you think?" I asked impatiently, knowing our lunch hour was almost over.

"About what?" He asked.

"About freebeer.ai. You know, the idea," I replied.

"Oh, I don't know. I've heard worse," he said.

"And?"

"And what?"

"And will you help?" I asked.

"Maybe. Find out if people are willing to pay, then we can chat," Ryan said, standing up to go.

"Okay. Got it. See you in a few weeks."

"Later."

And that was that. My long awaited lunch plan to pitch my business idea had come to an end. Ryan was not on board, but he wasn't not on board either. He wanted proof that this was going to be a good idea and something worth working on. I was a bit frustrated.

Ryan and I had worked together since 2003. We both worked at the same small company making networking chips. Later, I recruited him to be one of the first employees at my first company, Bigfoot Networks. After we sold Bigfoot Networks, I recruited him again to help me co found my next company, Karmaback. He even became my CTO at Key Ingredient when I took over as CEO there. That's

DOI 10.1515/9781501507083-003

more than 14 years of working together, and I'd helped him make him a lot of money. For all this, I get a "maybe" as a response.

If it's this hard for me to convince my longtime friend and nearly permanent business partner to get on board with my latest idea, imagine how hard it will be for me to convince others. This was going to be an uphill battle. I needed something. I needed evidence. I needed evidence that customers wanted free beer. I needed to prove to Ryan and others that my idea was good. I also needed Ryan, because he could code artificial intelligence systems, and I could not. No more maybes.

Good Ideas

In the last chapter, I discussed how to find a good idea on your own. What I meant was, however, a good *initial* idea. You actually don't know yet if it's good or not. What is good, anyway? Begin with the end in mind, as always. What's the goal? Did you achieve it?

A good initial idea is one that you believe in enough to overcome the first major hurdle: failure to start. That's all it has to do. It doesn't have to make you a billion dollars—it doesn't even have to make you one cent. This is why I stated in the last chapter that your idea should be an intersection of your passion, a burning need, and a complete solution. The only goal you had to achieve there is to start. Your next goal, however, will probably not be achievable with the initial idea. As an entrepreneur, you will have to constantly refine and adjust your goals and ideas. That's called *pivoting*, and it's one of the critical tools that successful entrepreneurs use to achieve success. I'm not saying you have to give up on your goals from Chapter 1—those goals are the long term goals. I'm saying you will need intermediate goals and ideas to meet them.

The idea you started your entrepreneurial journey with—whether from Chapter 2 or from before you opened this book—is fine, for you. The problem at this stage is that an idea just for you may not make you a penny. Being your only customer does not make for a very successful business. One of the first critical intermediate goals is to validate your idea. Validation is another key theme of this book, and validating an idea is important for many reasons. First, validating an idea can help you attract co founders (like me with Ryan), advisors or mentors, and early customers. Second, validating your idea can get you early revenue or at least some early customer leads. Finally, validating your idea is essential for getting financing or funding for your company. This chapter will discuss not only how to validate your idea, but also what to do if your idea sucks, which, as you are about to find out, is all too common.

So, the answer to what a good idea is depends on what stage you are at in your startup. At this stage, you need your idea to be good enough to attract customers or potential customers. How do you do that?

Validating Your Idea

Way too many entrepreneurs skip the step of idea validation. When they do, it always makes me cry inside. Skipping this step is such a huge failure that when this step is skipped, incredible amounts of money are wasted, and entrepreneurs often give up and never try again. How could that be? Imagine how you would feel if you thought you had a great idea, never validated it, but just went ahead and built it. Yes, built the whole thing, the *complete solution* that I previously talked about. How much money did it take to build that solution—thousands, or even tens and hundreds of thousands of dollars? This trend of building before validating (the if you build it they will come syndrome) has recently become widespread as startup accelerators have made it all too easy to meet the people who can help you build things. Of course that design agency or software firm wants to help you build it; you will be paying them! It's easy to fall into the trap of believing that you need to build a working prototype or even the entire product before you can validate your idea with customers. This is especially true when you think that the product or service is fairly easy to build, such as an app or a web application. Nevertheless, building that app usually ends up costing more than you think, and why spend any money developing something you aren't sure that real customers want? Ryan wouldn't write a single line of code for an idea that hadn't been validated with customers, not even for me.

The only way to be 100% sure that customers want your idea is to get them to pay for it. Chapter 4 will discuss the process of actually getting sales (or pre sales) for your product. Getting sales is the next level of validation after you have validated your idea. Before sales, though, there are a number of things you can do to validate your idea and convince you and your own co founders that your idea is good. First, interviews can be very revealing about your idea and can probably help you refine it more than you might think. Second, surveys can be incredibly effective at getting data about not only your idea, but also about whom your potential customers are and how they think. Finally, a very simple two page website can get you darn near Ryan irrefutable data that your idea is good. All of this would be enough to get Ryan to join my team and help me build an initial product. I know this because I did these three things and after seeing the results, Ryan did ultimately decide to build the AI that powers freebeer.ai. Let's look at each tactic in more detail to see what you might do in case you fail and find out if your idea sucks.

Interviews are fun. They should be, anyway. First of all, you are hopefully working on something in an area you are passionate about. An interview about something you are passionate about is really just an open chat with a like minded person who shares your interests. That makes it fun. In fact, the keys to a good interview are simple: find a good potential customer who shares the same hobby or passion that your idea touches on, and then make the discussion as open ended as possible. Your goal of the interview is to validate that the person has the problem you think that most people with that passion have and that they would be interested in learning more about a potential solution. If you have time, you can even run your solution idea by them to validate that they think it is worth pursuing, but this last point isn't really that important. Validating the problem is enough at this stage. You should try to interview at least three potential customers about the problem. Be sure to listen with an open mind. You may discover that what you thought was a big problem, isn't. This means that your idea probably sucks. However, you are also likely to uncover a larger, deeper problem in that area. At this stage, you may have already failed with your original idea, because it's clearly not the big problem you thought it was. This is why you have to ask open ended questions and get to the real problems in that passion area—it's where the money is, it's what customers want, and it's also the answer to this failure. Your idea sucks, but who cares? You've got a better one now, or at least, you now have a better understanding of the real problems that people face and are willing to pay to fix. If your interview showed that your idea sucks, simply *pivot* to the problem that everyone claims is a bigger problem. Remember that your idea will pivot many times along the way—this is just the first. Revalidate the new idea for the new problem, and then proceed to the next level of validation.

The next level of validation is a quantitative survey. The problem with surveys is that people can lie or give false responses. People will say that they want the service, they will pay for it, and they really need it. Studies have shown, however, that survey "intent to purchase" often does not correlate well at all with actual purchases.[1] Why would that be? Because saying that you would buy something and actually buying it is as different as fire and ice. Sure, you might get fired up about potentially buying something, but when it comes time to actually open your wallet,

---

[1] Lee, Myung-Soo, et al. "The Accuracy of the Conference Board's Buying Plans Index: A Comparison of Judgmental vs. Extrapolation Forecasting Methods." *International Journal of Forecasting*, vol. 13, no. 1, 1997, pp. 127–135.

it suddenly freezes shut. *Hmm. Maybe I don't want to forego beer, movies, or that nice dinner for this, after all.* People just don't do what they say in a survey. So, the obvious question is, why bother writing about it at all? It turns out that surveys are incredibly good at something else: getting to know more about your customer and how they think. The best use of a survey is to ask questions about their demographics, their psychographics, and their opinions about your marketing messages. This kind of survey is really designed to help guide how you talk about your product, more than understanding purchase intent. If you can get a better sense for how your target demographic thinks about your problem and solution, it can inform how you can present these to them. If you can get some insights into the common psychographic attributes (the things people like, for example) of your target audience, it can inform how you will be able to reach them. Finally, a survey is also a chance to show four or five different messages about your product and see which one attracts your target audience best. That's how and why you use a survey, not for purchase intent. I often combine this process with the next validation step in order to save time and effort. This step requires you to find at least 50, and ideally 100 people in the target audience in order to get statistically valid information. While it can be hard to get that many responses, especially for free, there really is no failing this step. You wouldn't abandon your idea based on these results because you aren't really asking go no go types of questions. You wouldn't ask, "Would you pay for this?" because they may lie with their answer. Instead you are asking questions about demographics and maybe even things like, "Which feature is most important to you?"

The final idea validation step is designed to answer, with some degree of certainty, whether people would likely pay. It's this important question that will finally decide if your idea is a good idea or not. It's not as hard a question to answer as it may initially seem, and I will describe in detail how to do it. The simple answer is to build a two page website where the first page is your idea, an offer, for sale, with a price. This first page has a big "Buy Now" button on it, where customers can buy the product. If your business is a service business, you might use a "Start Now" button or something else. Remember, the price must also be on that page because when customers push the button they are showing purchase intent at your actual proposed price. It's that purchase intent that proves if your idea is good or not.

The second page, which you can only get to if you press the buy/start now button simply says, "Sorry, this product/service is not yet available." You should then ask them to sign up to be notified with a one time e mail once it is available. It's often at this step that I introduce the survey mentioned above, since getting those 50 to 100 users to your site is required to get statistically valid data here too.

You might as well survey folks that get this far as well. That's it—with these two pages, you can determine with near certainty whether people are willing to pay for your product. How do you know? You know because they pressed the button, knowing the price, and with intent to buy. This demonstrates a real intent to buy, and it means more than a simple response in a survey. They don't know they can't buy it yet, but they pressed the button anyway. They also know the price, and they pressed the button. This validates your idea, your solution, and (maybe) the price you put there as well.

Validating Your Price

Price is one area in which you can fail. Not how you might think. You can put almost any price in there that you want, and you are not failing because as long as the price is above $0, you are still validating your idea and solution. The way you could fail here is by either putting a $0 price (a free trial, for example), or hesitating to get started because you don't know the price yet. Many startup founders get hung up on the cost of their product or service, how expensive it will be to make, or how unlikely they will be to actually launch, and therefore hesitate to do this early market validation. The problem with this hesitation is that you either end up skipping this critical step and going forward with a non validated idea, or you fail to start altogether. It's better to just put any price in there, make it $10 or $100, or some even multiple, rather than skip this step. I'll discuss pricing in more detail in Chapter 4, but for now, just price it similar to what people are paying today for an alternative; this is competitive pricing, and it is a very commonly used pricing tactic. Do not worry that your solution might cost more, do more, or cost less—just price it similarly and see how your test goes. The key at this step is to get it out there and see if the idea is any good.

Later on, when you are actually taking orders (which will be sooner than you might think), you will need to spend more time on pricing and think harder about it. For example, do you charge for shipping or not? What is your return policy? What is your warranty? Many price related questions will come up. For now, getting to the right order of magnitude (within 10x your final price) is all you need to do. That price will be close enough to determine if your idea is good enough.

Corporate Innovation

It is almost always better to ask forgiveness than to ask for permission. Being an entrepreneur, even inside a big company, means taking risks. One risk that may be worth taking is to go ahead and follow the advice of this chapter and do these interviews, do these surveys, and build this website, all without permission. If you can gather evidence that the idea is a good one, it's going to help you make a great case with your supervisors/management team. If you don't get the evidence, you can pivot to something else (as will be discussed later in this book).

One thing to remember though is that your tests should not contain branding from your company. Using your corporate logos on your test might skew your test results, or worse, get you fired. Until you have an official website and official approval, you should just keep your company name out of it. While you are at it, keep your corporate IT out of it too. Build this site at home on your own time, gather the data, and then present your findings when you go to get official approval and budgets internally. Most likely, nobody will care where or how you got your data, and if they do, you can say truthfully that you got it using an unbranded test page you built on your own time at home.

Building a Two Page Website

You might be thinking, *Well, I don't know how to build a two page website.* Look it up. Seriously, this is not something that you need to hire someone to do; you can do this yourself. This is your first test of self actualization that will reinforce the important self confidence that you will need to have and convey if you are to eventually become successful. There is nothing that you can't do, given time. This attitude will serve you well, and this is your first test. Luckily, building a two page website or landing page is incredibly easy if you know where to start. The place to start is with a free web hosting service with a visual editor, such as Wix or WordPress. Both of these services offer a free trial that is fully hosted, usable, and looks good. Most of my students think that Wix looks better than WordPress. While they may be correct when compared to WordPress' default templates, WordPress is ultimately more customizable and portable for long term use. Either one will work fine for your purpose here. You are not building your final, will last forever, must be perfect website. You are building a two page landing page test that you will likely pivot from or at least rework at some point soon.

To save you some time researching, here are some simple instructions for how to get started with Wix to create your two page landing page test. First, open your browser and go to wix.com. Click "Start Now." It will prompt you to create an account. It may ask you some questions, all of which you want to get through, just pick "other" or "skip" when asked. Start with the Wix Editor (not the ADI). You will be asked to choose a template. Do not worry if this step doesn't appear—just proceed with the template it gave you. If you get the chance to choose a template, pick one of the landing page templates. I like the product landing page (under launch), but any template will work. Choose it and press edit.

The next step is to delete any pictures that are there, because you will add your own. Simply click them and press delete. Add a picture of your own by hitting the plus sign (add) and choose a picture. You probably don't have a product or service yet, so your choices for a picture are to find a free to use picture from a service like Pixabay, or to take a picture of your own. If your product or service is really new, you may have trouble choosing a picture, so just pick a picture of someone smiling. This is always a good picture to have. For the example I created for this book, I decided to sell gamer hats.[2] I found a free to use picture on Pixabay of a young man wearing a hat.

Next you need to add the name of your product to the website. No name? No worries. Make one up. It doesn't matter and will likely change, anyway. Put the name at the top center of the site, replacing any text that is already there. Double clicking text in the Wix editor allows you to edit that text and any subtext below the main text on the page. You'll want to describe your product in as few words as possible. As an example, I just made a site for "Gamer Hats." Mine says, "Hats gamers love because they remind them of gaming."

Next, you need to edit or add a button that says "Buy Now" or "Start Now." You will link this button to the second page we are about to build, the *sorry page*. For now, just make sure that button is high up on the page and can be easily found. To edit the button that may already be there, just double click it. If there is no button, press the *Add* button and click the button to add one.

Next, add a price. Press the *Add* button and add text, a small heading, and drag it in. Next, you need to put this small heading near your "Buy Now" button. I like to position it right beneath the button. Double click that, and input your price. For my hat example, I put "$9.99 each."

Now, you need to make the *sorry page*. At the top of the Wix editor, click the "Pages: Home" button, and then press "+Add Page." Title the page, "Buy," and then add text: "Sorry, this product is not yet available." If you want to get fancy, you can add a contact form here (Wix makes this easy) and include the message, "Sign up for a one time e mail to be notified when this product is available." This way, you are collecting e mails of interested customers as well as tracking how people like your product. You need to go back to the home page now (click "Pages" at the top), and then hook up your Buy button to go to the new page you just made ("Buy"). Just press your button, press the link icon, and "Choose Page,"

---

[2] https://frtet9001.wixsite.com/gamerhats

and then select your new page. You are almost ready to start testing and tracking how many people press the buy button.

Speaking of tracking, there is one final step. Wix unfortunately does not add tracking by default, and this is what you desperately need. You want to know how many people see page 1 and how many people see page 2! The good news is that Wix makes it easy to add web counters to your page. Just go to "+Add," then "More," and scroll down to "Web Stat." Sometimes Wix will put the Web Stat under the "+Add Marketplace App" section so you may have to click around to find it. You want to add Web Stat to the footer so that it will appear on every page and track all your pages. To be safe, I also add the "Wix Hit Counter" to the buy page only (near the bottom, but not in the footer). This way, I get to track the views of the home page, separate from the views of the Buy page. If you know about or want to use the Google analytics tool, you can do that by simply adding custom HTML to your header or footer. Being able to add custom HTML for free, including forms and Javascript, is one of the best things about Wix.

You are ready to launch and ship it! You can mess with it for days or even years, but until and unless you hit "Save and publish," you are not really doing anything. I advise working on it for a few hours and then going live as soon as possible. Now that it's published, you can start getting visitors to your site and seeing how many people are clicking on your Buy button. You will soon discover that getting visitors to your site is quite a bit harder than building it was.

Getting Early Visitors to Your New Website

How are you going to get your website out there? You've built this nice two page website, and you maybe even spent three or four hours making it (don't spend too much more than that!). Now, you have to get people to visit your new website to see how they interact with it. Specifically, you need to get at least 50 potential customers to your new site in order to have valid data about your target customers' interest level. Are they pressing the Buy button? If you have only gotten 10 people to your new page, then you don't really have enough data to say either way. Maybe people pressed the Buy button, maybe they didn't, but you don't have enough data to indicate if it's truly a viable idea. You will need more potential customers to visit your site.

There are three methods of getting these 50 early visitors, and we'll cover them all here. In Chapter 6, we'll talk about truly scaling and getting people to your website, but for now we just need to get a few people there without spending any money. Not every business uses a website, so Chapter 6 will also cover other techniques to get customers to buy your products or services. For now though, these techniques are relevant if you don't want to spend any money or just want some quick feedback to determine if people are willing to pay for your idea or not.

The first technique is to contact your friends and family and ask them to visit the site. This method works great if your friends and family share your passion or hobby. In other words, if your friends or family could actually be potential customers of the product or service you've made, go for it. If they are not really in your target market for the product or service, you'll need to move on to the next technique. If you decide to ask friends and family, choose only those whom you think are potential customers; you want real feedback. Asking personally one to one will get you a better response rate—try Facebook Messenger or text messaging for the best response rates. Be sure to include the link to your new site's home page!

If you ran out of friends and family and do not yet have 50 page views on your website's home page, you are ready for the second technique. This technique involves some searching on the web for a forum, a Facebook group, or a Reddit subreddit (an online message board) that relates to your passion or hobby that can connect to your product or service. You can simply post the link into that web forum, group, or subreddit, and ask people to give you feedback on your new site. In the case that moderators delete your post, try reaching out with direct messages to users who post in that forum, group, or subreddit. Using online forums and groups like this works incredibly well and often gets my students many hundreds of visits from potential customers. Aren't you glad you asked people to input their e mail addresses on that "Sorry" page? All those visitors may someday become customers and having their e mail will help you reach back out again when you are ready to start shipping your product or service for real.

If forms and groups fail, then you may need to pay for some advertising—consider reading Chapter 6 as a guide. Your one last hope to get some free traffic to your website is the old fashioned way. Print out some fliers with a link to your website and a call to action such as, "Please check out this startup's new product." Then, go to a conference or an area where a lot of potential customers congregate, and hand out these fliers. Bring at least 100 fliers, and don't quit until you've handed them all out. For example, I would go to my local gaming stores and the mall and hand out fliers near GameStop. If you are asked to leave or to stop loitering, leave and go somewhere else. That being said, I like to tell budding entrepreneurs, "If you are not getting arrested or at least getting threatened to have the cops called, you aren't trying hard enough." I follow this up quickly with advice that as long as you follow the instructions any police officers give you, you will probably not get into any real trouble.

If all else fails, head to Chapter 6 and find out how to pay Facebook $25 to drive 50 visitors to your website. That's a small investment to find out if your idea is any good or not.

Quantifying Success: Do Customers Like Your Idea?

It's time to evaluate your success or failure. If you failed, do not worry—you are actually well on your way to success. If you succeeded, great, press on! Now the hard part begins: making money. How would you know if you failed or not?

The table presented at the end of this chapter is your tool to quantifiably prove if your idea is good or not, and whether you should proceed to building something that people can buy (the focus of Chapter 4). The success is related to the conversion rate of the people who press your Buy button. If the price is fairly high, then your conversion rate, as defined by your unique Buy page visits divided by your unique home page visits, can be lower than if your price is low. The higher the price, the more the purchase becomes a considered purchase. A considered purchase is one that a customer has to think more about and cannot make an impulse buy decision. A higher price means more things to consider, such as: *Is it worth it? Will my spouse approve? Do I really need this?* I believe a 2% conversion rate (or about 1 in 50) is adequate for a product that is a considered purchase. If your product has a low price (below $50), then it is more of an impulse purchase, and you should expect a 4% or higher conversion rate (about 2 in 50).

So, what do you do if your product had less than a 2% or 4% conversion rate? What if nobody clicked your Buy button? Something about your idea, the presentation of your idea or your price was not quite right. It's time to pivot. Remember, the whole point of this book is navigating your way to startup success. Guess what, you had a failure—great job, you now have information to help you navigate to success! So, how do you pivot?

First, reconsider your initial interviews. Were all your interviews glowing and perfect? If not, then you probably should have pivoted before you built your web page. Think hard about what your interviewers said, and see if you can glean an idea for a small pivot based on their initial responses. Not inspired? It's probably time for a few more interviews with potential customers to learn why they didn't (or wouldn't) press the Buy button. Maybe it's the price. It could also be how your picture looks, how you describe your product, how your site looks, or even just bad luck. Your goal now is to create a new hypothesis and a new product idea, and to modify your site accordingly to re test the new changes. It doesn't necessarily mean giving up on your idea, although a completely new idea is also a valid pivot. It does mean that you have to make a new two page site (or change your current one) and get 50 more people to come to the new site. Your second and third attempts at idea validation, however, are quite likely to succeed, because you learned from your first attempt! That's what it means to navigate toward success. Learn from the prior iteration and do it better the next time.

Degrees of Pivots

Going forward, this book will discuss pivots throughout each chapter. The whole idea of navigating your way to success is to fail, learn, and then pivot. The only way to truly fail and not eventually find success is to give up. Pivoting is a far better option than giving up. By pivoting, you are applying what you learned and getting continually better, then ultimately moving toward startup success. Beginning a startup is easy—heck, it's only the first three chapters of this book. Succeeding, on the other hand, is going to take a lot of hard work, failing, learning, and pivoting.

What is a pivot exactly? Well, it can be many things. The main idea is that it's a change, or something done differently in order to get better results. You avoid unnecessary spending of time and money on ideas that don't work by learning from what didn't work and adjusting as you go. If you can't get 50 people to visit your site as a first step, then you should really focus on improving your skills and messaging for attracting visitors. Trying a different tactic to get people to come to your website is an example of a pivot. If you did get 50 and they didn't click Buy Now, then you can use that fact and come up with a pivot idea.

A pivot can be as small as changing the color of a button, changing a tagline or headline, or even just a tiny variation of color or text in an advertisement. In a small change like this, you are hoping for slightly better results, such as more clicks on the new color of your button, more sales with your new tagline, or a higher click through rate on your advertisement.

A pivot can also be as significant as a completely new problem, solution, or even a different market altogether. This pivot does not mean that you had a big failure, but it indicates that you want to try something radically different. You may be choosing a big pivot over a small one because you have collected data or some piece of quantitative or qualitative information, perhaps from an ad test or an interview that has informed this change.

One way to think about a big pivot compared to a small pivot is to think of pivoting as a scale. A pivot can exist anywhere on the scale from small to large. Figure 3.1 depicts this scale and a demarcation between a large and a small pivot. If you are changing anything more substantial than price, then I consider it a large pivot. If you are changing price or anything else less substantial (color, shipping options, etc.), then I consider the pivot to be small. Why bother with these differentiations? Because a small pivot is really just an experiment or a quick hypothesis you can test, and you can quickly revert back if it fails. A larger pivot is usually something you need to stick with for a while, and give time and a few small pivots to see if it will work. For example, if you try a big pivot and it fails, should you immediately go back to the old idea that wasn't working in the first place? No. You should try a series of small pivots (such as color, tagline, price, etc.) to see if you can improve the new idea based on your big pivot. In contrast, if your small pivot fails, reverting back is usually the best response. You can also try something else—maybe even a big pivot.

In addition to the distinction of small versus big pivots, another way to look at pivots is by basing them on their type. There are many types of pivots, some of which will be discussed in detail in later chapters. The list I've compiled in Table 3.1 is based on my own experience and an excellent article from Forbes on the topic.[3] The idea of the pivot has become so mainstream that even Forbes is writing about it. Pivoting is now standard practice in entrepreneurship.

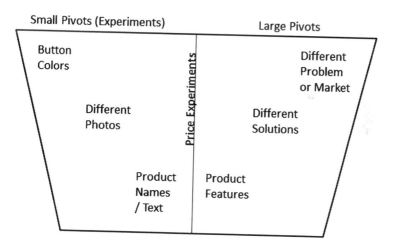

Figure 3.1: Scale of Pivots

---

[3] http://www.forbes.com/sites/martinzwilling/2011/09/16/top-10-ways-entrepreneurs-pivot-a-lean-startup

Table 3.1: Types of Pivots

Type	Description
Marketing	Small tests to attract more potential customers
Sales	Small tests to convert more potential customers into paying customers
Zoom in	Single feature becomes the whole product (cut back)
Zoom out	Product gets more features based on customer feedback
Customer Segment	Target a different customer group with your solution
Customer Need	Solve a different problem that customers revealed to you
Platform	Change from app to a platform or vice versa
Business Model	High margin, low volume to low margin, or high volume
Sales Channel	From online to offline, or direct to indirect
Growth Model	Viral, Paid, Sticky (Switching Costs), Organic
Technology	Cheaper, faster, or better. Leap frog or new science
Product	Same problem and market, but different solution
Pricing	Higher, lower, or a one time vs. annual/monthly subscription

The Story of Ordoro

Ordoro was founded in 2010 at the University of Texas at Austin. Co founders Jagath Narayan and Naruby Shlenker thought they had found a problem worth solving. Their idea was simple: they wanted to help print shipping labels for high volume eBay sellers and online retailers. Jagath was selling products on eBay himself and knew the frustration of dealing with all of these shipping labels and tracking numbers. As far as ideas go, it was a good starting point: the idea included something they knew (selling online), an identified problem (shipping labels), and a solution that would fix it (automating the shipping label process). The only problem was that it was an idea that customers weren't willing to pay for, they just didn't know it yet.

They competed in the UT Austin business plan competition (previously called UT Moot Corp, now called the Texas Venture Labs Investment Competition), and they got the first hint that their idea wasn't great when the judges (who are investors) promoted them to the finals, but ultimately didn't award them the top prize. Something was missing: customer traction and validation. Ordoro hadn't proven that real customers wanted the product yet, and that was something they desperately needed to do to convince the judges that their idea was a good one.

Fortunately, Austin, Texas has a great environment for startups, and Ordoro joined the Austin Technology Incubator (also loosely related to UT, but available to the entire Austin community). There, they started the real process of idea validation. They began with customer interviews, and quickly learned that they badly needed a pivot!

"I remember talking to these online merchants and hearing them say, 'We could care less about optimizing our inventory because what is really painful to us is getting orders out the door quickly and just keeping track of how much inventory we have on hand'" Naruby said about this early market validation.

Ordoro went on to pivot quickly to a full inventory management Software as a Service (SaaS) platform, offering not just inventory synchronization, but also order management and shipping label creation in one easy to use, easy to set up software solution.

This was just the first of many pivots the company had made and continues to make as they learn more about what their customers want and don't want.

"We are now avid validators. We try to validate everything we build into the software now. Every button, every feature all are validated by customers as being superior or necessary to the existing solution," says Naruby. "Rapid iteration and being willing to kill off branches of ideas that don't pan out have been the keys to our growth and success with customers."

They certainly have been successful! Since their founding, Ordoro has now grown to more than 1,000 customers, more than 15 employees, and secured more than $5,000,000 in investment. More recently, the company has begun generating profits, and that means an exit is potentially just around the corner.

It all started with customer interviews, launching, and pivoting their way to success. If they had built what they thought customers wanted before their interviews, Ordoro might not be where it is today: poised for a successful exit.

Conclusion

A good idea is one for which you have data or scientific evidence confirming that customers want to pay for it. The idea should solve a real problem, be based on something you love (or at least like), and be a complete solution. In order to gather enough data to test if your idea is good, you have to get it out there. You should collect data to support your hypothesis that this is a good idea. The best data to support your hypothesis is actual sales results. Since it may be a bit early to get real sales (see next chapter), then the next best thing is purchase intent.

You can determine purchase intent by making a simple website, or even by doing customer interviews or surveys.

It is likely, a good thing even, that you will determine that your idea is not good enough. Hopefully you also get some hint of what might work better. That hint and your failure should inform you as to what you should pivot to and try next. Learning and pivoting is the key to navigating to success. As a startup, your ability to rapidly react and pivot is one of your key advantages over larger incumbent companies. Pivoting during the ideation and validation phases is cheap and easy. Find that perfect combination of problem, solution, and market that motivates customers to get you above a 4% conversion rate on your Buy Now page. Use the tool provided in Table 3.2 below to help you determine if your conversion rates are high enough based on your minimum of 50 visitors on your website. When you start seeing people clicking on that Buy button, it's a great feeling of success. Use that feeling to propel you to the next step.

You want an idea so good that people are even willing to sign up with their e mail to be notified. If you have to pivot at a later stage, you had better hope it's a small one. Only during this idea validation phase can you pivot to completely new ideas, problems, and markets for very little cost. Later on, it becomes even more expensive both financially and emotionally to do big pivots, even when they are certainly necessary. If you try that big pivot now and listen to what your prospective customers are saying, it can save you later on when failure is more painful and costly.

Table 3.2: Idea Validation Tool

Item	Value
# of Unique Visitors to Your Home Page	A
# of Unique Visitors to Your "Sorry/Buy" Page	B
Calculated Conversion Rate (CVR) ("Sorry/Buy" Page #) / (Home Page #)	B / A = CVR
Success/Failure Condition Depends on Considered Price or Not[4]	If your Product Price is $50+, success = above 2% CVR If your Product Price is $49 or below, success = above 4% CVR

---

[4] http://nelsonschmidt.com/expertise/considered-purchase-marketing

Chapter 4
Failing to Ship—Again, what's stopping you?

To ship is simply to offer your product or service in such a way so that customers can actually pay you. The difference between validating your idea and actually shipping may be smaller than you think. In the last chapter, we discussed ways to validate or test whether your idea is a good one. We did this with quantifiable methods that can prove up to 90 to 95% of the way that your idea is good. We did not get to 100%. To be 100% sure that your idea is good, you have to actually collect money from a customer. Real dollars in your pocket prove that your idea is good and viable. Your idea may not become as big as you want (see Chapter 6), but it is definitely viable. You know this because you already got paid.

That is the difference between validating your idea and shipping. In shipping, you got paid. Ironically, as you will learn later in this chapter, sometimes shipping doesn't really mean actually shipping the product. It does mean getting paid for it, though.

The problem or failure that so many entrepreneurs experience here is that they never ship. They never open their hand and ask for money. Until you've asked for money from real customers, you have not shipped. Failing to ship, especially when you know your idea is good, is more common than you might think. There are many reasons why people never ship, but the biggest one is that they think it will take an investment to get to a shippable state. This thinking is backwards. In reality, you have to ship and prove customers' willingness to pay before most investors will consider investing. Catch 22? Read on and learn how to break this cycle.

The Story of the SmartPrompt Pan

We thought we had a good idea. We thought our idea was flawless. Our company, Key Ingredient, had amassed over 2 million recipes through user generated recipe sharing. We regularly got over 4 million page views per month on our recipe website. We were making money with advertising and product sales based on that heavy web traffic. So, of course, coming out with our own line of "smart products" was a good idea. We had a ready made audience (our site visitors), a working store (our e commerce website), and tons of recipes to use with the product. What could go wrong?

This was my third company, and the first one I didn't even start. I was hired as CEO to figure out the monetization of our traffic, and the idea to make and sell

DOI 10.1515/9781501507083-004

our own smart kitchen products was part of my grand plan. The SmartPrompt Pan was going to be just one of a line of products built that would combine products with our website and leverage our strength (our 2 million recipes).

How was it smart, you might ask? Well, we did some surveys to figure out what people wanted in a smart pan. People wanted it to display the temperature (of course) and indicate when to flip or add ingredients (a smart timer). People wanted it to display the recipe and tell them if the food was burning. People wanted the pan to know if it was boiling or not and for how long, as well as be dishwasher safe and have at least 1 year battery life. In short, people wanted it to have everything. There wasn't a single feature that our surveys found that potential customers didn't want. This is the problem with surveys—even the best survey design cannot easily solve this. How do you know what not to add to your product? That is the key question, after all. If you have to add everything, it will take a long time to build it, and you may not have that time (or money). So, what did we add? Well, everything, which nearly caused us to completely fail at shipping anything.

Our plan was simple: to get a prototype built in house as fast as we could, and then run a Kickstarter or Indiegogo campaign to get the presales to fund the production development. Our mistake was adding too many features, taking too much time, and almost failing to ship altogether. Ryan (yes, the same Ryan from the last chapter) was my CTO and he was tasked with actually building this behemoth. He started out simple enough, a temperature sensor, a small Raspberry Pi, and an old cellphone.[1] He built a little web page view and connected the cellphone's browser to the Pi. Suddenly you could see temperature of the pan in a neat little display. He took the extra step of getting an old black plastic box, sticking the phone in there, and taping it to the pan he bought at Walmart. Smart pan: done... Right? Wrong. His boss (me), in his infinite wisdom, wanted more, and that's where we got into trouble. We should have shipped right then and there, and we should have launched our Indiegogo with just those two features. We would have saved a ton of money and heartache, and we would have gotten to the right answer a lot faster. We didn't. We waited.

The first problem we had with waiting is that someone beat us to the punch. Three months after Ryan had his working demo, another company launched their own smart pan. All theirs did was display the temperature of the pan. Hell, they didn't even have a display built into the pan; you had to use your cellphone. That's so 2010. The fact is we were late. It had been three months since Ryan's

---

[1] https://www.raspberrypi.org

demo, and we hadn't launched anything yet. Why? Well, because Ryan was doing what I asked: trying to get all the features done. Here is a list of things he was trying to prepare *before* we launched our Indiegogo campaign:

1. Build a production looking non functional prototype (plastics design).
2. Get the working unit to work on battery power.
3. Get a companion device (a smart probe) working.
4. Get the software to look awesome and work well (design & coding).
5. Have the ability to click and send a recipe to the pan, and have the recipe show up on the pan's display.
6. Have the ability to detect times and temperatures in the recipe and program step by step timers (Artificial Intelligence).
7. Figure out how to make the whole product dishwasher safe.
8. Figure out how to actually get the pan and all parts manufactured.
9. Get a smoke sensor working for burning detection.
10. Get a motion sensor working for boiling detection.
11. Figure out how to do all this at a cost below the set price for the product ($149).

Okay, before you freak out about how ridiculous I was being, please bear in mind that we were trying to build what customers wanted. Our surveys told us the price and the list of features (prioritized). Our interviews told us that people wanted this idea and they liked it. We were pretty darned confident this would work, so why not invest more time and money into it?

The reason not to invest is that we were running out of money, and we were already too late. Ryan and his team actually were able to get all 11 of the items above completed in the next three months. It was really amazing—we were able to bring in a chef to actually cook with the device, live, for a demo video. My marketing team and I used the non functional prototype to make a kickass Indiegogo campaign video. We built a great landing page and put a lot of effort into the look of everything. Finally, six months after Ryan's first working prototype, we were ready to launch. We hired a PR agency, spent money on ads, and heavily marketed to our 4,000,000 visitors.

In short, we made every mistake in the book.

If you read the last chapter, you already know the first mistake we made. Where was our two page website with the "Buy Now" button and the "Sorry" page? We failed to fully validate our idea. We were going off of our big survey results to validate the idea. Sure, people would be willing to pay $149 for a product that did all those things, or so they said. But did they click any actual button trying to buy it? No. We never made that mini site. We failed there.

Our second mistake was adding too many features. We needed to get to the core of our product faster; what was the essential part? I think it was recipes, timer, and temperature. We could have finished all that much faster if we'd just focused on that. We didn't. We wanted to add all the features we dreamed up, partly because the survey said everyone wanted everything. See, survey's lie. We should have just used the surveys to learn about how our customers liked to say things, not if they wanted things. Surveys say customers always want all the things.

Third, we overspent, and I mean way overspent, on something that we had no idea whether it would actually sell or not. We hadn't sold one, and we'd already laid out $8,000 for PR, $10,000 in video expenses, and much more than that building all our marketing and website materials. Our total investment was probably well above $200,000. And did we know if it would sell even one unit? Nope.

So, how many did we sell? About 10—most of which were to friends or family, whom I think took pity on us. Why did we sell so few? I mean, we even ran ads on Facebook and of course our own site. We blasted an e mail to 2,000,000 of our users. We worked hard to get the word out, and yet we sold virtually nothing. Wow, what a failure. It was so tempting to give up at this point. As you may have guessed, we didn't. We persevered, and tried to get as much learning out of this as we could.

We asked our PR agents to send us a "What did the press say" report. We looked at the click through patterns of our ads and what comments people were making. We looked at forum discussions and e mail inquiries. We even ran another survey to see what people didn't like. There were three points that we learned fairly quickly. The thing I want to stress here is that we probably could have learned these points if we had just launched back when Ryan had his first prototype. Here is what we learned:

1. Nobody wanted our crappy looking pan that looked like it came from a discount store. People already have pans in their house and didn't want a smart pan at all.
2. Our price was too high. $149 was in the considered purchase range, and just too high for an impulse buy or as a cool little gift for the chef in their life.
3. Nobody liked the idea of the display actually built into the pan's handle. As it turns out, it being 2015, people wanted to use the phone they already have in their hand in the kitchen for this.

This story does end on a positive. We took this feedback and quickly pivoted the Indiegogo towards our other idea, the SmartPrompt Probe. The probe was only $50, made for a cool gift, and could attach to any pot or pan. We even ran some two page website tests with this idea to get validation on how it should look and function. It was a much simpler product in so many ways, and when all was said and done, we sold hundreds of them. Not thousands, as we had hoped, but selling hundreds was still a success. I am confident that if we had started out with a small test, as in Chapter 3, and then launched a smaller product faster, we would have gotten here faster and had more time to get well beyond. Our hundreds of sales was great validation, and the feedback we got from early users was positive and informative as to how to make it even better. Key Ingredient had recently been acquired by Groupe SEB (a French cookware company) and this project was an attempt at corporate innovation inside our now skunkworks operation. The Groupe SEB management, a $4 Billion Euro company, didn't agree. To them, 100 sales was a pittance and they wanted bigger results. Corporate innovation can be very challenging at this stage because big corporations are usually used to big financial results, not small ones where we intend to keep on pivoting until we get it just right. Groupe SEB eventually pulled the plug on the project. Fortunately, the project didn't get canceled until after we shipped out all 100 those pre orders. The team and I are quite proud of that.

I still have and use my SmartPrompt Probe almost every week. My wife loves it too.

Minimum Viable Product

My definition of *minimum viable product* (MVP) is a product or service that has the fewest features and least amount of polish needed for customers to want to buy it and that you could actually ship. Some other authors, most notably Eric Ries, believe an MVP can be viable even if its only job is to collect data or test pricing. I prefer to call that a *minimum buyable product* (MBP) because although it may be buyable (and someone may actually buy it), it's not viable because you are not yet able to truly ship it to a customer.

"The minimum viable product is that version of a new product which allows a team to collect the maximum amount of validated learning about customers with the least effort." —Eric Ries, Startup Lessons Learned.[2]

If you take Eric's definition, then the market validation you did in Chapter 3 is actually an MVP of your product or service. I don't think it's far enough, though, and that concept hides a critical point. Until and unless you are actually accepting money from customers, you have not yet shipped. You are only toying with the idea.

---

[2] http://www.startuplessonslearned.com/2009/08/minimum-viable-product-guide.html

A lot of people may be confused as to what an MVP truly is. The confusion stems from the word *viable*. To be viable, it means that someone somewhere must be willing to pay for it. The problem with this definition is that until you actually ship it, you don't know if anyone is willing to pay for it or not. The other problem with the word viable is that it sort of implies that it will meet your financial goals. That's not at all the most likely case. Much more likely is that either nobody will buy it or that it will be a trickle of sales. This is actually a normal and good thing, not a bad thing. You have to fail in order to succeed—at least, that's the point of this book.

Because of the flawed thinking that your product must be a huge success right out of the gate or else it wasn't viable, people often delay the decision to launch until they think everything is perfect and ready. We all—and you know from the story above that I am included—feel the pressure to hesitate to launch and try to make sure everything is perfect. Remember, the first launch of a product doesn't have to be good enough; it just has to get you data toward what will eventually be good enough.

This is why I like MBP better. Buy ability is simple: Can someone pay or not? I'm not saying that they will pay for it, but could they? Can a customer type in their credit card number and give you money, or not? Launching, shipping, and getting past this first step is about making it possible for people to pay you. There are lots of ways to do that, but for many people, they are holding back. They either don't know how or are afraid to ship.

There are a lot of reasons you may not have shipped, and this chapter will cover many of them. Regardless of the reason, however, if you haven't shipped yet, you are failing. To get over the failure, just ship it already.

What's stopping you from shipping and accepting money from customers?

Reason Number One: Being Beholden

The first reason that people don't ship, or even try to ship an MBP or MVP is that they are afraid of being beholden. You see, once you've accepted money for a preorder, you are beholden to actually ship them a product. That's scary. But I am here to tell you there is nothing to fear. You can always refund the money. You can always declare bankruptcy; you can always say you are sorry, things happen. 9% of Kickstarter projects fail to ship anything.[3] This doesn't include the

---

[3] https://www.kickstarter.com/fulfillment

projects that ship only partial units, messed up or non functional products, or only ship the t shirts. Nearly half of all Kickstarter campaigns also do not ship on time, based on their estimates. In fact, if you are really worried about being beholden, you should really consider doing your MBP preorder on Kickstarter or Indiegogo. These platforms include the legal terms of service that limit your legal exposure if you fail to ship. Where you can, and some have, get into trouble is if you use the proceeds of the Kickstarter on something other than trying to ship. You wouldn't do that, though—you want to ship! You want to ship at least an MVP, and later on in this chapter, I will share with you five techniques you can use to ship an MVP for cheap. That said, your feeling of being beholden is still true even in a Kickstarter or Indiegogo campaign. You know these are real customers who gave you real money, and you really do want to please them.

Being beholden is not just for preorders and Kickstarter projects, however. You are also beholden to customers to whom you ship an MVP. You are beholden for potential problems (customer service), potential returns, and potential lawsuits. I will discuss legal issues later in this chapter, but for now, understand that shipping a product can be scary. It makes you beholden to please your customer, if only because you will want to. What happens when your product breaks or fails to satisfy? While it may seem like your death knell, if handled correctly, it could actually be your saving grace.

If a customer gets an MVP and is not satisfied, it's the perfect opportunity to open a dialogue about what the customer liked and didn't like. Instead of just automatically accepting a return, ask to arrange a phone call with the person so that you can learn more about their problem. What you may think is a real problem could just be a personal issue, like they didn't have as much money in their bank account as they thought and needed to return it in order to pay rent. Alternatively, and more commonly, their issue is a user error or a trivial fix, and they would settle for a repair. You may find out they actually love it, but it broke in some way. That learning, that key insight from a real user, is exactly the point of an MVP, after all. The key is to take the time and simply ask the customer to speak with you in more detail about their problem. Don't make it optional. Say, "We'll gladly accept your return, but we really do need to know more about your issue before we can issue you a return authorization. Can we set up a time to call you to discuss the issue at your convenience?" Most customers, especially those who know they are buying from a startup, will understand. Sometimes, just making that call, being nice and having that open discussion, and really wanting their feedback, will lead to the customer accepting a repair or even canceling their return request. In exchange, you got the data you need to make your product better. That's worth a few returns.

Worried about your total exposure? Limit your risk by only allowing 10 or 100 units to be sold. Go out of stock after that and accept preorders again. This way, in case all 10 or 100 of your products are bad and get returned, you have limited your financial exposure to just 10 or 100 early adopters. Early adopters of products and services are more forgiving of flaws anyways, so your risk is already somewhat mitigated. Remember, being an entrepreneur is about taking risk, and if you want to truly do this, you have to get over your fears. The fact is that you are beholden to customers who preorder, and you should think about how you will refund them if needed. You are beholden to customers you ship to, and you need to think about your return process and your total exposure. You can limit your warranty to as low as 30 days in most states, but that won't limit your desire to please customers. Being beholden is a good thing: It challenges you to make your product great, make your customer service experience great, and overall, to grow into the huge success that I believe you can and will be.

Corporate Innovation

One of the biggest challenges with doing corporate innovation is that the concept of a small launch is almost inconceivable. Big companies are setup for scale, and so are experts at big volume production and big volume sales. This means that corporate management may want to take your validated idea and then invest for a year or more to get it into volume production and an oversized launch, all before you've sold even one product (or serviced one customer).

If your organization works like this, you may have to grin and bear it. You've already gotten something amazing accomplished even by getting the company to do this innovative launch. In fact, you did it so well that they are ready to invest big. Well done.

That said, understand, your launch is still at risk. Until you actually have dollars and feedback from real customers, you can't really predict results. What's worse is that you also don't get insights into how to take your early product, make small pivots and improvements, and eventually make it big. You are rolling all your dice on that one big shot. That is not the entrepreneurial way.

To help mitigate this risk, one thing you could try is to agree to the big launch, but plan a series of *marketing studies* along the way. These marketing studies are actually just mini releases of work in progress products at various stages to real customers (hopefully paying ones). It's a slightly different vernacular, but the feedback and pivot process results can be the same.

Reason Number Two: Not Good Enough

The second reason that people don't ship, or even try to ship an MBP or MVP is that they are afraid that their product or service is not good enough. They think that they have to add more features, more polish, make the user interface (UI) look amazing, and make everything work flawlessly before they can ship. This can be an even bigger problem for companies that are building new and amazing technology or who are working as corporate innovators inside a bigger organization. They believe they have to actually get the technology fully working in order to ship it. They are wrong.

Remember, buy ability means that customers are able to pay you. You do not need a working technology in order to do that. You don't even need a prototype, an actual product, or anything at all. All you need is the ability to accept payment somehow. Building that is actually easy and cheap, as you'll see in the next section.

What does this concept imply? Well, first it implies that you don't need investment to start asking for payment. While it may still take investment dollars to build that new enterprise software app, medical device, or microchip technology, you don't need that investment to launch your MBP. In fact, as we will discuss in Chapter 7, getting financing is often only possible if you do have an MBP and have proven that customers are willing to pay.

It also implies that customers themselves may be able to fund some or all of your development. What I am saying is that an MBP is opening your hand and letting customers put money into it. What happens if they do? Well, you have some money you can use to build the product. This is why platforms like Indiegogo and Kickstarter are doing so well; they are proof customers want the latest and greatest and that they are willing to pay for it!

So, what is good enough? I think it is helpful to break down the MBP from the MVP and answer this question.

The MBP is good enough if it strongly conveys your problem, and has enough detail about your complete solution such that a customer understands what they will eventually receive if they pay you. It must also have a price and some method of payment. This is why I like crowdfunding platforms—they allow you to list out your problem and solution in enough detail that you can put a price on the various levels of solution. I also like that they allow different *rewards* for different levels of pay, as well as stretch goals. These things allow you to potentially offer more features, but also make you focus on the minimum feature: the minimum buyable product.

An MBP does not have to use a crowdfunding platform. It can be a *preorder website* or even a "Buy Now" website such as the one we made in the last chapter. All you have to do is link that "Buy Now" button to a real payment solution (these details will be discussed next). Your MBP could also be a slide deck or even just a verbal sales pitch. The key to either of these is that you are describing the complete solution, the price, and are asking for money that day. Not money tomorrow, once it is ready, but that day. Here's a closing script of a verbal sales pitch to illustrate my point:

"Our product isn't quite ready yet, but we are taking preorders today to line up which customers will get our first production run. Would you like to place an order today?"

Here's another version:

"We are looking to establish our launch partners, and are asking for a 25% payment with the remainder to be paid upon delivery. We expect to deliver by the end of the year. Do you want to put down $25,000 to hold your place at the top of our launch partners?"

Do you see how you asked for money? It didn't even have to be the full price. Even a 25% pre payment on a $100,000 sale is a 100% signal that you have an MBP. It's buyable.

So, how is an MVP different than an MBP in terms of the actual *good enough* metric? Well, *good enough* is probably less than you might think. Good enough for an MVP means that the viability of the product has also been established. A viable product is one that people can buy, so it is an MBP, but even more. It needs to have all the same capabilities as an MBP, but it should also be ready to ship in some state, right now. An MVP cannot be just a preorder, under my redefinition of the term. An MVP needs to be a product or service that is ready to be immediately delivered (or served). As you'll see later in this chapter, there are a lot of ways to actually build an MVP quickly. For now, understand that the word *minimum* has an important meaning here—it *means* minimum. Not every feature, not every nuance, not final packaging, maybe not any packaging. Some people argue that it should *look good* regarding the user interface (UI). I disagree. I think it should *look good enough*. That is to say, it is usable and doesn't make you want to puke. That's a pretty low standard. Whether you are selling software, hardware, or a service, the MVP is simply the minimum you have to put together in the fastest possible way to have something you can actually ship to a real customer.

How do the MBP and MVP relate? The answer is simple. Start with the MBP, ship that. If you get preorders, or at least very strong interest, go ahead and proceed with the MVP as fast as you can and ship that to customers. If you don't get any preorders during the MBP stage, I challenge you to think hard about this question: Since you know your MBP failed, do you really expect your MVP to succeed? Or should you perhaps pivot?

Answering this question—heck, even just asking it—means you are getting it. You are becoming a true entrepreneur and you are well on your way to navigating towards success.

Reason Number Three: Not Knowing How

I want to start this section with a brief story. At UT Austin McCombs School of Business, I started a new entrepreneurship class called Healthcare Technology Commercialization Practicum. This class was designed to identify budding healthcare technologies at UT Austin and to help their inventors create business plans for launching these technologies into the marketplace. One of these technologies could potentially end all long term effects of traumatic brain injury (TBI). In other words, cognition loss, motor loss, memory loss, and worse would be a thing of the past. With this simple pill, getting a concussion could potentially be a minor injury in the future. There is only one problem: even the inventor isn't sure that it will work. In any healthcare technology, there is a lot of technical validation that has to happen before you can even consider coming to market. I am not just talking about the FDA, which ensures that your product does no harm. I also mean in hard science, where you have to prove your technology not only works, but also works with human subjects and to the level you suggest. Even the dosage has to be micro optimized in a controlled study. It's a massive hurdle, and one that, to my students, seemed impossible to overcome.

Yet, every day, scientists and companies do overcome these hurdles. It takes time and money, often in the form of grants, but these obstacles are surmountable. At the core of the TBI drug, there is already hard science that is promising. The question is how do they build an MBP? It's a question I asked my graduate students, and they struggled to answer it. In fact, they couldn't.

This story demonstrates that building an MBP, let alone an MVP, can be hard work. Most people have no idea how to do this. Whether it be technical skill or business knowledge, building an MBP or MVP can be difficult.

When my students read this, they will finally have the answer. The TBI drug company, which, sadly, may never be formed, could have built an MBP and an MVP within the semester if they had followed this advice. Here's how they (and you) could do it.

To build an MBP is actually fairly simple. Remember, the requirements are to describe the problem, describe your solution, and open your hand for money. How would that work for the TBI drug company? Very similar to how it would work for you.

All you have to do is create that two page website described in the last chapter. The home page or first page of that website should describe the problem: cognitive loss after a traumatic brain injury. The home page should then list a price. For a new drug still in development, it is not only hard to know what your production costs might be, but it is actually illegal to sell it (FDA regulation). But who said anything about costs? And who said you have to sell your product? For an

MBP, you can sell something else—something that isn't yet your product. For example, you could sell an existing product, such as ice packs, and you could say this: "100% of all profits from the sale of these ice packs will go toward further development of this drug." Then mark up your ice packs, which you can get from Amazon or Costco, by 100%. You could also just as easily ask for donations. You don't even have to be a charity. "We are asking for non tax exempt donations of a minimum of $100, all of which will be used for the development of this drug." This is just the tip of the MBP ideas. You could also make a presentation and pitch it to corporations for grants. You could make a GoFundMe account and ask for donations there. The possibilities are endless as long as you focus on opening up your hand to let people put money into it. You'll be surprised when they do!

Let's get technical for a minute. For those readers who think they are not skilled enough to build a website that can accept payment, let me help you out. You can do it. Do some online research. Or just read the next paragraph!

To create a button that accepts payment is far easier than you might imagine. The first step is to create a PayPal account. If you already have one, it's probably a personal account. For lots of legal and tax reasons (all discussed in later chapters), I suggest creating a new PayPal account just for business purposes. Start with a fresh Gmail account and set up your new PayPal account as a free business "payments standard" account.[4] It just takes a few clicks and you'll have the new business account. There are no wrong answers to the sign up process, and you can change your company type from sole proprietorship to something else later. Next, you need to go into your PayPal account and select "tools" and then "all tools" from the top menu. If only one tool shows up, you have to press "next" to see all the tools. You want to use the tool called PayPal buttons. Open that tool and make a new button for each product or price you want to offer. Once again, there is no wrong answer—just be sure to input your price. Once you get to the code section of your new button, click on the e mail tab. This has a link in it that you will use on your website. Next, you need to copy the link inside the e mail tab and connect it to the "Buy Now" (or similarly named) button of your website. Instead of that button going to the "Sorry" page, you are now taking orders and accepting payment. Yes, it really is that easy. If you have trouble with any of this, I've even created a little video for my students that can walk you through this step by step.[5] Welcome to your new MBP!

---

[4] https://www.paypal.com/us/webapps/mpp/product-selection
[5] https://youtu.be/E9-rHLqmkr0

Okay, you got your MBP, some customers paid you, and now you want to ship them something. I advise that you do try to ship them your MVP. Even if you intend to ship them a more complete solution later, you should ship them the MVP as soon as you can. So, how do you build an MVP? There are lots of ways, many of which will be discussed next.

MVP Requirements

In addition to being something you could actually ship to customers, there are three critical elements an MVP needs to have. First, it needs to have a built in measurement capability. In other words, you will need some way to capture whether or not your customers like and use your product and what they would like changed. For software, just install Google Analytics. Google Analytics can be installed into a website with a simple copy and paste.[6] Google Analytics can also be installed into any software application, be it server application, desktop application, mobile app, or even embedded applications through their simple API.[7] For hardware and services, it can be challenging to think of this step, because, well... it's hard. Don't skip it. Even if you just print out little cards with a customer satisfaction survey URL that you can build for free in Google Forms, you need to do it.[8] This feedback will be critical to understanding not just what customers are saying they like about your product, but also what users' actual usage patterns are.

Second, all MVPs need to be designed with iteration in mind. Instead of shortcutting as fast as you can to the shippable product, take the extra one or two hours it takes to document the process you used to build it. While you are building it, identify tools and systems that you are using and keep good records. This will allow you to eventually expand operations and hire someone else to build more units, but also allow you to think about doing each step better in the future. Also, when you do get that feedback from real users about your MVP, you can make small changes to your overall process rather than starting from scratch. In software, this also means building in modularity to your code. In hardware, modularity is also important. With luck, this will not be your last production run, nor

---

[6] https://support.google.com/analytics/answer/1008080?hl=en
[7] https://support.google.com/analytics/answer/6317479
[8] https://gsuite.google.com/learning-center/products/forms/get-started

will it be the final form of your product. Document what you do now so that you can reuse it later.

Finally, and most simply, you need to allow customers to actually buy your MVP. That means your MVP needs to have built in payment. Without payment, you didn't really ship anything customers can buy. This step will seem easy for most of you—after all, you just read the section on MBP, and know how to do it with a PayPal button. For some of you, however, you will know that this is harder than it seems. Why? This is hard because maybe your product is *free* like a social network, or has a *free trial* like a game or app, or isn't complete enough to ask for money yet. Bullshit. The whole point of MVP is that it is worth money. Either you truly haven't built enough, or you are just too nervous about it being good enough. You should reread the section above about your MVP being *good enough*. One more thing you know you need to add is the ability to let people pay you. Even if it's set up as a donation inside your new social network, it's still a way for people to put money into your hand. If you never open your hand, you will never know if people will pay. If nobody pays, nobody cares, and you need to know this! It's a failure you know how to fix. It's a pivot(al) moment!

Types of MVP

There are many ways to build a minimum viable product. Note that I am not talking just about a minimum buyable product—building an MBP was discussed in the last section. I am talking about a full on MVP that you could actually ship to customers. This section will describe five different types of MVPs and how to actually build them.

The first method is called the *switcheroo*. In the switcheroo, you are offering something you can actually ship now, but the proceeds from which will help you build what you really want. As an example, previously I talked about the traumatic brain injury (TBI) drug. I suggested selling ice packs (which you can buy in bulk from Amazon or Costco) at an inflated price, and explaining that the proceeds help with the development of the drug. This idea isn't limited to drugs and medical devices. You could do it for anything. For example, if you were hoping to build a new kind of keyboard that uses AI to fix typos in real time as you type and can communicate with you (which is a product I just made up), but you don't have a real prototype to sell, then you could use a switcheroo. You would build a two page landing page about the new AI keyboard, talk about its core features, and then offer to sell a decent keyboard (say, a $20 Dell keyboard) for $30. Explain that the Dell keyboard ships today and they can get a $10 discount when your full product launches. It's a switcheroo, but it funds the development of your true keyboard. Most importantly, you generated revenue on your idea and demonstrated that it really is viable.

Similar to the switcheroo is the *down payment MVP*. In this method, again, you would build that two page landing page (with payment capability) and ask for a partial payment to reserve their order. This is technically a preorder, and thus is actually an MBP, not an MVP. Sometimes, though, this may be your only real option.

To make something a real MVP, remember, you have to actually ship the customer something. One of the coolest ways to ship something is to do it by hand. This MVP method is called *concierge*. For a hardware (physical) product, it means building it—or a version of it—by hand. This can take longer and may cost more, but in return for this extra cost, you get to say that you actually shipped one, and, more importantly, you get actual feedback from a real user. You also probably get a product champion out of it.

For a software product, a concierge MVP means that instead of coding the full project, you only code part of the main user interface (UI). This UI connects to a human who does the actual work of the app. You are simulating intelligence of software by using a human to do the actual work. Instead of creating that amazing algorithmic technique for scheduling doctors' appointments, for example, you fake it out by having a human figure out the scheduling problem. To the user of the app, it seems like the software is doing it. At scale, this software concierge technique can be extended, still with real humans, to a human worker farm. What? Yes, there are virtual farms of humans out there just waiting to pretend to be software for you. Many of the best apps out there actually use these human worker farms to deliver seemingly amazing capabilities. Image recognition, transcriptions, translations, and more all happen by humans, though we think it's a computer doing it. The most popular virtual farm of humans is called Mechanical Turk.[9] For as little as $0.25 you could get a human to slot in that patient into the doctor's schedule at the optimal time—no algorithm required. Most concierge MVPs are hard to scale up later because it's just you doing the work. Using Mechanical Turk is one way to build future scalability into the product or service right from the start.

For a service, the concierge MVP is just what it seems. You personally do the service for the customer. You drive over to their home. You pick up their dry cleaning. You go and drop it off to be cleaned. You pick it back up and return it to the customer. You are the concierge for your new dry cleaning app. Want to

---

[9] https://www.mturk.com

make a business that teaches people how to speak a new language? You just became a teacher. Want that in an app, by the way? Use a service like Twilio to make it using a text message system people can use on their phone, well in advance of actually building a full on app.[10]

The next MVP technique I will describe is *the cobble*. The cobble MVP is the cobbling together of already available parts to make a whole. For example, do you want to offer a solar powered laptop? Sure, future iterations of your laptop (generations 2, 3, and 4) will probably have your own plastics design and maybe your own solar cells. For now, though, start shipping today by cobbling together commercially available parts from sources like Amazon, Digi Key, and Alibaba.[11] You ship all the parts to your house—the solar panel you got from Alibaba, the laptop you bought from Amazon, and the wires and voltage converter you got from Digi Key—and you wire them up and you ship that bad boy. No engineering degree or plastics design required. You ship them to order, one at a time. You don't buy 1,000 and then put them up for sale. You buy one, take a picture, put it up for sale, sell it, and buy parts for a second one. One to show and one to go is the tried and true method of getting the money you need to build the next one.

Finally, building an MVP can seem tough without a technical co founder. Sometimes, though, you need to have actually sold something in order to attract a technical co founder (for example, Ryan—not that I'm bitter about it). So, how do you do it? You don't have much money or skills, and you don't know where to start. In this situation, you need to consider some light outsourcing. The outsource MVP does take some money, but not as much as you might think. You may even be able to pay in stock. The first step in considering outsourcing the research and development work is to, again, focus on the minimum you need to be able to ship. You certainly don't want to pay someone in cash (or stock) to build more than you need. Most people add too much and don't trim enough. Consider a cobble or concierge MVP technique combined with an outsource MVP to reduce costs and feature sets further.

Next, you need to find some potential partners who will build your MVP on the cheap. Your town may have a Facebook group for startups, which is a great place to start. If it doesn't, you can use my town of Austin's Facebook startup group—they won't mind.[12] There are tons of lurkers there who are just waiting for a startup to ask for help with something, and then they will pounce on them with

---

[10] http://www.twilio.com
[11] http://amazon.com http://digikey.com http://alibaba.com
[12] https://www.facebook.com/groups/austinstartups

offers. It's a place where you may even be able to get work for stock. Craigslist is still used for this purpose (small contracts), so don't knock it. I've personally found machinists willing to build models out of metal, and coders and designers willing to do UI work, all on Craigslist. Finally, consider Upwork or Fiverr.[13] Upwork and Fiverr are two great websites that give you access to an entire world of freelance contractors willing to do work for rock bottom prices. It does not mean low quality. Most of these freelancers are actually employed full time at the bigger shops and use Upwork or Fiverr to supplement their income. You can find the good ones by their reviews on the site. You can find freelancers to do just about any coding, hardware, business, and operations tasks you can think of. Notice how I've focused on freelancers rather than contract shops. Freelancers may, occasionally, accept stock in lieu of pay (or partial pay). Freelancers are also usually much cheaper than full on contract houses (like design or coding agencies). Another great thing about a freelancer, especially one in your town, is that you may eventually be able to hire them full time. At a minimum, you can keep going back to that same freelancer, which is something a contract shop cannot usually offer because they rotate people and have attrition. The trick to managing a freelancer or a contract shop is to be very clear about your needs, the deliverable, the pay (try to get a fixed bid), and to keep the project as small as possible. As extra incentive, you can offer the promise of future work if the small project works out first. It's a good way to build a relationship. Start small, and then grow, even if that means a few iterations before you have a shippable product.

Reason Number Four: Legal, Ethical, and Moral Guidelines

Is it legal to ship food to another country? Is it legal to prepare packaged foods in your personal kitchen? Are you allowed to sell tobacco, firearms, or alcohol? The answer to all the questions above: probably not. If you have legal concerns about whether or not you are allowed to ship your product—especially as it relates to food, medical drugs or devices, or the big three (tobacco, firearms, or alcohol)—then you need to have that answered. Find out what these rules and regulations are as they relate to your business. You need to figure it out, and the good news is that you can probably research it online. A simple search for one of those questions above will usually give you an answer. If it doesn't and you are still not sure,

---

[13] http://upwork.com

you can also use one of the many online legal services like LegalZoom to get a quick and simple answer to these questions.

For most business types in the United States, however, you do not need a license. This makes it easy to start a business. For example, you do not need a license to sell software (unless it includes professional services like law or taxes), nor do you need a license to build products. If you are bundling products that other people make, you don't even have to worry about FCC regulations (which are something you do have to worry about if you are manufacturing your own devices). For almost every kind of software, hardware, and product out there, you will not need a license to sell it. You don't even need a corporation (as discussed in Chapter 2), because, as a US citizen, you can get a sole proprietorship for free with your social security number. You should generally look out for things that involve the government. Food, drugs or medicine, guns, alcohol, and professional services are the main things you'll need to get more legal advice about. When in doubt, do some web research or ask a lawyer.

Ethically, you may not think that your product is good enough. If so, see the prior section, "Reason Number Two: Not Good Enough." However, if your ethical dilemma is that you think your product might cause physical harm to other people, please do us all a favor and stop. Don't ship. Before shipping, do the research and testing needed to ensure that nobody is going to get hurt. You can't unhurt someone. The exception to this hurt issue is if you are afraid you might offend someone else. Offending or hurting someone's feelings is a moral issue. The legal protection of free speech makes it legal to hurt someone's feelings—hey, they don't have to watch your commercial or read your ad! Possibly offending or hurting someone's feelings is not a reason not to ship. It might mean that your product is edgy enough to actually get some traction! You can't please all customers, but you should please your core customers.

If you are worried that you might be violating another person's patent, trademark, or intellectual property (IP), this could also be an ethical issue. Here is how I would resolve it. Do I *know* that I am violating another person's patent or IP? If so, stop. Figure out a way around the problem, or do something else. If I don't know *for sure* if I am violating, and I didn't just blatantly copy someone else's work, then I would ship it despite my fear or worry. Yes, you might get sued (see Chapter 8), but more than likely, if someone detects this and shows you that you did wrong, they will first send you a cease and desist letter (a threat to sue), and you will simply stop and avoid getting sued. It's happened to me, and it was not a big deal.

Morals are based on the norms of society. The legal boundaries of society are usually what guide business decisions, not moral ones. For example, if you are building a new virtual reality (VR) porn application to provide a lifelike sexual experience to your customers (a huge new market, by the way), you need to consider both the legal and moral sides of this. If you think that pornography is immoral, you probably started the wrong business, so you should just stop. If you are concerned, however, with how someone might inappropriately use your new technology, I would argue: Isn't that your user's moral issue and not yours? If you are building a new weapons system for the US government, you have already crossed your own moral bridge. You aren't the one deciding how the system will be used, so you will need to stop fretting about that. On the other hand, there are legal boundaries that you must consider when building these VR technologies or weapons. You should have worried about these issues of morality long before you actually started building an MBP or MVP.

Lastly, are you feeling bad about the high (or low) price of your product offering? Why feel bad about that? Hey, an MBP or MVP is a test—people will either pay or they won't. It's not a moral question, it's a market question. Moral questions are important, but they should not mar the progress of technology and innovation for those who are working within the law. Use law as your guide if you have any confusion about this topic.

The Real Reason You Didn't Ship: Fear

Fear is a fire that will burn up the best ideas and turn them into ash. Entrepreneurship is about taking risks, pushing boundaries, failing, and eventually succeeding. You cannot let fear guide you or you will never navigate to success. You will have to try and fail many times in order to gain the critical insights that will ultimately lead you to success. Remember, if you haven't spent a night in jail for your idea, you might not be trying hard enough. I mean, try getting arrested for loitering outside of a trade show you didn't pay to exhibit at. Try that for fear.

The fact is, almost every reason you didn't ship was because of fear. You were afraid of being beholden, and you were afraid of not being good enough. You were afraid of not knowing how to start. You were afraid of getting sued or hurting someone's feelings. You have to get over these fears, and the best way to do that is to simply ship it already! I promise, once you have shipped that MBP and then that MVP, it is going to feel great. You'll start failing faster, which means you are getting closer to success.

Koffie: Fresh Coffee Delivered

Koffie was going to revolutionize coffee drinking. Imagine showing up to work at your usual time, and when you get there, a young college student is standing there holding your hot cup of coffee. Not just any coffee, but fully organic, fair trade, amazingly fresh, delivered into your hand coffee. Oh, by the way, you can pay for a monthly 20 cup subscription and get a big discount, or simply order with your phone to have it delivered within 20 minutes. Does this sound too good to be true? To me, it sounds just like a great idea.

Koffie was the brainchild of one of my students in the fall 2016 course, "Lean Startup Essentials." Jimena was one of my brightest students. She understood every topic, had brilliant ideas, and was incredibly capable. She took to the lean startup concept well, and probably also read the textbook for the class, *The Lean Startup* by Eric Ries, in its entirety (you can never really tell if students read a book or not). She had this idea from the very beginning of the semester, especially since our 9:30 am start time was the perfect time to have a cup of coffee. She would see me come into class carrying my coffee, and dang it if she didn't want one too! Hey, we all did.

Jimena is a coffee snob. That's not a bad thing—it means she's passionate about coffee. She wanted coffee with full flavor. She detested Keurig and other instant coffee makers. She wanted the real, roasted, ground coffee, fresh today. So her idea struck home not only with me, but also with the whole class. Where was this Koffie app?

Jimena was no slouch—she knew from my class that building an app would be hard, and that a way around that was to build a website. Students are required to build a site in my class, and Jimena spent extra time and effort to build an amazing looking site. The dark brown colors and wafting aromas of coffee were practically swimming off of her web page. There was only one problem. There were no buttons—just a "Coming Soon" at the bottom. For someone who wants some coffee now, this can be really frustrating.

For her idea validation, she eventually did hook up a "Buy Now" button to a "Sorry" page. Jimena and I went back and forth on the price to display on her page, and we eventually settled on a high price, only to offer the coffee now. For $5.55, you could get this extra large cup of coffee delivered to you anywhere on campus in about 20 minutes. At my suggestion, she restricted her market and audience to the UT campus, since my plan for her was to actually give this a try.

Even at a high $5.55 price tag, she got a lot—close to 20%—of clicks on her Buy button. People wanted this. This idea was prime time. Even better, potential customers—mostly students at UT Austin, but not her friends—were giving her their e mail addresses on the "Sorry" page to be notified when it was ready. Her idea was the most validated idea because it had the highest click through rates of the class. Where was my Koffie, though?

A long battle ensued between Jimena and I about the next step. She had e mails addresses of customers. She had found a free way to reach UT students: Facebook pages. She brewed coffee herself every day. Her first class wasn't until 9:30 am, and her professor (me) told her that it was okay to be occasionally late. Nevertheless, she refused to launch an MBP or MVP, despite it being one of the homework assignments of the class (she got a B on that assignment). She would not link a PayPal button. She would not accept orders for her obvious MVP. Why?

Jimena was afraid. She was afraid to launch an MBP even without coffee, because she didn't think it was possible and that people would not prepay to be the first customers of Koffie. She didn't think people would pre order coffee, but she was wrong. I know at least one person who was ready and willing to pay to try her coffee: her professor! I suspect other students in the class would have pre ordered it as well.

"Jimena, you could just offer people to pay $5.55 for a token to be traded in for a free order when you eventually launch. They are preordering with this just like anything else in the class," I said.

"I don't know. I mean, nobody will do that," said Jimena.

"They will, and I will! Come on!"

We would go on and on like this, sometimes one on one before class, and sometimes in front of the whole class (who were on my side, by the way).

"Okay, fine. Don't do an MBP. Let's do an MVP. I'll help you. I'll be your first customer. I'm not joking. And I'll be the easy one—your last order of the morning and you just bring mine to class," I said. I wanted coffee, especially the kind she was planning to offer. Oh, that rich aroma!

"Nobody will want to pay that much," she said.

"Well, you don't know that yet, and besides, I'm telling you that I will. Not to mention all the people who clicked your idea validation Buy button and were sad to see that sorry page," I replied.

"Well, I think I will need money to get started," she said.

"Jimena, you already make a pot of coffee for yourself every day. Go steal some cups from Wendy's," I said. Okay, granted, that was probably not great advice, but hey—if you aren't getting arrested, you aren't trying hard enough.

"Yeah, well, I don't know. Don't I need a license? And I can't pay anyone to deliver coffee," she said.

"To sell coffee? Not that I'm aware of. I'm pretty sure you don't need any license. You can quote me on that," I replied. "And anyway, you can just say you are only available between 8 and 9:30, first come, first served," I replied.

"But delivery..." she started.

"You can deliver it. You told me that you've got a bike. You can just deliver the orders one at a time, or batch them. Jimena, you can do it," I said.

"It'll be a lot of work," she said.

"Yeah, so?"

"But what if some customers don't get their coffee?"

"Don't accept the order unless you are sure you can deliver. Just reject each order you can't fulfill and quickly reply, 'Sorry, I cannot deliver to you today. Please get your order in sooner for tomorrow,'" I said. "People will understand and get their coffee their normal way."

"Yeah, but won't I have to build a whole, like, ordering system?" she asked.

"No. Just make it that PayPal button. They pay, and you see the order in seconds. You text them when they want it, they tell you, and then you decide if you can do it. If not, reply with an apology message and refund their PayPal. No software needed—it's fully concierge," I explained.

"Hmm, let me think about it," she would say.

So it went, on and on throughout the semester, and as you may have already guessed, Jimena never shipped. As it turned out, she already had a difficult and time consuming day job. Her day job was being a student, and I can't rightly blame her for being unwilling to sacrifice grades to make me some of her delicious looking Koffie. I don't blame her for making the decision to focus on her studies and not launch. It's not the kind of *risk tolerant* decision that an entrepreneur needs to make, but it was a good decision for her. A more risk tolerant student would say that it *might* impact their studies, but that it's worth the risk. Besides, I always explain that running a startup is like getting a 4 year college degree every eight weeks!

Three Analytical Tools for Shipping

For many of you, having read this chapter, you know when to ship. The answer is now. Don't wait. For the rest of you who are on the fence, the end of this chapter offers you a ship ready checklist. Use this checklist as permission to ship it. Table 4.1 at the end of this chapter shows this ship ready checklist, which is very easy to use. If you can check the box up to the MBP, you can ship the MBP. However, I urge you to try to keep checking boxes past the MBP line if you can. You may be able to skip the MPB phase altogether and go straight to an actual MVP. An actual MVP is better because it makes you more beholden to the customer. Ironic, isn't it? That one of the reasons you aren't shipping is because of a fear of being beholden, but in reality, being beholden is actually a desired state. This means that you are doing this thing, so no more excuses. Many entrepreneurs have found success by being beholden. If you can't check the boxes past MBP, go ahead and ship the MBP, but don't wait—start working on that MVP too, even as data begins to roll in about your MBP. There is always time to pivot later, but there is no time to waste.

Whether you have shipped your MBP or MVP, it is now time to get some more traffic to that page. Using the marketing techniques from the last chapter (initial traffic) and also Chapter 6 (scaling marketing), you need to drive customers' attention to consider buying your MBP or MVP. Just having an MPB or MVP out there is not enough to get any sales, and it's also not a fair experiment. You need to get real customers there to see if they will buy—it's the whole point of shipping. By the way, during your idea validation phase, did you perhaps collect e mails on your "Sorry" page? If you did collect e mails, now is the time to e mail those folks and let them know they can place a preorder (MBP) or an order (MVP).

Once again, as with your idea validation test, you need to drive at least 50 people to your site or MBP/MVP. 100 visitors are even better. 1,000 visitors are better yet. Why at least 50? Remember, without a sample size of at least 50, most statistical science is useless. It would also be great if all 50 were actual real potential customers that are not family or close friends. Non potential customers (for example, men visiting your women's clothing shop) are not representative of actual customers, and should not be counted among the 50 people or be part of your experiment. Friends and family are great, and hey, money is money, but they also should not be added to your 50 count or your experiment.

What is this experiment? Launching your MBP or MVP is the experiment. Shipping is not the end—it's only the beginning. Everything you do from now on in this book is actually just an experiment. You need to get at least 50 samples, see the results, pivot, and repeat. That's navigating your way to success. I offer two tools to judge your MBP and MVP experiments, respectively.

The MBP assessment tool provided in Table 4.2 looks very similar to the idea validation test, but is in fact trying to assess something other than just a good idea. You are trying to assess buy ability, and so the metrics are a little different. Note that we are not trying to assess viability—that's the second tool. Simple buy ability is just answering the question: Did someone buy it? Not just someone, but a real potential customer that you didn't know before you started the experiment. If you have determined buy ability, it's time to move on to an MVP. I want to say something now that may get me into trouble later, but I hope not: If your MBP experiment succeeded, it's probably worth investing some of your own money into an MVP. There, I said it. Certainly, you can use the funds from your MBP experiment to fund development and production of your MVP. You can also use the results of your MBP experiment to attract co founders, investors, and even that one big investor you already know: yourself. You can now potentially invest more of your time and money into your startup because you *know* that it's a buyable idea.

Did your MBP fail? That's almost better than your MBP succeeding. You've learned, at a very low cost, that your idea is not as good as your initial validation led you to believe. When push came to shove, your customers who liked the idea before were, for whatever reason, reluctant to put down actual dollars and preorder. It's time to pivot. Since you tried idea validation already, I suggest trying a few small pivots before you consider big pivots. Small pivots to try would be the price, design or style, and trust. If your price is above $50 (in the considered purchase price range), you might try asking for a partial payment to hold their place in line (don't call it a layaway, but a preorder down payment). Make it just $20, or something less than the full price. You could also try structuring your price differently by making it a subscription or cutting features and making it cheaper. Consider the design, style, and overall look of your site or sales materials. Do you think it is high enough quality, or does it need some work? Consider adding real pictures of you working on prototypes. Consider using Wix's many gorgeous templates and adding more detail to your page. Make sure that the "Buy Now" button and price are big and above the fold, so customers don't have to hunt for them. Finally, think about trust. Do you trust yourself? Yes, obviously, but how will you convince someone else to trust you? How could you build more trust for a buyer who is putting down a preorder? One idea is to include more details about yourself on your page, including your picture, your backstory, or even your CV/resume. Making your company have a real trustworthy human behind it can go a long way toward convincing people to buy your products. Also, consider launching on a different platform (like Kickstarter) or adding trust symbols to your page (Visa logos). Put up some of the early feedback you got from your interviews and idea validation data. Why not? It'll contribute to people being able to trust you. Once you've done a small pivot, you need to get 50 more people to your site or into your sales funnel. Welcome to the startup treadmill—this is the job. Only after two or three iterations of small changes would I suggest a big pivot. A big pivot (such as a different product) probably means going back to idea validation, but not necessarily. You have probably gotten good at building MBPs by now, so you could possibly start here this time.

Okay, either your MBP is working, or you jumped straight to MVP. It's now time to assess viability, and this could get a bit tricky. It is important to note that assessing viability does not test scalability. Scalability is the ability to grow consistently to the full size that your goals imagine. We can't do that test yet, because you are not necessarily using scalable methods to attract your first customers. Instead, to test viability, consider using the assessment tool presented in Table 4.3, which uses conversion rates and price to offer a formula for viability. This formula will give you a sense for your viability, and will also give you a number to shoot for in your scalability test (presented in Chapter 5). Viability comes down to four factors: *customer acquisition cost* (CAC), *customer lifetime value* (CLV or LTV), *serviceable addressable market* (SAM) size, and *costs of goods sold* (COGS). After your MVP experiment, you should be fairly able to accurately estimate all four of these numbers to assess viability. CLV right now can be estimated as the sum of money you expect from a customer, whether that be just this one sale (purchase price), an estimated 1 year of subscription service (don't go beyond that), or some combination—for example, expected repeat purchases within one year after the first purchase (like the Koffie example mentioned previously). You can also estimate SAM by simply calculating the total number of potential customers in your target customer demographic and multiplying it by the CLV you just calculated. Your COGS are simply the variable costs of production to provide one unit to a customer. COGS should never include overhead costs (like your salaries or office space), nor should COGS include costs of development or R&D, such as paying contractors to design something. It should only be the costs to produce the unit, such as the web hosting costs (for apps) or the costs of the actual parts that go into the unit.

Lastly, the results of your MVP experiment should also give you a hint at an initial or estimated CAC. CAC is calculated as the amount of money you have to spend to get one customer to actually buy your product or service. It is usually calculated as total amount spent divided by total quantity of unique customer orders. However, since it is likely that you are using methods from Chapter 3 (free methods) to acquire customers, it would not be a good indicator of eventual CAC. You will need to estimate this using a different formula. The formula uses either leads or clicks. A click is a potential customer who clicked on an online ad and went through to your website where they could make a purchase then and there. A lead is a potential customer you might reach through any other method, not an online ad. I suggest estimating that it will cost you $1 per click (a reasonable long term goal). To calculate CAC for clicks then, you simply divide the cost per click ($1) by your conversion rate. So if you had a 10% conversion rate in your MVP experiment, your CAC would be $10. If you are not using a website for indirect sales, you will have to use a lead generation cost estimate instead. I suggest using $100 per lead as an estimate for how much it will take to get a lead. Direct sales, and thus lead generation, is almost always more expensive than online or indirect sales. Calculate your CAC by dividing your $100 by your lead conversion rate (based on this test) to get an estimated CAC. For this example, that would be $100/10%, resulting in a CAC of $1,000. Viability, as shown in Table 4.3, therefore comes down to this: Can you make enough money through sales to achieve your goals while remaining at least marginally profitable? Considering the COGS plus the CAC, is this number less than the LTV? If so, is the SAM big enough to achieve your goal? If so, you are viable! Congratulations, it's time to print money (see Chapter 5)!

Is something breaking your math? Is your conversion rate too low, for example? If so, it's time to address that item and fix it before you try to scale up, which is the subject of Chapter 5. This means you will most likely need to do a new MVP test after a small pivot. It could be a big pivot, but hopefully not. Just like with an MBP failed test, the first thing to ask yourself is whether you can improve your conversion rate. Could a small pivot—such as price, design, or trust—lead to even a 1% increase in conversion rate? If so, that could substantially lower your CAC, and possibly make you viable. Is your SAM too small? Consider expanding your potential audience to a new market. Maybe women over 50 would like your new scarves, after all—it's time to run an experiment and see. Your MVP experiment needs to now validate the new market and its conversion rate, and then you can combine (average) your two experiments together and sum up your SAMs to get a new SAM. You've just expanded your market. Sure, those women might cost more to acquire (lower conversion rate), but you are hopefully still profitable on those sales and thus you can include them in your SAM. If your SAM is achievable and is enough to give you what your goal was (from Chapter 1), then you are viable. Not necessarily profitable yet, but viable.

Consider trying ways to lower your COGS. Consider raising prices, or making more offerings such as a software subscription to go along with that hardware device. See how that raises the LTV and thus suddenly makes you viable? Well, now you have to test whatever you just changed. If you have changed the COGS by making the product smaller, you have to test that for viability. If you changed the LTV by offering software too, you have to test that and actually determine who pays for the subscription as well. This is the new entrepreneurship. This is data driven decision making. This is navigating your way to success. You will get there. Just don't be in a hurry to "scale up," and especially not if you are not making profits on the sales you are doing today. It's a recipe for bankruptcy. Iterate in the MVP phase to save future heartaches and failures, and from going back to the drawing board. Once you find that magic combination of LTV > COGS + CAC is the time to hit the gas. That's when you should go and do the scalability work described in the next chapter!

Table 4.1: Ship Ready Checklist

Item	Answer
Is your idea validated?	Yes → Proceed No → Go back and validate (Ch. 3)
Do you think that, given time, money, and talent, your solution is eventually a real possibility and nobody would be harmed?	Yes → Proceed No → Reconsider solution. Go back and validate (Ch. 3)
Are you able to accept payment (credit card, cash, check, or invoice)?	Yes → MBP ready. Launch it! No → Set up payment, open your hand, then launch MBP
Can you measure how many leads (i.e., visitors) and how many sales you got?	Yes → Proceed No → Figure out a way to track leads and sales, then proceed
Within 2 months of an order, can you ship the customer something (even if it's not the full solution or a final form of your product)?	Yes → Proceed No → Consider different MVP types, and put something together
Do you have a way to collect customer feedback and then iterate your solution from here, based on that feedback?	Yes → Proceed No → Consider survey, or collecting customer contact information
Have you overcome your fears? Are you ready to start learning and pivoting your way to success?	Yes → LAUNCH MVP! Don't wait! No → Think about your reasoning, but launch MVP anyway!

Table 4.2: Minimum Buy ability Assessment

Item	Assessment
Did you get at least 50 non friend/non family potential customers to see your offering (site, pitch, etc.)?	Yes → Proceed No → Keep driving traffic/getting leads. See Ch. 3 or Ch. 5
Did you get a sale/preorder (even just one), from someone you don't personally know?	Yes → MBP passed! Congrats. Build an MVP now No → MBP failed! Consider small pivots/big pivots, and retest

Table 4.3: Minimum Viability Assessment

Item	Assessment
Did you get at least 50 non friend/non family potential customers in your demographic to see your offering (site, pitch, etc.)?	Yes → Proceed No → Keep driving traffic/getting leads. See Ch. 3 or Ch. 5
Calculate conversion rate (CVR)	(Quantity of Sales) / (Clicks or Leads)
Calculate estimated customer acquisition cost (CAC)	Either: $100 / CVR [for leads] or: $1 / CVR [for clicks]
Calculate costs of goods sold (COGS)	Sum of all costs that go into making one unit (e.g. parts) (Not including development or overhead costs!)
Calculate estimated customer lifetime value (LTV)	Price * # of re purchases up to 1 year or subscription charges for up to 1 year
Are you per unit profitable? (CAC + COGS) < LTV	Yes → Proceed to SAM test No → MVP failed. Pivot to get better CVR, COGS, or LTV
Calculate your SAM	SAM = Total Number of Reachable Customers in Your Target Demographic(s) * LTV
Is your SAM greater than your personal goals for the business (from Chapter 1)?	Yes → Viable business! Proceed to Chapter 5 and SCALE UP! No → Pivot target market. Consider different customer demographics or adding more customer demographics to expand SAM, then retest the new/expanded market with new MVP test

Chapter 5
Nobody Cares—What can you do about it?

"And, you can get people to do stuff on social media for your brand for next to nothing," I said, for the third time that day. It was 2009. I was sitting in my office at the Austin Technology Incubator (ATI) in the very old MCC building in north Austin. ATI is a UT Austin incubator that provides cheap and sometimes free office space for young startups like mine. They also provide guidance and help you refine your pitch, all with the goal to help you get your business funded. Funding was not on my mind that day; I was trying to build a company without funding. I needed customers to do that.

"Harlan, that sounds great. Let me get back to you next week," said Min Liang Tan, the CEO of Razer, a gaming hardware company. Min and I became friends while I was CEO of my last company, Bigfoot Networks, which was also a gaming hardware company. We would see each other at trade shows, and were always looking to do some kind of deal together.

"Okay, great. Just let me know if you have any questions," I replied.

"Gotcha, no problem. Later," he said.

I knew I lost the sale. Whenever someone says, "Let me get back to you," it's actually a very polite no. For some reason, the people I had been relentlessly pitching my new startup idea to, simply were not getting it.

Karmaback was the brainchild of my two co founders, Ryan and Rajat, and I. We had dreamed it up because social media was exploding, and we thought that meant a new way for companies to sell their stuff. It took us about three months of coding and design to build the website for Karmaback. The idea of it was simple: have companies put swag in our *reward points store* and pay us a monthly fee. The companies would get likes, comments, and shares of their products and company on social media. We would motivate their customers and fans to earn points by "liking" their pages, "commenting" on their postings, "sharing" their postings, and entering their sweepstakes. We built the first like button for web pages about a year before Facebook did it. There was only one problem: Nobody cared.

No, I don't literally mean *nobody*, but just most people we were talking to. It just didn't blow them away or excite them enough to sign a deal with us. Our initial validation calls went well. Initial customers were excited about the offering. We even had a few paying customers. The problem was, it was taking too much time and too few people were buying compared to how many we were contacting. Our conversion rate sucked.

DOI 10.1515/9781501507083-005

For months, I had been calling everyone I knew who ran companies. I hit up every marketer I knew. After hundreds of calls, I had only a few sales, and they weren't very big ones. My Rolodex was running dry. There was something about our offering that people just didn't understand. Didn't they want social media to buzz about their company and product? What were we missing? Why didn't anyone care?

It was time to change my tactic. It was time to get desperate. It was time to ask some open ended questions. Frankly, we were desperate. I had been living off my own savings for more than six months and my co founders were growing frustrated from getting no pay and our very slow traction. Engineer types will quickly become uninterested in working with you if they don't see solid traction and results soon.

I picked up the phone for round two of the same people I had already called. Slowly calling each of my prospects again, I took a different approach. I had recently read an amazing sales book called *SPIN Selling*, and I was going to take the approach of asking questions.[1] *Do these companies even know what social media is?* I wondered.

"Hi, Jacob. It's Harlan," I said, as Jacob from EVGA, a video card manufacturer, picked up my call.

"Oh hi, hey. I'm kind of busy. What's up?" he asked, wary of another sales call from me after our last awkward exchange.

"This isn't a sales call. I know you are probably not perfect for Karmaback. I was just hoping to get 10 minutes to talk to you about your problems in social media, so I could understand what to build next," I said.

"Sure, what do you want to know?" he asked. Jacob's a good guy—he'd give me 10 minutes, even if it did still sound like a sales call. People generally respond better to requests for help than they do to requests for money.

"Just really quickly: What kind of social media are you doing now?" I asked.

"Oh, we're doing the page thing, getting our fans to like us and posting stuff to our social media, like deals and stuff," he said.

"Right, neat. What problems are you having with that?" I asked.

"Well, mostly, it's tough to get people to like our page, so we're thinking we might just stop investing in social media altogether. Harlan, that's why we probably won't do Karmaback. It doesn't make sense if we can't even figure out our Facebook page," he said.

---

[1] http://fastai.com/blog/2013/10/11/spin-selling-for-engineers-how-to-teac

I know that when they say my first name like that, it's not good. He thinks I'm still trying to sell Karmaback.

"I see, no worries. I'm not trying to sell Karmaback at all, honestly, I'm just trying to understand what problems people are having," I say.

"Right. Well, we've tried some contests and sweepstakes, as everyone is doing to drive page likes, but they don't let us require the page like, so it never works. Our gamer customers just keep gaming the system," he said.

"Oh, right. So, you are running contests and sweepstakes? How are you doing that?" I ask. Sweepstakes were already going to be part of our own platform, so I was a little frustrated that he didn't say this on our last call. I realized that I didn't ask. On our last call I had spent the whole time talking about my own solution, and asked virtually no questions.

"We use WildfireApp, but they are so expensive to white label, and they want to charge us an arm and a leg just to require liking our page in order to enter the sweepstakes."

"Alright, cool. What if you just paid by the page like? I mean, wouldn't that be fairer?"

"Yeah, that'd be okay. Pay for results, right?" he laughs.

"Right, like fifty cents a like?" I ask.

"Yeah, that sounds fair and doable. Could we cap it at 10,000 likes?" he asks.

"Sure."

"And it's white label, right? Not Karmaback labeled?" he asks again.

Wait, what is this? Am I selling right now? I don't know when or where this shifted into a sale. We don't have the solution he's asking for. We can't white label a sweepstakes. We can't charge by the like. We don't even have our sweepstakes system working yet. What am I doing?

"Sure, but can we put a minimum on it too? Say, $1,000?" I say, realizing this is quickly turning into a real deal.

"Let me check with my boss Joe, but yeah, probably. That shouldn't be a problem," he says, sounding actually excited.

"How often might you do these sweepstakes?" I ask in a last attempt to make this a sale that I can do.

"If this first one goes well, we'll probably do them biweekly," he says.

Then it hits me. I'd be making between $2,000 and $5,000 every two weeks from just this one customer. That's ten times more than our entire platform was going to generate from one customer per month. Holy shit!

"Alright, that's great. I'm sure you'll get the results, as long as you offer a good prize," I say, as if I know something about this.

"Yeah, we'll offer one of our high end motherboards. Will that work?" he asks, as if I know.

"For sure. I mean, gamers will do anything for free stuff," I say, which I've said dozens of times on our previous call, with no results.

"You're right. Okay, let's do this. I just sent Joe an e mail and he replied that we are good to go," he says.

Just like that, I am in a new business.

Just like that, I am on a deadline.

Just like that, our entire company has pivoted to a pay for like sweepstakes platform, all by just asking small simple questions. Time to get coding!

How to Know Nobody Cares

You might be starting to think nobody cares about your product/service/company. People are clicking, but you are not getting nearly as many sales as you would like. People are taking your call, but very few are biting. How can you decide that nobody cares, and what can you do about it?

In the prior chapter, we discussed the minimum viable product (MVP) and the minimum buyable product (MBP) in detail. That chapter also contained a tool to help you determine viability (CAC + COGS < LTV) and buy ability (just one sale). These assessments are good for very early stage companies, but quickly become frustrating as you try to scale. Once you have been slogging it out with your startup for six months, barely treading water, or starting to drown, those few sales stop being as motivating as they used to be. What you need is money—enough to pay for some noodles, at least. Sure, you passed the MBP, just like Karmaback did. And yes, your MVP assessment passed too, for your initial sample of 50. However, since then, you've had little progress. The occasional sale is not enough to live off of, and even those sales have started to slow down. You have started to think: maybe nobody cares.

Stop! You don't know that yet. You only *think* nobody cares. It only *feels* like nobody cares. To truly know, there is only one thing you can do: ask.

Just like I did when I called my list of prospects back and asked them questions, so should you. How many? A lot. I ended up doing about 50 similar calls, and eventually, it just became my sales method. Ask questions until the offering is obvious or not.

You are trying to understand and get to the bottom of two things. First, you need to figure out if the problem you are solving is real and important enough to your prospects. It may be that you need to go back to Chapter 2 and re think your problem statement. It may also be simpler. The second thing you need to understand is the objections or issues your customers are having with your offering. In short, why aren't they buying it? You can't go out and ask that though—it's usually too complex, and customers may not even know. You need to develop questions to get to the truth in a friendlier way. These questions and the asking process may be slightly different for B2B compared to B2C, however, so each one should be approached slightly differently.

Business to Business: Customers Don't Care

Most business to business (B2B) sales involve higher prices, bigger commitments, and longer non standardized buying processes. Getting B2B sales, therefore, usually involves human interaction of some kind. If no humans are involved in your sales process, you might consider checking out the next section (B2C). Because your business is so automated, the B2C process might make sense for your B2B business. For most B2B companies, however, there is a human interaction by phone, e mail, or in person that ultimately leads to a sale. This is the process for you.

The process of uncovering whether your problem is big enough and what objections customers are having is truly as simple as asking. Develop a set of questions that you will ask either by phone or in person. Set up the call or meeting, ensuring that the prospect understands it is not a sales call, but a product development call. Then, ask the questions and collect the data. As always, 50 customer interviews is a good number to shoot for. You might be tempted to act with fewer than 50 interviews, but be wary. The reactions from just a few customers could send you on a pivot and down a road that leads to satisfying only those few customers, when, if you had finished the interviews, you could have figured out a pivot that would address a lot more customers than before.

To develop good questions and have usable data, you need to think through and understand your sales process. Business to business sales with human interactions are usually imagined as a sales funnel. Figure 5.1 shows an example of a sales funnel. You first get some leads, probably through advertising or trade shows. You then qualify those leads as being actual potential customers. Next, you contact those leads by e mail, phone, and/or in person with the goal of getting them to the next step of the funnel: to request a quote (in my example). Then, you deliver the quote and request a purchase order. Once you get the PO, you've made the sale. The key thing you are trying to figure out (in addition to the size of the problem) is where in the process of the sale is the customer getting stuck. More often than not, it is in the first step of the funnel: getting the customer to request a quote or reply to the first contact request. Why, though? Why aren't they interested? What is the issue? Is it not a problem for them, or do they have some objection? Could it be your approach? You'll need to ask them to find out the answers. It could be anything, and it will probably surprise you.

Table 5.1 includes some of the questions I have asked to figure out why customers aren't biting. You can use these, adapt them, and add your own. The key thing is to try to form open ended questions—that is, questions that allow the response to be free form and unbiased. "Do you have a problem with x?" is a bad question because it's a yes or no answer. "What kinds of problems do you have with x?" is a better question because it is open ended (although it is also leading them). "What problems do you have with x, if any?" is best, because it is open ended, but also allows them to say that they have no problems at all.

There are three categories of problems to ask. First, you need to establish if you are talking to the right person. These are qualifying questions, and if you already know the answers from prior talks, don't ask them again—it's annoying. Second, you need to determine if they have the problem that you are trying to solve, and how big it is. Finally, you need to ask about the buying process and what objections might come up that would prevent or slow the sale from going through. If you can uncover these three things, you can devise a pivot that could unblock a whole bunch of your sales funnel at once!

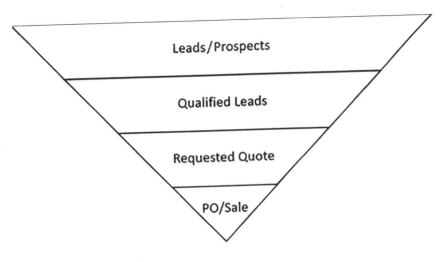

Figure 5.1: Typical Sales Funnel

Table 5.1: B2B Objection Discovery Questions

Question Type	Question
Situation Question	What is the buying process for products like x at your company?
Situation Question	Tell me about yourself and your role in the buying process.
Problem Question	What is happening with x right now, and what is your current solution/ provider?
Problem Question	What kinds of problems do you have with x, if any?
Problem Question	How frequent and severe are those problems in terms of dollars or effort?
Objection Question	Where do deals like x usually get stuck in your buying process, and why do they usually get stuck there?
Objection Question	Who or what group usually has the biggest objections about x?
Objection Question	What kinds of objections, if any, does your team have for our x?
Objection Question	How would you suggest we change, either in how we talk about our x, or what x is, to overcome these kinds of objections?

Business to Consumer: Customers Don't Care

If your customer acquisition process involves selling to end consumers (B2C), more than likely, you don't have their phone, e mail, or address. Even if you do, it might be a bit annoying to them for you to contact them when they decided *not* to buy your product. How did you even get that information if they are not your customer? For some B2B companies, this is also true: you take your orders online or through some reseller, and you rarely, if ever, get contact information for non customers. If this is the case, then you may have a hard time following the B2B method outline in the prior section. Consider this process instead.

You still need to get to the core of the issue: Do people have the problem you are solving and why aren't they buying your solution? What are their objections? The difference is that since you can't call your prospects back, you have to ask the customer why they decided not to buy right at the moment that they are about to leave your site or store. Capturing customer information from customers, who have decided not to buy, before they leave, can be difficult. There are three techniques to try, in order of difficulty, from hard to harder to hardest.

First, you could try to implement a survey system. To do this, you would set up a button called "Not Interested? Tell Us Why" on the home page of your website next to your "Buy Now" button. The downside of this is that it could discourage sales. Another way to do this is with some Javascript coding. You would detect the mouse when it's about to go up to the navigation area. This is called an *exit pop up*, and there are several online services that you can easily build into your website without knowing how to code.[2] The key is that the pop up message needs to ask them to take a short survey to tell us what they think of our product/service, with a survey link. The best surveys are incentivized to increase the rate at which people take the survey. Simply state that 1 in 100 survey responses will randomly win a prize, such as a $50 gift card. That's how you incentivize it. Be sure to ask for the user's e mail address at the end of the survey in order to enter for a chance to win the $50. Then, you pick one at random and send them the $50 gift card through Amazon. But what does the survey say?

Your exit survey should ask similar questions as the B2B questions in Table 5.1. Make them open ended, and let the customer fill them out. Obviously, you probably don't need the problem questions, but you should instead ask demographic questions. You want to make sure the feedback you are getting is from customers in your target group. If you are targeting millennials, but your survey responses are from 50 year olds, you need to ignore the feedback outside of your target group. In fact, that may be your problem—you are attracting the wrong audience! See the next section for a discussion on this. Demographics questions are easy and canned. Add the questions that really help you determine whether this is a user in your target group or not. I advise sticking to simply asking for their age, sex, location, and income.[3] Be sure to allow the users to click "prefer not to answer" on all those questions. In my experience, they will answer anyway, and feel better that they had the option not to. Asking questions about race/ethnicity or anything else too personal will likely get you a lot of uncompleted surveys and frustrated people.

If a survey won't work for you—for example, if you sell through a reseller like Amazon—you have only a few options left. You still need to figure out why people aren't buying, but you won't be able to ask customers you got naturally. Instead, one option is to create a marketing campaign that attracts potential customers to take a survey. On the survey, you present the product (including the price) to them and ask them for feedback on it. It's the same survey as above, but you got these potential customers through some other means, such as advertising or perhaps some survey service like SurveyMonkey.

The last resort for getting this non customer feedback is to put feet on the street. You may have to go out there, literally on the street (outside of farmers' markets, shopping malls, stores, etc.) and incentivize folks to check out your

---

[2] http://blog.wishpond.com/post/93315626207/5-exit-popups-you-need-to-know-about
[3] https://infoactive.co/data-design/ch04.html

product, hear your pitch, and do your short interview or survey. Take notes—this can get expensive. In this kind of situation, you'll need to have merchandise (usually called swag) or some kind of raffle to incentivize people who participate in the survey. T shirts or USB drives work well. Remember, in all cases above, you need to get to 50 target customers to get the feedback you need.

Which Customer Are You Targeting, Anyway?

You think nobody cares, but do you really want everyone to care? Is it even possible to get everyone to care? The answer is no. If you have something to sell that everyone cares about, it's probably water or electricity. Only utilities and commodities are things everyone needs, and even then, you'll have a hard time convincing everyone to care about your commodity. People can live without pork or even electricity.

In fact, in order to please one group of customers, you will almost certainly have to piss off another group. Just ask any politician anywhere. For example, my latest startup is called freebeer.ai. It's an artificial intelligence website that, when you sign up, helps you find events near you that will have free beer on tap. The number one complaint I get is, "Why don't you have free wine?" My answer, as snide as it seems, is often, "Because it's called freebeer.ai, duh." I am serious about that. Freebeer.ai will never help anyone find free wine. It's not what we do. We explicitly reject wine drinkers, in favor of our beer drinking friends. Why would we do that?

As soon as you start to try to please everyone, you start down the road of displeasing the very customers you were hoping to attract. Sure, I could very easily offer free wine. It's the same AI code, after all. However, our marketing message would be watered down (no pun intended). We'd suddenly start showing people in fancy clothes at a dinner party. No, that's not what freebeer.ai is about. Freebeer.ai is about helping dudes (our target market) who are poor (or cheap) to score some free beer. That's the brand we have, it's our message, and it's what attracts our target audience. In fact, our refusal to find free wine makes the free beer crowd love us even more.

Explicitly rejecting or ignoring the feedback of the wrong customers is critical to finding startup success. What if the free wine crowd started asking us for cheese? Should we start offering free cheese? It's just a path to obscurity, confusion, and failure. Some of the best examples of companies that tried to please too large a crowd and failed badly include: AOL, MySpace, and Coors Rocky Mountain Spring Water (yes, water failed). Want to know the best example of doing it right? Twitter. Twitter only allows those 140 characters. No exceptions. That's what they are about. Sure, it would be easy to allow users to do more, but they don't. They don't care that not everyone likes Twitter. They know that some people do, and this is their target audience. Their beachhead audience is still their top audience: reporters.

There are two key ideas here. First, regarding collecting feedback about your product or service (the last two sections), you need to make sure that the feedback you are getting is from the customers you want. Don't be convinced to release Rocky Mountain water from non Coors drinkers, as they are not your target audience. Coors drinkers want beer, and so do freebeer.ai users.

Second, the reason you might be failing to get traction (nobody cares) is that you might not be reaching the target audience for whom you built the product or service. Freebeer.ai was built for beer lovers and cheapskates, not wealthy wine drinkers. It's why we don't advertise in *Wine Enthusiast* magazine! In fact, if your intuition or your surveys/interviews lead you to realize that a lot (more than 25%) of your responses are coming from an audience you didn't expect and never intended the product to be for, your problem may not be your product, but your marketing tactic.

Pivoting on Marketing and Attracting Potential Customers

Up until this point, I have assumed that you have been able to get decent numbers of people into your customer funnel. Regardless of if those people are B2B leads or just clicks to your website, you are getting people's attention, but they are for some reason not buying like you think they should. If this is not the case or if, as mentioned in the previous section, you are attracting customers outside your target audience, then you have a marketing problem.

Marketing is technically defined as driving customers to take action through use of the 4 Ps of marketing. *Product, place, promotion,* and *price* make up the 4 Ps, which are like levers of control to drive customer action. The textbook definition includes the 5 Cs, which are ways you can push or pull on the marketing levers. The 5 Cs are *customers, collaborators, competitors, climate,* and *company.* I like to think of marketing as a formula:

$$\text{Customer Action} = \text{Need} * (\text{Product [5 Cs]} + \text{Place [5 Cs]} + \text{Promotion [5 Cs]} + \text{Price [5 Cs]})$$

Notice that the formula above includes need. Need is that tangible, true thing inside an individual that you can only hope they have. You can only influence whether they feel the need to buy your product—it also has to be inside them. This is the reason that poor people don't buy silver tea sets, and rich people don't care about the price of hamburgers. Poor people don't need a silver tea set, even if they could afford it. A regular tea set is just fine for them, thank you. Rich people couldn't care less about the price of hamburgers—even free range, grass fed, expensive beef is of no consequence. Poor people, however, do care, and they buy what they can afford or what fits their situation. Once our basic needs are fulfilled, we move on to other needs: the need for human contact, the need for experiences, the need for relaxation, and so on. Maslow's hierarchy of needs[4] is a far from perfect way of describing this concept, but it does serve as a good place to start thinking about customer needs in a new light. Your job in marketing is to find the right customers that are most likely to have the need that your product or service answers, to reach them (through promotion), and motivate them to take action (buy).

In order to get customers to take action, you need a good marketing plan that can be executed in a way that is always looking to optimize. I will break this process down into seven steps.

Corporate Innovation

This book takes the view that marketing is more than just advertising. In fact, marketing is an essential component of corporate innovation because it includes things like who the customer is, what they want, how they think, and how your innovation should be created to satisfy both the customer and your corporation. The concepts described in the following seven steps should not be skipped by corporate innovators. Understanding and having answers to these marketing ideas will be essential in convincing your organization to ultimately fund and proceed with your innovation.

Step 1: Proactive Marketing

The best time to start thinking about marketing is before you've shipped anything. At this stage, you can work on making your product remarkable or worthy of being talked about. You can add social sharing, viral ability, and referrals to the product. You can create products that have the marketing within them.

It has been demonstrated that the best form of marketing is word of mouth marketing.[5] The main reason for this is the same reason that Facebook sharing is

---

[4] http://psychclassics.yorku.ca/Maslow/motivation.htm
[5] Brown, T. J. "Spreading the Word: Investigating Antecedents of Consumers' Positive Word-of-Mouth Intentions and Behaviors in a Retailing Context." *Journal of the Academy of Marketing Science*, vol. 33, no. 2, Apr. 2005, pp. 123–38. CrossRef, doi:10.1177/0092070304268417.

so effective—people tend to interact with similar people. Sales managers tend to know other sales managers, and get kudos for sharing insider tips, like that new sales tool you made. Skateboarders hang out with other skateboarders and get "mad cred" for showing off their new frictionless air wheels you invented.

How do you get to this stage, though? How do you get customers to tell other customers about your product or service? The first step is remarkability. You need to create your product or service to be so targeted to a specific customer type that they get social credit for having found it and for sharing it with their peers.

Got their attention? Now, make it easy for them to spread the word. If it's online software or an app, build in the sharing buttons for users to share things to social media. If it's an offline product, add some kind of handout card to the box that they can give to friends to tell them how to get one too. Consider giving points or merchandise to reward your most loyal customers for finding you more customers. Feeling devious? Build forced virality into your product like the old *Farmville* games. It doesn't have to use Facebook, but you could make the product more useful and powerful if more people use it—that's virality too.

Step 2: Begin with the Customer in Mind

From the start, think deeply about the specific kind of customer who would truly love to buy your product or service. Don't just consider their age, gender, and geographical location (demographics), but also consider what they do, how they think, and what they love (psychographics).

A common technique is to develop one, two, or (at maximum) three customer personas or fictional people with made up names. These people have a face (which you can borrow from a Google search), they have demographics, and they have psychographics. The reason you choose two or three is to try to include just a few personas that are a good match for your product. The ideal number is just one persona, because then you can be very targeted and thus very interesting and appealing to that one persona. If you have two or three, hopefully they share some commonalities that you can market to. If it takes more than three, your product is probably too bland and boring, so retry.

Now that you've got the personas, it's time to build your product positioning statement. Figure 5.2 below shows the construct of this statement, and it's up to you to fill in the blanks. The main idea is to try to make it clear who the customer is and why they would want your product in context of the competition. See, those 5 Cs and 4 Ps are popping up all over the place!

_____ is a _____ that does _____ for _____ .
(product)   (category)   (core benefit)   (target customer)

Unlike other _____ products, _____ does _____ .
                  (category)   (product)   (unique benefit)

Figure 5.2: Product Positioning Statement

Step 3: Measure, Measure, Measure

How will you know what marketing technique is working if you are not measuring it? Each and every thing you do to try to attract customers, whether it costs you money or not, should be tracked to see if it worked. You may ask, "Why track free attempts?" Because nothing is ever free. It takes time to write those tweets on Twitter, to hand out fliers, and to make phone calls; everything has a cost, even if it's just a trade off of time.

Measuring digital is easy, and I would be surprised if you're not already doing it. Google Analytics has made it easy to track traffic sources, clicks, and sales. It should be your go to for tracking anything that has an internet connection, including apps, websites, and even some physical products. Most digital advertising platforms like Facebook and AdSense will also allow you to track digital sales. This is essential and incredibly valuable to determine what works, what kinds of messaging are effective, and where your sales are coming from. Determining not just what is bringing people to your site (ads of half clothed models can do that easily enough), but what kind of messaging is actually bringing people to your site and what are they doing once they get through the sale.

Beyond digital, though, every marketing effort should be measured. Trade shows can be measured using business cards in a fish bowl, and then using follow ups to see who buys. Billboards can be tracked with unique URLs just for that campaign. Every phone call, print ad, and TV ad should be measured not just for "reach" or how many people see it, but also for action. Whatever action you wanted them to take needs to be attributed back to the marketing effort you started. The ultimate action, in all business, is sales. You can always ask your customer how they heard about you when you make a sale. This is the least you should be doing.

Step 4: Offer Win Win Value

What is value? Value is what the other person gets out of the transaction, minus the cost that they paid. For this reason, you cannot charge a price that is equal to the value, because the customer is more likely to just keep their money in their pocket—there is nothing in it for them. Give them one cent? Still, barely worth the effort they must make to open their wallet. You need to give them a reason to buy, and that reason is value to them, in their frame.

Figure 5.3 below shows how this value compares to price and cost. Notice how the value of the item has nothing to do with the cost. In fact, nobody except you cares about the cost. Even investors don't care about the cost of your product or service, at least initially (more on this in Chapter 7). The key idea here is that there needs to be enough value above the price for your product to be bought, and it has nothing to do with cost.

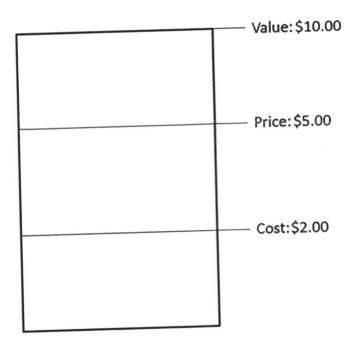

Figure 5.3: Pricing Based on Value

To illustrate the concept of value based pricing, first consider the light bulb—that cheap item you buy at the grocery store. It is incandescent because it uses a filament and emits a lot of heat. In fact, the heat makes it wear out fast and the filament can break easily. Assume that $0.50 is the average price of a light bulb at your local grocery store. Now, how much value does that light bulb have? At night, when it's dark, it is valued at maybe $1.00, for this example. See, it was easily worth it to buy that light bulb.

Now consider one of the new compact fluorescent light bulbs. These light bulbs last five times as long, use less energy, emit less heat, and don't require changing as often. Value? Hell yes! Not just the $1, but one could also argue at least $5 of value, since it's like buying five of the regular kind in a row. The value is probably higher if you also include the frustration factor in changing a light bulb. Also, lower energy costs are a real thing—when I say lower, I mean 1/5 of the energy. Add it all up, and you can easily say that the value for the compact fluorescent light bulb is $10.

What price should you charge for the new compact fluorescent light bulb?

If you chose $10, you left nothing for the customer. It was too high, so nobody bought it.

If you chose $5, you are closer, but still wrong. You will capture some early adopters, but people used to paying $0.50 may still not feel like it's worth it, since they can just buy five regular light bulbs for $2.50.

As it turns out, around $2 per bulb is nearly perfect. It is not quite five times the price of the original light bulb, and it leaves at least $0.50 of perceived savings to the price conscious folks who are price shopping.

The average price at launch of the compact fluorescent light bulb was around $5. Today, you can find them for about $2. Notice the cost of the bulbs has nothing to do with the price.

Step 5: Be Understood in Understanding Customer Needs

To communicate value, and thus convince someone that they are getting value when they buy your product or service (B2B or B2C), you must understand what your customer needs. This understanding comes from step two above, and continues throughout the life of your startup.

Once you know what they need, you have to put it in a form that they will understand that you understood it.

What?

You need to demonstrate to the customer that you get it, and that your solution solves it. The best way to communicate this is not by describing your product—that doesn't tell them either of these things. Instead, you have to describe the benefits of your solution, not the details of your solution. You have to show them what they will be like once their need has been solved. You have to show them how they will be a hero for solving the problem. In short, you aren't selling solutions, products, or services, but you are selling a happier, more respected, more awesome them.

Consider a series of examples to illustrate this point. First, imagine poor, wimpy Arthur of the Camelot tale. He is just a boy, not even a man. And there it is, a sword in a stone, Excalibur. Do you want to buy it? No. You already have a sword—you have five. But this sword is special. Why? It can make you a king. The entire sale of the sword is not the sword, but the fact that the person who holds it will be king. That's worth $2 for a try at pulling it out, eh?

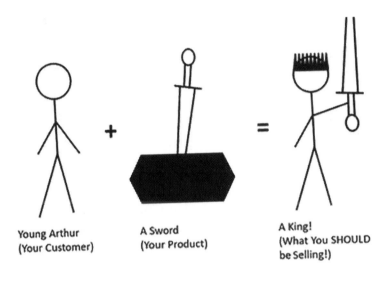

Young Arthur | **A Sword** | **A King!**
(Your Customer) | (Your Product) | (What You SHOULD be Selling!)

Figure 5.4: Marketing to Arthur of the Camelot Legend

To continue the examples, you are not selling mushrooms to Mario—you are selling Super Mario, the guy who can break bricks with his head, jump super high, and never die.

The best real world example of this is any Apple, Inc. advertisement. Consider the advertisement for the iPod. Remember the awesome dancing silhouettes with white earbuds sticking out. Instead of being lanky and boring, they can dance! Move on to the iPhone ads, and now, you can dance, walk on walls, ignore the dirty streets, and take amazing, picturesque photos of wildlife in the forest. They are not selling you a phone, they are selling a version of *you* that you want to be: freer, happier, and dancing, even!

What does this mean for you and your startup? Everything. If it seems like nobody cares about you, it could be that you are not connecting with your customer. You are not showing them who they will be once they have your product or service. You are not making them a hero or a king. It's time to try it. Talk about the benefits of your product, what it will personally do for them, and talk less about your features. They might start caring enough to actually wonder, "Gee, what are these features that get me this benefit?" If they do, you've got them! They suddenly care.

Step 6: Synergize the Message

In Step 3, I talked about measurement. It is important to measure, and in fact, it is essential to understand what to invest in and what not to invest in. Unfortunately, marketing is more complex than that. There is evidence that it can take three or more sources of exposure for your brand (ads, social media, etc.) before a customer becomes aware enough to consider taking action.[6] This fact is especially true in a higher priced item, rather than a low priced one that could be an impulse buy. A customer might start thinking about it when they see it once in a Facebook ad, and then talk it over with their spouse after reading a review, and then forget about it. Three weeks later, they might see a Google ad, and finally take action by purchasing it. This process of discovery, consideration, and purchase is a cycle that you need to think through for your product or service and for your particular customer type and channel. Even a consumer product might have a sales funnel to traverse—just ask my wife, when I wanted to spend $3,000 on a new surround sound system. I had a whole buying process after that idea, which I did smartly run by her first.

Since you need to consider the buying process of your customer, your marketing efforts need to work together to get your customer all the way to the action (sale, subscription, first order, free trial, etc.). Short, simple ads need to drive attention and interest, but if your pricing is off (say, $3,000), you might consider asking for a customer's e mail address as they browse your site. Collecting e mails is a great way to get permission to reach out and get one more marketing reach for almost no cost to you.

---

[6] Pechmann, Cornelia, and David Stewart. "Advertising Repetition: A Critical Review of Wearin and Wearout." *Current Issues and Research in Advertising*, vol. 11, Mar. 1988. ResearchGate, doi:10.1080/01633392.1988.10504936.

Video content on your site, or on YouTube, will allow people to learn more about your solution. More specifically, it will allow them to discover what they will be like once they have your product or service (see Step 5). Reviews and testimonials can be used to help customers get over the most common objections and to build trust with your brand and product or service. Press, articles, and even white papers can help overcome objections and might lead to yet one more reach. When a customer starts searching while they are researching if they should buy your product/service or not, you want them to find answers outside your own website and from trusted other sources.

Your social media campaign is all about the increasing chances that "almost customers" will become "real customers." That's why putting social media links on your website is so important—it's like collecting an e mail address. It is yet another way you might reach a customer once you've started down this multichannel pathway.

Finally, comparable products and pricing might make sense to help your customer compare your product to alternatives. You don't have to put buy links for competitor products, but talking about how you are better, or, better yet, how they will be better if they buy your product and not the competitor's, will help seal the deal.

All these efforts work together and help facilitate your customers' buying decision. Your approach should be multichannel and considered. You may need to experiment to find the right marketing mix, but it is almost never just one thing.

Step 7: Sharpen the Marketing Saw through Experimentation

Experimentation in marketing and all things startup is the key to eventual success. Not everything you try in marketing will work. The good news is that since you installed measurement capability, you will be able to tell what works and what doesn't.

This search of finding new and better ways to reach customers and convincing them to care never ends. You will launch in new markets to new customers and with new products and services as you grow. You will also likely reach plateaus of growth where you can't seem to grow more. These plateaus are only broken up by constant experimentation with marketing.

Each of the steps outlined above can be tested and adjusted. Digital marketing is so incredibly useful because this testing can be done quickly using random samples to groups of 50 or more. The Google experiments tool that I explain how to set up and use in my blog is particularly effective at testing content, buttons, messaging, and more.[7] Most advertising platforms allow for simultaneous advertisements to run with different messaging and graphics. All of this is how you evolve over time and get better. You are getting sharper the day you decide that you will measure your marketing efforts and cut those things that do not lead to results or at least make an impact.

Marketing when Nobody Cares

Along the seven steps of effective marketing I have just outlined, you may have noticed one or more areas where you might have realized you could do better. That is the point. The reason nobody cares is not because they dislike you, it's because either they have never heard of you (most likely) or what they have heard is not interesting or compelling enough for them to take action. In our multichannel world, it is possible that they have not heard of you *enough* and need to be reached in more than one marketing channel, be it Facebook, TV, Magazine, or some other marketing channel where they might also hear about you.

In the case that nobody cares because you are not reaching enough potential customers, you need to do better at getting the word out. It's time to start experimenting with other methods of getting attention and being noticed. The next chapter will cover ways to scale up your marketing once people start caring (e.g. when sales are flowing). However, in this early stage, it is possible and even likely that you don't have enough money to invest in the advertising you will be able to afford later, such as TV and Magazines. Now is the time to test every free marketing idea you have ever heard or read about. Table 5.2 below is a list of some of the free marketing and advertising ideas you can try to get the word out.

In the case when people are coming to your site or they are becoming leads, but they are just not converting into sales, it's time to try pivoting on messaging. Consider Step 5 from above, and reframe your offerings in terms of benefits and how you can make them become a king. Consider adding trust symbols like security icons and Visa logos. Consider adding testimonials and videos. You need to create a multichannel experience that guides customers to take the next appropriate action, whether that is "Get a Quote" or "Buy Now."

---

[7] http://fastai.com/blog/2014/06/18/3-ways-to-do-google-ab-testing-or

Table 5.2: Free Marketing/Advertising Ideas

Ideas for Free Attention
Search engine optimization (website and/or blog)
Community outreach to bloggers
Community outreach through guerrilla marketing on other people's websites
Standing outside of trade shows (unpaid)
Standing on the street near a store (unpaid)
PR: Contacting media about your story
PR: Contacting media to request a review
Social media: Getting fans/followers through contests, tweets, posting in Facebook groups, etc.
Social media: Driving action through social postings
E mail marketing: E mailing leads you generate from your organic traffic

The Big Pivot

As has been described before, a business pivot is when a startup changes direction in response to some key learning. When nobody cares, the first temptation is to pivot strong and fast to something completely different, and ignore the fact that few have heard about it (more promotion needed) or what they hear doesn't *interest them* (benefits and value). It is always important to make sure you have really tried to get the word out and communicate your benefits and value well before you consider a big pivot. Try a series of small pivots first and you might just crack open that tide of customers just waiting to become heroes by using your product or service. However, at some point, you may need to take more drastic action.

Remember, the 4 Ps and 5 Cs of marketing are about more than just *promotion*, which is what advertising is all about. It's also about the product, the price, and the place. Price is not really a big pivot; it's something easy enough to try very quickly, even with a simple Google experiment. Product and place, however, are big pivots worth considering only after you've fully tested your ideas and gotten feedback from actual customers that you got something wrong.

A product pivot is easy to understand; it's simply changing your product offering to better fit what customers want. Most people think this means adding more of what customers want, but in reality, a good product pivot should be about moving toward what customers want *and* cutting what they don't really care about. If you are doing a product pivot, it is important that you go back to

Chapter 3 and start the validation process over again before you over invest in your new product idea.

A place pivot is more complex because you are using the same product, the same price, and the same promotion, but your customers just buy it somewhere else. Place pivots can be beneficial when your brand is very young and not yet established. For example, if you are selling glassware like whiskey glasses, you will probably have trouble selling them through your own online store. Put them on Amazon, however, and at the right price, they might sell very well indeed. Similarly, a new place could add legitimacy or ease the buying process in a variety of ways. Putting your products on eBay sends one message, and putting your products on Etsy sends another. Where on eBay your products were considered *used*, on Etsy, they are considered *repurposed* or handmade.

A place pivot could also open up access to customers you could not reach before. Working with resellers or agents, for example, could mean opening accounts where buyers, such as B2B buyers, only deal with a few limited sales agents. Getting set up in distribution could also help you reach a broader set of customers faster—for example, being set up with Pepsi distribution could let you reach hundreds of thousands of restaurants, grocery stores, and gas stations. A place pivot is the same thing as a channel pivot, the two words are interchangeable. Channel/place pivots where you have to get a partner, such as resellers or distributors, are more risky than direct sale channel pivots. Resellers and distributors will take percentage points off of your sale—from 5% to as high as 30% such as in the Apple iTunes Store or Google Play Store. You also have to convince the reseller or distributor to partner with you. While *collaborators* is one of the 5 Cs of business, in my experience, it's also one of the most risky—it is out of your control and could take a long time to *secure* that partnership deal.

Regardless of what you do as a big pivot, remember, if the customer or the product changes, you'll need to revalidate. This is why avoiding a big pivot and trying a bunch of smaller ideas first is usually a good idea.

The Story of Spredfast

In 2008, social media marketing was in its infancy. Everyone knew that Facebook and Twitter were going to be important, but very few companies had figured out how to capitalize on the new opportunities. There were challenges, too. Customers wanted to engage with companies in these new mediums, but companies didn't know how to interact in these public settings.

Ken Cho and Scott McCaskill, the founders of Social Agency, Inc., had an idea. They would create a company that would act like an advertising agency, but focus on all things social media. Their plan was to use their clients to pay for the development of more automation tools to serve those clients, all while allowing the customers (B2B) to interact with them like an agency. Social Agency, Inc. was born, and nobody cared.

The problem was there: Companies were struggling to figure out what to do with the new world of social media. In addition, social media was hot, it was attracting a ton of investment, and everyone wanted to be part of the rising market tide. When Social Agency hit the street, early customers around the Austin area— where Ken and Scott started Social Agency—got it. They liked being able to talk to Ken and Scott and the team. They appreciated the guidance as well as the work they got from their agency. The problem came later, when Ken and Scott were looking to go national and to attract more customers. Nobody cared about a social agency. The concept wasn't resonating. It was time to pivot.

In about a year, despite early traction with Social Agency, their team decided to change tracks. They pivoted. Their pivot was small, but it ended up being exactly what the market wanted. They did not fundamentally change what they did; they still helped companies figure out what to do in social media and how to execute it. They simply rebranded the company (a surprisingly easy task), and started talking differently about what their company did.

Spredfast was born, and by 2010 had acquired a lot more customers, many of them outside of Austin, and had even secured $1.6 million in funding.[8] The messaging, even the name, switched to the benefits of working with their team, and not on what they do. They took a classic case of "what we do for you" and turned it into a "what you get when you work with us." You get literally spread... fast. Spreading fast on social media was exactly what customers were looking for. The Spredfast team developed the tools and techniques to help companies do just this, and to help them quickly claim and keep their strong market share position in the new world of social media.

Today, although Ken has moved on to found another startup, Spredfast continues to grow and be one of the largest startups in Central Texas. Ken stepped down as CEO in 2011 (a story for Chapter 12), but stayed on until the merger of Spredfast with Mass Relevance in 2014. At that time, Ken was able to take a sizable exit for himself that was enough to fund his next venture and more. His newest venture, People Pattern, continues to grow as it finds its niche in the world of big data and social media to find audience insights.

---

[8] https://www.bizjournals.com/austin/blog/techflash/2013/12/spredfast-closes-225m-funding.html

The point of the story is two fold. First, Ken and Scott did not give up when early customer patterns started to show that nobody cared. Instead, they kept going, talked to customers, and found out that their solution wasn't the problem—it was how they were talking about it that was hurting sales. Their brand and messaging pivot was the key to unlocking customer success, and ultimately, financial success for the co founders and their team.

Analytical Tool: Dealing with Apathy

Apathy is when there is simply a lack of caring. If your customers are apathetic about your product or service, there could be a number of reasons why. Your job is to get to the bottom of them and to experiment with new ideas, new messaging, and new ways of reaching potential customers. Table 5.3 offers a tool to measure the learning you are getting from customers, assign a value to that learning, and propose the next experiment to make. In general, if you have earned at least 1,000 points of learning and have still not started gaining the traction you desire, it is time to consider a big pivot and to go back to Chapter 3. It's not the end; it's just a new beginning. The only way to truly fail at your startup is to give up altogether. All other mini failures along the way are simply learning points that you get to feed back in to the next cycle. These points will add up in the end, and offer you a reward for your hard work.

Table 5.3: Apathy Learning and Suggested Next Experiment Table

Customer Learning	Value of Learning	Suggested Next Experiment
At least 100 potential customers interacted with your site/call/lead.	100	How many sales did you get?
You made at least 1 sale per 100 qualified leads.	1000	Stop! 1% means that people probably do care. Experiment to reduce your customer acquisition cost or increase your lifetime value.
You interviewed 10 customers or prospective customers about their apathy.	200	Great. What did they say?
You surveyed at least 50 customers or prospective customers about their apathy.	300	Great. What did the surveys say?

Customer Learning	Value of Learning	Suggested Next Experiment
Surveys/Interviews said: Not enough value compared to price.	300	Experiment with lower price (if possible) or increase value (perhaps by just talking about it differently).
Surveys/Interviews said: Problem is not big enough.	200	Experiment with different messaging that focuses on benefits instead of features.
Surveys/Interviews said: Not sure if they can trust you.	300	Experiment by adding trust symbols, reviews, and testimonials.
Surveys/Interviews said: Competitor is entrenched such that switching to new offerings is too burdensome.	300	Experiment by offering free trials or working with partners. Consider trying a different target customer set.
Surveys/Interviews said: Solution incomplete.	200	Experiment by lowering your claims, or targeting a different customer set that would appreciate your "simplicity" more.
Surveys/Interviews said: Just don't understand.	200	You clearly have a messaging problem. Try breaking up your benefits from your features. Lead with benefits, and then provide a "how it works" section/part of your pitch.
Customers are too hard/expensive to reach effectively.	300	Consider trying a new channel (place) or a new customer segment that is easier to reach.

Chapter 6
Somebody Cares—Yippee! Now what?

"Ten thousand players in two hours?" Chris asks excitedly.

"Yep, we got a YouTube review from one of the game reviewers and players are flocking to try out our free game," I reply.

"And how is our LTV looking so far?" Chris asks.

I just look at him askance. He knows it's too early to tell.

. . .

Forty eight hours later, Chris and I sit once again at his desk discussing progress with Night Owl Games' new title, *Dungeon Overlord. Dungeon Overlord* is a new kind of web based game that is built inside of Facebook and with social gaming in mind. Unlike the more casual games like *Farmville, Dungeon Overlord* was designed for real, competitive gamers. The plot is that you control a dungeon filled with evil creatures that you can send on raiding parties against other player's dungeons. It's a player vs player game designed to push players to play constantly or spend money to keep up.

It is also completely free—that is, unless you want to buy something. You can buy boosts, things that speed up waiting times as things build, and even skins to make your creatures and dungeon look cooler than your friends'.

"How are we looking?" Chris asks from his swivel chair, having just typed some line of code. Chris was the CEO of Night Owl Games, but he was also one of the best coders on the team. He had me there to take care of marketing and sales.

"Chris," I start, looking sad, and then suddenly looking happy, "actually, we're looking great! Lifetime value after just two days of all those new players is well over two dollars on average and rising. The best part is we have about 100 whale players who seem to have already learned the best things to buy and keep buying over and over."

Chris just smiles.

"Retention rates are just okay though. We are holding at eighty percent second visit retention and fifty percent third. I wish retention were little higher on the third visit, but I have some ideas for e mail marketing to fix that," I say.

"Okay, so, let's call our investors and start driving players to the game," he says.

"On ads?"

"Yep. You can do it, right?" He asks.

DOI 10.1515/9781501507083-006

"Well, yeah, I know how to set it all up, but I've never spent the kind of money you are talking about. Fifty thousand dollars a month will drive a lot of players to the game," I say, excitedly.

"Yep, and you have to keep those LTVs high too. We can't afford to let those slip," he says.

For the next year, we did just that. We attracted over a million players to the game, and maintained customer lifetime values (LTVs) at a profitable level. Somebody cared and we hit the gas hard. The payoff was there. My only regret was not hitting the gas even harder. Eventually, Facebook changed its algorithms and ads become more expensive than LTVs. It was a wild ride while it lasted, though.

The Startup Journey/Phases of the Startup

Up to this point, most of the failures I have been sharing are about getting started. Getting started, however, is only just the beginning of the startup journey. In fact, I like to think of the startup journey as a roller coaster. Figure 6.1 below illustrates what I mean. Unlike other roller coasters, this one has many loops back onto itself. The startup journey roller coaster also has several ways to "get off the ride," some good and some bad.

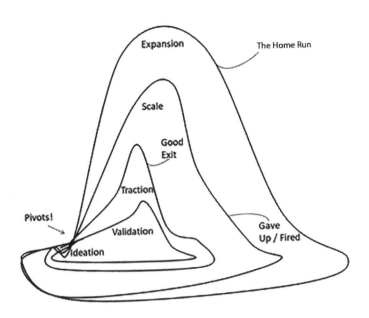

Figure 6.1: The Startup Journey Roller Coaster (Phases of the Startup)

Each phase of the startup journey is depicted as an increasingly tall roller coaster path. The higher the phase, the further you can fall. During the ideation phase, it's easy and fast to pivot, and it's not very far to fall. During the validation phase, it's still pretty easy to pivot and the fall doesn't hurt. Once you hit the traction phase (Chapters 4 and 5) your fall is further, and it can be painful to implement a pivot, especially if you have to go back to ideation or validation. There are many stories of a good exit during the traction phase, but they are usually just lucky. Most investments and acquisitions in today's markets happen in the scale phase. It's the scale phase in which you use investor money to scale up. Scaling up is what you should do when you are getting traction, and it's the subject of this chapter. Sometimes, instead of an investor, you take a nice exit instead. A good exit during the scale phase is an acquisition or sale of assets to another company.

Beyond scale is expansion. The difference is that you can scale up one product, but to expand, you need a line of products. Most companies don't have an *initial public offering* (IPO) with just one product; they need a line of products and services, and they also need to have expanded into new markets. You don't have to have an IPO to have a home run exit—you could also be acquired for billions. I define a home run as anything over a 10x return to investors and founders.

Every loop back is a pivot. When you learn something or something isn't going right at whatever phase, it's a pivot. You simply adjust what you are doing depending on what you have learned. Sometimes the pivots are small, and sometimes they are large. As long as you are still on the ride, you have a chance. The only way off the ride is to give up or be fired, both of which I will cover in later chapters. For now, it's important to understand that a good exit, a home run, or a give up/fired pathway exists on every loop of the startup journey roller coaster. And of course, running a startup really is like a roller coaster. You will have ups and downs, high and low moments. As long as you are not giving up, the ride continues. No matter how high up you are though, ignoring critical facts and failing to pivot means giving in to *sunk costs* and almost certainly means you are destined for a crash.

How to Know Somebody Cares

In the last chapter, I showed you what to do if nobody cares. In Chapter 4, the formula to check that nobody cares was introduced as (CAC + COGS < LTV). With that formula you can be per unit profitable, but that may only be enough money to pay for noodles. Small scale testing is great for determining if nobody cares, and you should continue market research and validation at all phases. However, to know that somebody cares and that it is time to scale requires quite a bit more data and work.

To know that somebody (your target customer) cares, you need to have figured out at least one method of repeatable customer acquisition that involves profitable sales. A profitable sale still means that (CAC + COGS < LTV). What is new here is that you seem to be able to repeatedly get customers using the same method over and over again. The quantity and frequency of sales will vary greatly based on your startup type, pricing, and target customer. To know if you've got a repeatable customer acquisition flow, it needs to work at least five times. Five sales may not seem like a lot, and it may not be if you are spending a lot of money or selling inexpensive items, but it should be enough to give you and your investors a signal that you are onto something. Especially if you maintain (CAC + COGS < LTV), investors will see your five sales (and counting!) as validation that your customer acquisition flow seems to be working. You have traction.

Failing to Scale or Failing at Scaling

Once you are hitting traction by confirming that somebody cares, you have a choice to make. You can keep going slow and steady, and working hard to maintain your current growth rate. You can also try for an early exit, especially if you've already been approached as such. Or, you can shoot for the moon, and see how big you can scale up your customer acquisition and growth. There are risks and rewards with every path.

If you decide to go slow and grow organically, you may soon find that you are failing to scale. In other words, you may fail and stagnate (stay small) or even start to decline in growth rates. There are lots of reasons for this, the main one being competition. Failing to scale often means leaving the market open for fast followers to come and capture the market from you. Fast followers are competitors who see what you are doing and, within a few months, are able to work around any intellectual property (IP) you may have built up and can use their surplus of money to out market or out advertise you. Once you've lost the market to a competitor, it is much harder and more costly to get it back. First mover advantage is just that—you pay less to acquire your customers for your product or service because you were first. Everyone after you has to battle you because you are already entrenched. No first mover advantage lasts forever, however. Products wear out, fashions go out of style, and that new startup down the street just invented something even better than what you have, which now gives them the advantage. It does last a while though, because your brand has earned credibility and those products you sold are still working. If you can outmaneuver the competition on that new innovation they just announced, you can maintain your first mover advantage even further. It all hinges on your decision and ability to move fast, grow fast, and capture the market. If you leave too much of the market un-captured, the market will become fragmented as competitors battle it out for your customers. Fragmented markets usually mean it costs more (higher CPA) to ac-quire customers.

Many companies decide to raise money from institutional investors at this point to empower their scale up. It takes money to scale and capture market share, and investors are attracted to investment deals that they are convinced will be able to grow even faster with their investment dollars. Failing to scale isn't necessarily failing, however. It is possible to go the long haul, keep your equity for yourself, and just grow organically. Depending on your business and your goals, this strategy may be best for you because you can sometimes earn more in a small exit or achieve your goals better without outside investors. Once you take investor money, you will need a bigger exit in order to make the same amount of money for yourself.

If you decide to scale, you may find that you have trouble actually scaling the channel you thought was working before you tried to hit the gas. Also, hitting the gas without first making sure that someone cares (e.g., getting traction) is not advised. In both cases, what may happen is at small scale, and your customer acquisition worked. When you tried to spend more and more money, however, that customer acquisition method you thought was working so well suddenly doubles and triples in CPA. Now, you start losing money by getting customers, and a vicious cycle could ensue in which you try harder to spend money in that way, but keep losing more money. It's a fast way off the ride, because you are bleeding cash.

What is probably happening when you are failing at scaling is that you are pursuing the same customer you did before. That small, targeted niche market that loved you before still loves you, but there does not seem to be as many as you thought. Your conversion rates are going up, and you are not connecting with the audience at the same rates. In order to continue to grow, you have to get past the early adopters and "cross the chasm" to reach the audience that isn't as will-ing to take risks on a new startup.[1] Sometimes, this is just a change in how you talk about your product (messaging). Adding more reviews and testimonials can help, as can putting your product or service in places where customers feel more trust (Amazon or Home Depot, for example). In addition, growing beyond your

---

[1] Moore, Geoffrey A. Crossing the Chasm: Marketing and Selling Disruptive Products to Main-stream Customers. Harper Collins, 2002.

early adopter niche may require you to reach them differently. Groupon and Woot, as examples, are ways to reach beyond the early adopters and into the types of customers who want a good value or bargain. Regardless of this, you will need to experiment with all of this as you scale, and keep an ever watchful eye on the conversion rates and CPA. If you can test and react fast enough, you will be able to continuously scale and expand on your customer acquisition channels and methods to keep CPAs down. At that time, it's time to think about a possible exit, or about that new product or service launch (expansion phase).

Another reason you might fail at scaling up is because advertising does not usually scale linearly. When marketplace advertising is used, such as Google and Facebook advertisements, you don't actually get a discount in cost per advertisement—instead, you pay more per ad than before. The reason for this is that your ads start to compete more with other companies' ads because your reach interferes with theirs. As a result, your CPA goes up even if your conversion rates stay the same because CPC has gone up. If your CPA goes up, you will need to work hard to try to increase your conversion rates while lowering your CPC. Figure 6.2 below illustrates this concept of what may happen as you try to scale up in a single channel very quickly. The way to keep the cost per click or cost per thousand impressions (CPM) down is to try direct or bulk purchasing. Buying banner ads on a site directly, for example, will usually be cheaper than trying to buy the same number of ads via the Google ad marketplace. Spending money in multiple advertising channels will also spread the cost burden of competing ads and allow you to potentially scale that way. In short, you will have to look for new ways to spend advertising money and probably will not be able to rely on the method that got you through the traction phase. If you can figure it out, move fast enough, and test, you will scale. If you scale, or even start to scale, while keeping profitability high, you may have opportunities to exit, or else it is time to start planning for expansion.

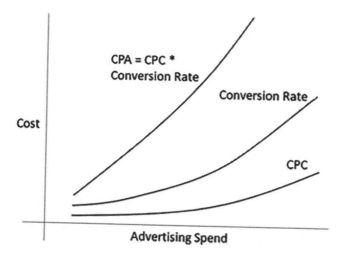

Figure 6.2: Rising Costs as You Scale Advertising Spend

One of the ironies of scaling up is that you become more attractive to potential acquirers. The reason for this is that scaling up means you are gaining more market share and also attracting more revenues. Your profile as a company will also be higher as you gain recognition in national press. You suddenly end up on the radar of acquirers and they have to decide to buy you or compete with you. They cannot ignore you any longer. What is the irony? In order to scale, you probably have to take investor money (see the next chapter for more details). If you do, they will want a bigger return than what acquirers are willing to pay right now. In other words, while everyone might make a little money with an acquisition at this stage, your investors may actively block it because they want a chance at the magical 10x or even 100x return on investment. In fact, your success will make them feel like they should "let it ride." It is at this stage that many founders get frustrated with their investors. "Why can't we all just make a nice 2x return, and make me a millionaire?" many founders wonder. It's one of the worst ironies in the startup world: Now that you've made it, you can't sell. You'll have to try for expansion, which is yet another chance to fail. If you were able to get here without too much investment, let's say less than 50%, you may have the power to force the sale anyway. My advice would probably be to take it. That is, unless I am an investor—in which case, I might think, *Gee, let's let it ride, I might be able to get a 10x return out of this instead of a measly 2x return on my investment.* Sick, isn't it?

Hitting the Gas

We may be getting ahead of ourselves by thinking about exit. It is tempting to do so, though, and it can actually be useful to help you when the roller coaster is on a downward hill. Before that exit can happen, however, we have to scale. To scale, it means hitting the gas on what is working, and on experimenting what might work. You have to do both, or else the rising costs of customer acquisition (CPA) will eat your profits and you will fail at scaling. Testing will show how to combat this rising cost and allow you to stay ahead of it. Hitting the gas means increasing spending in both areas, testing and when you find something, increasing spending until it starts to almost become unprofitable (CPA + COGS = LTV) to do so.

As you increase advertising, you are expecting to increase sales. As a result, you will also need to start hiring or contracting more people to help you. Hitting the gas is also about scaling up the team that can deliver the results you need. Someone to help you manage marketing or run marketing, a CMO or marketing director, can be a big help, as the area you need to grow the most is your customer acquisition. Outsourcing production, shipping, and other logistics is usually the best approach to dealing with those issues. Amazon, for example, has a program called "Fulfillment by Amazon" where you can warehouse in their three big regions and ship to almost anywhere with two day shipping.[2] This affects not only sales you get on Amazon, by the way, but also sales from anywhere else, including retailers or sales from your own website. Chapter 9 will discuss more about hiring and the challenges therein. For now, bear in mind that you will probably need to scale your team as your sales scale. Note that I said as your sales scale, not as your advertising spend increases. Without the sales to support the larger staff, you will need to keep your team small and lean. As many dollars as possible should go into your marketing efforts, and you should only hire when you are overwhelmed by sales (see Chapter 9). Until then, you or your co founders need to be the ones hitting the gas on your advertising and sales efforts. It is surprisingly easy to do this on the two largest platforms out there: Google and Facebook.

---

[2] https://services.amazon.com/fulfillment-by-amazon/benefits.htm

Test Advertising

If you have not been using advertising to acquire customers up to this point, it is time to start testing. Your mission is to systematically try as many systems and types for ads as you can find, and try them out one after the other. To do an ad test, you will have to think, *Measure, measure, measure!* You need to install conversion tracking at a minimum from Google.[3] Google Analytics has a very simple conversion tracking technology that lets you send it conversion events to track, as well as web tracking data. If your website is not your main source of sales, but rather sends you leads, then you track the lead form and not the sales form. You may also need a tool like Salesforce to track your sales funnel. You don't have to use Salesforce for this, however—you could use a free shared Google Sheet (spreadsheet) instead. You do need to track where your leads came from, though, so that you know what marketing works.

If you start with a budget of $100, you can measure how many leads or clicks you get from any given ad system and type. Once you have 50 to 100 clicks or leads, you can measure conversion rate from that source as the number of sales divided by the number of leads you got. You can also measure CPA for that channel only as your ad spend divided by the number of sales you got. If you got zero sales, try something else.

The top three advertising channels to test are Facebook ads, Google search ads, and LinkedIn ads. Once your testing shows promise, now you need to test scale. To test scale, you should increase budget, adjust, measure, and repeat. It's the adjusting part that is needed to keep control of CPAs, however.

Corporate Innovation

Many corporations are organized into departments like marketing, engineering, finance, sales, and so forth. While this structure helps make it easy to know one's roles and responsibilities inside an organization, it is not always a good structure when it comes to corporate innovation. The problem is that individuals are far too tempted to *pass the buck* down stream to the next department in the line. Engineering leaves marketing to marketers, marketers leave sales to sales, and so on.

In order to do corporate innovation right, innovators need to stay with their innovation all the way through the product's lifecycle. The marketing of the product and the sales efforts are every bit as important as the idea and creation of the product itself. In fact, they are all connected into creating something of value, something that customers want, and the ultimate success or not of the innovation. Read this chapter with an eye toward learning what marketers should be doing to understand customers, how to reach them, and how to scale results once the paths to customers have been mapped.

---

[3] https://developers.google.com/analytics/devguides/collection/analyticsjs/events

Scaling Facebook Advertising

Advertising on Facebook is different than using Facebook for your social media efforts. Social media marketing is about engaging with your customers and fans to get and keep them interested in you and what you do. It is quite different than growing customers and getting those fans in the first place. In addition, social media marketing is generally difficult to scale, and most companies realize this only after they actually try to do it. How do you consistently add 1,000,000 new fans per month?

The answer is that you can't—not even Kim Kardashian can do that. Instead, in order to grow your fans and, more importantly, get sales, you'll need to advertise. Could you scale up a company without spending on advertising? Maybe, but I've never seen it. You can start a company and get some sales without ads, but eventually you'll have to start spending money on marketing to reach new customers.

Fortunately, Facebook makes it easy to spend money on marketing. In fact, you can pay Facebook for a lot of things, including new fans, spreading your posts out (boosting posts), and generating clicks.[4] However, you should not pay Facebook for things that don't eventually lead to sales, or else your CPA will go up. You're wasting money and not getting sales for it. Generating clicks is the thing that will most commonly lead to sales in a direct and scalable way. Where do those clicks go? They go to your landing page where you describe your product or service and make your pitch. It's your landing page that you will get your first conversion: a sale, a request for quote, or a lead (e mail/phone). That conversion either generates a sale or leads to a sale through your funnel. This works exceptionally well for consumer products where the price is low enough for the purchase to be an impulse decision. When the purchase is more considered, like B2B or large consumer purchases, you'll need to think about the sales process and get the information you need to level up the customer.

Facebook ads work like this: You set up your target audience and your ad, you make a bid for clicks, and you spend money based on how many clicks Facebook sends you. It's that easy. They will spend only up to your budget, and will not charge you more per click than you are willing to pay. The challenge to Facebook advertising is in setting up the audiences (you will need more than one), then crafting ads to fit those audiences and getting them to click through. Simply increasing your bids in one audience will not lead to better results—it will only

---

[4] https://www.facebook.com/advertising

lead to higher CPAs. To get more sales, you need to expand the audiences you are targeting and craft ads that fit each audience independently, potentially even crafting the landing pages where you send those clickers.

Setting up an audience is easy. You simply choose demographics (age, gender, location) and psychographics (interests, pages they like, and online activity), and the combination of those two things form an audience toward which you can target your ads. The trick is to get a decent sized audience (about 100,000 at a minimum), but not too big (1,000,000 at a maximum), and then create an ad that is targeted to that audience. When I browse Facebook, I routinely get ads for *Top Gun* t shirts. Why? Because *Top Gun* is my favorite movie (I pressed like on the *Top Gun* movie Facebook page long ago), and I am a male over 40 years old, so I get ads for this. In addition, I have clicked on similar ads and bought the dang t shirts in the past, so they just keep sending them to me. They've figured me out, and yes, I would and will buy more in the future.

Setting up the ads themselves is also pretty easy. You simply figure out what messages you think will work and you make five or six ads with various images and messages in them for each target audience. Remember, advertise benefits, not features! After that, you tweak every day based on what people are clicking or not clicking. I've found that ads with red in them usually get more clicks. Ads with deals in them also tend to get more clicks.

Once you start getting clicks, then you can expand your budget, up and up, until you start to see diminishing returns and lowering CPAs. It's then that you need to target new audiences and try new messages again. It's a daily chore, but one that is necessary to keep control as you scale.

Scaling Google Advertising

Google has at least three types of advertising on offer. Video ads are for YouTube pre roll advertisements; it's a modern form of television advertising. Video ads are usually about getting *brand impressions*, rather than sales. Brand advertising is usually not part of a good scale up plan because it doesn't lead directly to sales and can thus negatively impact CPA. Google AdSense allows you to place banner advertisements on other people's websites algorithmically. AdSense places the ads based on the content or text of the page matching keywords and phrases you configure. If you sell fishing rods, for example, you would target AdSense ads to the keywords *fishing* and *angling,* and then your banner ads would show up on sites like fieldandstream.com and similar fishing sites. Google AdSense also lets you geo target and target based on some user demographics. In that sense, Google AdSense ads are similar to Facebook ads, just on the broader web. AdSense ads are worth testing and may yield similar results to Facebook ads, depending on how well you target and how good your ads are. Google search ads, on the other hand, are a totally different kind of beast, and are worth looking at closely as part of your scale up efforts.

The difference between Google search advertising and Facebook advertising is first in the mindset of the potential customer. A Facebook visitor, or even a fieldandstream.com visitor, is there to read Facebook or the website they came to see. They are not there to look at ads, so the ads are an annoyance. In fact, they may even have an ad blocker and never see your ad to begin with. Google search ads, on the other hand, target customers who are actively searching for something. Whether that is a search for a brand, a solution to their problem, or if they are just shopping, they are in the mood for an answer. They are open to being advertised to if you have the answer they seek. If they are shopping, they are actually ready right now to consider you, and will respond to offers and promotions even more than if they are reading their Facebook feed and happen across your promotion. For this reason, scaling up Google search advertising is an important and potentially highly scalable technique worth testing.

You can scale up any types of Google advertising by increasing targeting, budget, and/or bids. As mentioned before, only increasing budget will not usually get you more clicks or leads, because competitors are already consuming clicks from the marketplace. You could bump up budget and bids, and if you have room in your LTV equation, you can do this a little, but CPAs will creep up and could start to eat away at profits after a while. In order to scale Google ads without pushing up CPAs, you will have to focus on targeting.

Targeting ads on Google is handled differently for each type of ad. For all three ad types, you can do some limited demographic targeting, but it is limited and not nearly as accurate as Facebook's demographic targeting. Geo targeting works well because it is based on IP address (they know where you are generally). The rest of demographics targeting on Google is murky. Think about it this way, do Google users log in every time, and if they do, is their birthdate known by Google? Sometimes, yes, often, no, so Google tends to guess. On the other hand, Facebook knows not only your birthday, but also other information, such as your anniversary or your parents' names. For YouTube ads, you can also target based on topic, interests, placements, and keywords. YouTube videos are categorized (by topic) and have descriptions (for keywords), and your ads are placed on ones that have a match to your keywords or topic. For Google AdSense ads (banner ads placed algorithmically on other websites), placements and keywords are available. Google's computers read every website and scan them for keywords that might match what you program. Placements in both cases are simply specifying the website, web page, video, or video series you want your ads to show on manually rather than algorithmically.

For Google search ads, the ad type that I believe is the most important, you target based primarily on keywords. The idea here is to think of phrases that people type when they search. Those phrases, and words within them, become your keywords. Your text ads will match those phrases as answers to the search question. For example, you might be selling flashlights. You target the phrases "best flashlights," and "top flashlights of 2017." You then create an ad for each phrase (a separate ad group for each) to say, "Learn why ACME builds the best flashlights," and "See a list of the top flashlights of 2017." The first link goes directly to your best flashlight where you describe (using the word best) why your product is the best. The second link goes to a different page, probably a blog article on your site, that lists what you believe are the top flashlights, even if the top three are your own products. This is how you run a Google search ad campaign. You simply answer what people are searching for with answers you want them to have.

Scaling of all these ad types on Google can be challenging. You have to log in every day and add more keywords, placements, topics, and ads. You can't simply increase the budget and bid, as you will both run out of potential customers searching for that answer, and your CPA will creep up until it is no longer profitable. In fact, you also have to turn off any ads or keywords that, after 50 to 100 clicks, are not delivering you sales results. This is why it is so important to install those conversion tracking pixels that Facebook and Google provide. They can show you not just your overall conversion rates, but also the conversion rates and CPA of each specific ad.

Other Advertising

There are many other types of advertising to test, both online and offline. For the online types, there are two paths: direct advertising and marketplace advertising. Direct banner placements onto the websites that seem to be best for you, is an example of direct advertising. For direct advertising, you work directly with the online site that you think is good for you and work out a deal with them. Marketplace advertising usually scales better, however, because in a marketplace, you can advertise on many sites without striking as many deals with individual sites. Google is an example of a marketplace for ads. Facebook and LinkedIn are hybrids of marketplace and direct. They offer a marketplace for their own sites, making it easy to set up ads there without making any human contact or special contract, but still focusing on their own site. LinkedIn is a good one to test if you are a B2B company. With LinkedIn, you can target people's jobs and work experience, as well as demographics. LinkedIn also lets you try *message ads*, where you are advertising by sending people messages to their inbox. These techniques can be good for reaching, for example, restaurant owners in Austin, Texas, in case that is a potential audience for your B2B business. One LinkedIn technique that I think works well is to not ask for the sale right away, but to offer knowledge. If you can offer knowledge to someone, they are more likely to check it out. After they are done looking at your free knowledge you can give them your product/service pitch. It's similar to Google search ads in that regard; you are giving them an answer to a question they might have (knowledge), and as a result you get to give them your pitch. They will likely be more receptive after you've given them this knowledge. As an example, consider a LinkedIn sponsored message targeting those restaurant owners. Instead of saying, "Please use our cleaning service," you might put a message that says, "I wanted to share our top five tips to help you pass restaurant inspection." That message will get more views and clicks. Tip number five is, you guessed it, to use a cleaning service like ours to virtually guarantee a pass.

Offline advertising is generally a bit trickier because it is more difficult to track. If you are going to test offline advertising, you will need a tracking strategy. Here are my two best tracking strategies for offline advertising. First, try to push them online. Get them to submit their e mail, or type in a special URL so that you can now track them digitally. A special URL on a billboard, for example, will allow you to track leads and identify who visits your site from the billboard. Collecting business cards and entering them into your database (or spreadsheet) after coming from the trade show you just attended is another way to import the data into your online systems. The second technique for tracking offline advertising is to ask after every sale, "Where did you first hear about us?" This simple question can get you the data you need to associate what advertising is working offline.

In my experience, offline advertising has not been a very CPA effective means of customer acquisition. I have tried television ads, radio ads, magazine ads, trade shows, and direct mail. This does not mean they aren't worth doing. In fact, everything is worth testing. These channels are also good at getting to the magical two or three exposures it takes to drive an action. They might see your ad in a magazine, and then see your online ad and click it. Did the magazine play a role? Yes. Was it trackable? No. Sometimes, you can measure sales results in the presence of brand advertising (like a magazine ad) combined with online ads to see if the online ads work a little better. For most startups, however, your funds are likely better off going into the channels that you know (i.e. have measured) deliver results.

Non Advertising Growth and Scale

Up until now, this chapter may have given you the wrong impression. Marketing is not just about ads—that's only one of the Ps (promotion). The other 3 Ps are product, place, and price. Also, don't forget about the 5 Cs: customers, competitors, collaborators, climate, and company. These factors are also potential ways to scale up your sales. Remember, we're scaling sales, not marketing. Results are what matter, not definitions.

Many companies can scale up by exploring new channels, not just new advertising mechanisms. Getting your product onto the shelves of Best Buy is itself a marketing expression (and a big challenge, by the way). Dealing with retailers is complex, cuts deeply into margins, and can be quite demanding. The rewards of retail, however, can be very high, leading to massive upticks in revenues and growth. Online retailers like Amazon are worth considering right away. Pursuing distribution agreements and considering sales representatives are other ways to reach retail quickly. Retail is not the only channel to consider when exploring growth options. Partnerships (competition or collaborators) can also lead to new sales channels. This is especially true in B2B markets where a competing or collaborating company has an incomplete solution and, when combined with your offering, makes the offering more complete and compelling to customers overall. Other sales channels to consider are direct sales (hiring salespeople), franchising, setting up your own stores or outlets, licensing, affiliate sales, catalogs (mail order), telemarketing, and more. Table 6.1 shows a list of channels to consider, why to consider them, and the estimated cost of doing business in that channel. The sales channels you try depend entirely on your product or service, the cost of the channel, and how you think you might best be able to reach customers. During your scale up phase, your goal is to find more ways to reach customers with your product or service, because you will eventually have some problems, and new channels can help overcome them.

Table 6.1: Sales Channels Comparison

Channel	Why to Consider	Typical Deal Structure
Online Direct Sales	Fast to set up. Keep all margins.	4% credit card fees
Online Retailers	Fast to set up. Keep good margins.	8% to 20% transaction fees
Affiliates	Decent margins.	10% affiliate fee & 4% credit card fee
Retailers	Big reach. Marketing built in.	30% to 50% to retailer, possibly more if distributor is required
Distributors	Sometimes needed for retailer. Sometimes helps get retailers.	4% to 12% warehousing & other fees
Sales Representatives	Helps find buyers (direct customers or even retailers).	$2K–5K/mo. fixed fees & commission (5% to 10%)
Direct Retail (Your Own Brick & Mortar)	Marketing built in. Customer service + brand quality control.	$100K–$200K/year & build fees ($50K) 4% credit card fees
Direct Sales	Complex sales & relationship building/customer service.	Salesperson: $100K/yr. & commission (5% to 20%)
Telemarketing (TV)	Marketing built in. Easy sale, but needs video proof.	50% revenue shared with TV studio. Sometimes fees as well ($20K–$100K)
Catalog	If you have lots of products/variations.	Printing fees ($2K+) & 4% credit card fees
Partnerships	B2B and value added deals.	10% to 20% margin from bundling
Licensing	Incomplete product/service.	Totally different deal structures
Franchising	Rapid geographic expansion.	Essential systematized licensing

Speaking of reaching customers, geographic expansion is another thing to consider for many startups. For service businesses, launching in a new city is an obvious and important way to scale sales. Opening new geographical locations is critical for these kinds of businesses to grow. Figuring out how to open new cities, states, and even countries in a cost effective and timely manner is essential to becoming the world dominating company you want to become. Every company should consider geographical expansion at some point. Even just launching your online product in a new country or a new language could greatly expand sales of your product or service.

Exploring new markets with your solution is another way to scale sales. A new market is different from a new geography or channel, in that it is an entirely different set of customers. Those customers might be in the same location and channel, but would never have considered your product or service if you didn't include them in your marketing (messaging and advertising). This technique sometimes even means creating a new version of your product or service in a subtle way, but not overly tuned for that market. As an example, my company Bigfoot Networks built network cards for online gamers. We were clearly a gaming company. However, we explored the idea of selling network cards to day traders, as well (under a slightly different name). Both groups want lag and latency reduction, but the target is so different that we had to try each one separately. The day trader market never materialized for us, but it was worth a shot.

This list in Table 6.1 is by no means comprehensive. When you are considering growth and scale strategies, the key is to consider all 4 Ps and 5 Cs and look at each one as a direction in which to attempt scale. The key word here is *attempt* scale, because you just don't know what is going to work until you try it. You should be systematic and try as many methods as you can, measure everything in an order you think is most logical, and find what works. Once you have two or three strategies working, try pushing on those channels to deliver you ever more sales and spend more in those methods, until they break or peak. Then, to scale more, you must try new experiments in new methods of customer acquisition until you are growing again. That's scaling, but it's really called experimenting, and it never ceases.

Watching Out for Roadblocks, Bumps, and Crashes

As you scale up your sales, slowly and steadily experimenting, you need to watch out for roadblocks, bumps, and crashes. A roadblock is rapidly approaching if your CPAs are going up. This is usually signaled early by rising CPCs or decreasing conversion rates. As the CPA economics go up, you run the risk of unprofitable sales. Unless you believe your LTVs will go up in the near future, you have hit a roadblock and need to back up, slow down, and think about going a different way. What are those different ways? Consider different marketing techniques, sales channels, geographies, and markets, for starters. The point is you may have hit saturation in your given channel or marketing technique, and it's time to look for new ground. Continuing to focus on this technique and think you can get more out of it is probably not going to be successful unless something about your product or service changes too. At Night Owl Games, we hit this roadblock when Facebook changed its algorithms for Facebook games, to no longer show viral game invites to users. Our CPAs went up dramatically, because we lost a lot of our viral effects of getting a new player. Advertising games also became more competitive because it was pretty much the only way to get players at that point, and CPCs increased. To get around this roadblock, we pivoted to a different sales channel. We made a deal with an international distributor to launch the game in a different country under a new name. That deal turned out to be extremely lucrative and effective and helped the company to succeed well past its roadblock.

A bump is when you seem to be unable to spend more money in a given channel, despite the fact that your CPAs are still good. In other words, you are increasing your budget, but it's not being spent. This is incredibly common in both Facebook and Google ads, where the bidding system puts you in direct competition for a set amount of ad inventory. Even when you increase your CPC bids, however, you could still have problems spending your entire budget. To get over this little bump, you just must expand the audience you are reaching with your ads. For Google, that means using new keywords and possibly new demographics. For Facebook, expanding your audience usually means making new ad groups that target different demographics and/or psychographics. It doesn't mean you must target new customers or markets, but it does mean looking for new psychographic words that might suggest that Facebook users would like your products or services. In both cases, you are essentially getting more reach not by spending more, but by targeting more users with your ads. It's a bump but it should be fairly easy to overcome with daily ad management.

A crash is something else entirely. If your LTVs are going down, and customers are not spending (or converting into paying customers) the way that they used to, you are in deep trouble. You will need to act fast to figure out what is happening. Consider interviews and the other techniques described in Chapter 5 to help you figure out what is going on. The problem with this kind of crash is that it is not necessarily related to the experiments you are running to scale your sales. Unless you are targeting a new market (and thus, do not really know the LTV of the new market), hitting a crash like this where LTVs are going down means something else might be going on that is unrelated to your scaling sales. You might have a new competitor, bad reviews, or something else entirely. You should pause your ad spending if your (CPA + COGS) starts to get close to your decreasing LTV. It's time to go back to testing LTVs and fixing that part of your business rather than focus on scaling. The roller coaster continues.

The Story of Burpy

In 2013, Burpy.com was founded by Aseem Ali, a student at the University of Texas at Austin. His vision was to build the Uber for groceries. He would find drivers from Craigslist who were willing to go to the grocery store, shop, and deliver what customers had ordered, all in about an hour. He was, of course, his first driver. He would manually go to the grocery store, look at prices, and type in products until his fingers got tired. Customers would place orders on his website, and he would drive, buy the orders, and drop them off. It was enough to get started and discover product and market fit. People in Austin, at least, wanted Burpy.

The problem that Aseem faced, however, was how to scale. How do you scale up in Austin first? Then, how do you economically launch in new cities where you don't live or have in depth knowledge about these locations?

Burpy and Aseem were able to begin to see scale in Austin by leveraging three distinct marketing vehicles. First, Burpy capitalized on search trends in the Austin area for grocery delivery by launching a series of Google search advertising campaigns answering the question, "Does my grocery store deliver?" The best part of their campaign was that they could target people searching in the Austin area, which was his only area of delivery at launch. Next, Burpy was able to get local press to take an interest in his story as he built something that was similar to Uber, but unique to Austin. The PR campaign got him awareness and good validation that his search advertising campaign could leverage to create successful conversions. He tweaked his business model to simply mark up the product sales and greatly reduce delivery fees (to $0 in many cases). Finally, Burpy developed technology that would automatically add items to their inventory and used it to expand their shopping offerings to cover the entire store. This, combined with their excellent SEO campaign, led to many customers finding Burpy when they needed specific items delivered. This SEO strategy of having lots of products and web pages all for specific items or answers to specifically searched questions is called a long tail SEO strategy. Burpy used this long tail strategy effectively to attract new customers who are searching for specific items to be delivered. After fine tuning the Burpy website, adding live chat and adding zip code search, Burpy eventually figured out a growth strategy that was working for Austin.

At the same time, Burpy started getting national press. Companies like Amazon and Instacart were entering the grocery delivery market, and that also gave Burpy some nice national exposure. The only problem was that Burpy was only available in Austin, which greatly limited the value of this exposure. Their true growth strategy had to be to geographically expand. They needed to launch in a new city, and fast!

By the end of 2013, Burpy was experimenting with launching in new cities such as San Antonio and Houston.[5] The challenge with these expansions was that

---

[5] http://www.siliconhillsnews.com/2013/12/07/burpy-expands-to-san-antonio-and-houston

the grocery store landscape was different, and Burpy had to rely more on their web scraper software to see what was available in those areas. They had to build their website to allow for zip code search and product inventory customization by area. Their biggest challenge, however, was hiring and keeping good Burpy drivers. Just like Uber, Burpy initially went on a Craigslist strategy to try to hire drivers in these new regions. It was not scaling well. It was hard to get drivers without personally being in the area. Burpy finally unlocked Houston and San Antonio by hiring regional managers to oversee drivers and inventory. Since then, Burpy has had tremendous growth and success.

Today, they are setting their sights beyond Texas. Unfortunately (or fortunately) for Burpy, however, they are presently capital constrained for further expansion. They have taken very little investment dollars so far (just $200K), and that small amount has been the bottleneck in their growth rate. They are trying to grow the business organically without taking on more investment so that they can control when and if an exit might happen in the future. Since they are profitable, they can also choose to harvest their own profits without worrying about growing for a big exit. Limited funding, though, means that Burpy cannot expand as fast as they otherwise could, and that they are ever more vulnerable if Amazon or Instacart should truly decide upon a nationally inclusive grocery delivery system. Should Burpy get a big investor to help them go national and capture the market? Should they position themselves for IPO or acquisition? Go back to Chapter 1 if you think you have the answer to this question—I, for one, cannot answer it. I don't know Aseem's personal goals! What I can say, though, is that the scale they have proven so far certainly should make it possible for Burpy to get a big investor should they want one.

Chapter 7
Oops, We Ran Out of Money—Funding and finance

"What the hell are you doing?" Mike asked, with a shocked look on his face. He was wearing a matching black suit just like mine, but with a t shirt underneath, instead of a collared shirt. The t shirt had, like always, a Bigfoot creature with "Bigfoot Networks" printed on it.

"I'm taking a selfie," I replied.

"What the heck is a selfie?" he asked. It was only 2006, after all, and selfies hadn't yet taken off like they would years later.

"It's a picture of myself," I said casually, positioning the camera so it could capture the whole room with Mike in it behind me.

"I get that, but why?" he asked, still dumbfounded, and quite a bit annoyed. It's how you get when you travel so much with someone. Mike and I had logged about two dozen trips all over the country. We had spent all that time sharing a car and a hotel room. Our wives thought we were crazy, but the reality was that we were out of cash. Our fledgling company, Bigfoot Networks, had no money. Any way we could save, we would.

"Well, Mike, I want to capture this moment right here. Do you know how rare this is?" I asked in reply.

"Well, it's our first time, and you're jinxing it," he said, genuinely frustrated.

"Come on, you know it's as good as done. Cali said so. All we have to do is not mess up in there," I replied, gesturing toward the windowed room where more than twenty people sat waiting for our grand entrance.

"You're nuts," Mike said.

"Yeah, but I'm right, too. We've had more than 50 investor meetings over the last year, and this is the first time we've ever been invited to pitch to the whole partnership to finalize a deal. This could be it, man. Cali already showed us the term sheet if the partnership agrees. It's $8 million dollars, man! Aren't you excited?" I asked.

"I'm scared as hell," Mike said.

He had every reason to be scared. Although we had been meeting with this investor for more than three months and had over a dozen meetings and calls, it was not a sure thing. We had to impress the entire partnership to get through the final vote. We already had a partner who wanted to sponsor us, which meant it was likely a 90% sure thing, but it wasn't 100%. After experiencing 49 rejections (both soft and hard no's), Mike and I were exhausted and elated. This was the moment. I still have that selfie. I also still have the ATM slip with the $8 million balance.

DOI 10.1515/9781501507083-007

Corporate Innovation
This chapter may seem to be about startup fundraising. In reality, it is about financial planning, building a great business pitch, and convincing others to back you. These three things are incredibly important in a corporate innovation context. In order to cause change to happen in a corporation, whether it is a new product, a new service or a change to some internal aspect of an organization, you will have to convince others to join you in your quest to success. This chapter gives you tools to help you convince others that your ideas are worth pursuing. You might need to convince people to join you on the team, invest in your idea, approve your budget, or simply approve the project. Remember, corporate innovation requires dedication to think across departments, from product, to marketing, to sales, and yes, even to finance. This chapter will help you convince anyone in your organization that your quest is worth pursuing/funding/doing.

Managing Cash

This chapter is all about money. It will cover everything from spending money to making money, and especially securing investors. Before I can get to investors, however, a few things should be made clearer about money in a startup. In a startup, money is only one thing: cash. It's not receivables, payables, balance sheets, or inventory. In a startup, the only thing that matters is cash, and how you manage it. The reason is that only cash (which should be kept in a bank) is useful for getting through to the next month, and hopefully to that moment when you either start to make profits or secure that needed next funding. In a pinch, you can delay paying your payables (which are like loans that come from suppliers), so ignore payables when thinking of cash. You cannot force receivables (money owed to you) to pay up, so you can't count on that as cash. Your balance sheet and inventory are not cash, because it takes time (that you usually don't have) to sell inventory or your limited assets. Cash is all that matters. It can pay for that last minute flight to Boston for that partner meeting, just like it did for Mike and me. The key is that you need to keep a close eye on your cash and do everything you can to keep your cash burn at a minimum.

Keeping an account of your cash is simply called *cash accounting*. It's not like big corporate accounting—that's called *accrual accounting*. Instead, cash accounting is more like balancing a checkbook. To do it right, all you have to do is keep track of your running cash balance by entering every bit of cash you spend as a negative, and every bit of cash that comes in as a positive. Because companies (and individuals) have to pay taxes, it's important to keep track of what it is that you spent money on, and where that cash came from. Investment, even from parents or friends, is not taxed to you or your business when the investment is made. Instead, the investors will get taxed when they get a return on their investment, and pay tax on the amount gained.

Table 7.1 below is an example of a simple spreadsheet for keeping track of your cash. I use Google Sheets, but any spreadsheet software will do. Simply add the date, amount, the name of the person or company involved, and a description when cash comes in or goes out. Remember, cash that is supposed to be paid doesn't get recorded here, although you should keep track of that elsewhere and pay your bills on time, when you can. Also, cash that is forthcoming doesn't get recorded here, either. Your monthly *cash burn* is the sum of the prior month's cash outlays (spends). Your expected monthly cash burn is what you predict cash burn will be next month (higher or lower than the previous month, and an explanation why). If your expected monthly cash burn will bring your bank account to zero or negative, you are in trouble. In fact, most startups try to make sure they have at least three months of cash burn available in their balance at all times. Most startups, however, rarely have that luxury.

Table 7.1: Simplified Startup Accounting (The Checkbook Spreadsheet)

Date	Amount	Person or Company Involved	Description
1/23/2018	$500.00	Self	Personal investment
1/30/2018	−$250.00	Best Buy	Parts to build product
2/5/2018	$50.00	Customer 1: C. B.	Sold 1 unit to C. B.
Cash Balance (Running)	$300.00		

If you are nearing negative, it's time to take action. First, consider fundraising (see later in this chapter). Second, see if you can sell some inventory or generally get more sales quickly. Even if you can move inventory at a big discount, as low as its cost, you could end up saving your company. Remember, inventory is stuff you already paid for, so selling it at its cost means bumping up your cash! You should also consider slow paying people. Slow pay bigger creditors first, and employees last. At one point during our mad scramble to raise our $8 million round at Bigfoot Networks, we asked all employees to voluntarily take deferred salaries until we could raise the needed funds. We had 100% participation in that program, and I'm still proud of that. It showed my team was committed to our mission and believed that we would eventually be successful.

Building a Financial Plan

Speaking of running out of cash, how did you get here in the first place? It's clearly a failure, and a big one. In fact, if it goes on too long, and you cannot pay your creditors, you will have to declare bankruptcy. You'll need a lawyer for this, and most startups will never come back from it. It's one of the ways to get off the ride, become fired, and lose your company. Your creditors, whether they are banks, suppliers, or the electric company, will have first dibs at the assets and remains of your company, in the event that you default or go bankrupt. If they eat away at too much of your assets, you've got nothing left, and you may as well start over. It's not the end of you as an entrepreneur (although it will be much harder to get a loan in the future). It's just the end of this startup. It would be better to avoid this situation in the first place by initially establishing a good financial plan. It's also an essential piece of information that you will need for investors to consider investing in you. They want to know what will happen if you are successful. How big will you get? They also want to know what will happen if things don't go quite right. Internally, all investors know that you'll have to fail a little on your way to success; how much cash you have determines how big or how many times you can fail until success.

There are three kinds of financial plans to consider, but you can make all three. The first is a top down financial projection. By default, since it is top down, it is an optimistic projection. This kind of projection is the least useful for planning and investor purposes. In my startups, I only use this plan to get a sense of my total market size, which is something that investors do want to know about. The other two types of financial plans are both bottom up models in which you actually consider how you will get these mythical customers to pay you (e.g. marketing). There are two types, because you will make two versions—one for investors (which assumes that you get investment), and one for your own planning (which does not make that assumption). The bottom up models will be covered later in this chapter. For now, let's look at top down financial projections.

In order to make a top down financial projection, you first have to figure out your TAM, SAM, and SOM. The next section will discuss how this is done, but for now, realize it's going to give you a huge number (like a billion dollars). A top down financial projection makes the assumption that somehow, month after month, you gain a certain percentage of this market through sales, and it becomes your revenue. From there, you subtract costs and expenses, and you are left with profits. The reason that top down is not overly useful is it doesn't really show you or your investors how you will get those sales. It just magically happens. This is how companies end up getting a marketing budget that is a percent of sales. It's just not realistic for a startup in which all your money should be going into getting sales or servicing those sales (once you have a product or service available to sell, that is). Calculating your TAM, SAM, and SOM is useful because it makes a great and helpful slide in your investor PowerPoint presentation.

TAM, SAM, and SOM

A top down financial plan is not generally useful. Determining a startup's TAM, SAM, and SOM, however, is incredibly helpful for investors to understand your market potential. These are acronyms that are used generically in the startup world. A *total available market* (TAM) is the total global market size of the opportunity, ideally expressed in units you could sell. The TAM potential revenue is then calculated as the dollars you could make—unit sales multiplied by unit price—if you had 100% market share. Some people incorrectly specify TAM as the total market of an industry (such as the gaming industry's total size), but that is the total gaming market, not your total market, which is what investors want to know. If you got every customer in the world to pay full price, how many dollars is that? That's your TAM potential revenue. To calculate TAM correctly for the gaming industry, as an example, instead of taking the total gaming industry size ($91B in 2016[1]), take the total number of PC gamers as the total units of a game you could sell—around 711 million.[2] To calculate the TAM potential revenue, take that number and multiply it by the full price of your game (say, $50). For the PC gaming market, you get $35 billion as your TAM revenue potential. In the footnotes, I have cited the sources of the market sizes. Citations like these are essential to making your TAM, SAM, and SOM believable.

A *serviceable available market* (SAM) is very similar. The difference is that you are going narrower with your targeting, either geographically (say, all of Texas, or all of the United States), or by target customer (say, only targeting avid PC gamers). An example of a SAM for the PC gaming market is US gamers. About 100 million gamers in the United States play PC games making the SAM $100 million and the SAM potential revenue $5 billion.[3]

A *serviceable obtainable market* (SOM) is narrower yet, and is supposed to reflect the actual customers that you will be able to reach in the short term

---

[1] https://venturebeat.com/2016/12/21/worldwide-game-industry-hits-91-billion-in-revenues-in-2016-with-mobile-the-clear-leader

[2] http://www.pcgamer.com/there-are-711-million-pc-gamers-in-the-world-today-says-intel

[3] https://venturebeat.com/2017/07/04/the-future-group-changes-both-game-shows-and-live-events-with-mixed-reality

(without opening new locations, for example). Avid PC gamers are an example of a SOM. Avid PC gamers play online games the most, and are therefore the most likely to buy a network card that reduces lag (the product that my company Bigfoot Networks made), so they are Bigfoot Network's SOM. As an example SOM potential revenue calculation, there are 17.3 million avid PC gamers in the USA.[4] Multiply that by $50 and you get SOM potential revenue of $865 million, a very respectable number. Investors generally want to see SAM potential revenue to be at least $1 billion. SOM potential revenue can be much smaller. The smaller and more targeted your SOM is, the better, because it shows investors that you truly know who your beachhead customer is. If possible, keeping SOM potential revenue between $10 million and $100 million is best because it shows if you succeed only in the SOM, you'll have a nice sized business, if not a massive one.

TAM, SAM, and SOM are generally shown as potential revenues to investors and often done using concentric circles, as shown in Figure 7.1. Remember to cite your market size information. If you want to build out a full on tops down financial model (not recommended), you would start with your SOM potential revenue number and then magically *get sales* of a few percent per month until you are profitable. The problem with this approach is that it does not show how you will really get those sales. As a result, a tops down model is not very useful to anyone, so I never bother with it.

---

[4] https://www.gamespot.com/articles/us-gamer-population-170-million-npd/1100-6214598

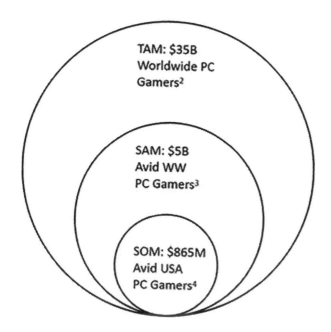

TAM: $35B
Worldwide PC
Gamers[2]

SAM: $5B
Avid WW
PC Gamers[3]

SOM: $865M
Avid USA
PC Gamers[4]

Figure 7.1: Examples of TAM, SAM, and SOM Revenue Potential Figures

Business Models

Before I can show you how to make a bottom up financial model, it is important to first consider the various business models that a startup might use. Your business model (how you make money) is crucial to bottom up modeling because you will need to be more precise with how you get customers, how they pay, and what it costs you. It's what makes bottom up modeling so much more useful. It exposes the variables and key levers that affect your eventual profitability, or your bankruptcy.

Table 7.2 shows a listing of many types of business models and their definitions. Each model impacts the bottom up financial forecast significantly, because this implies several different possibilities. Figure 7.2 shows the three axes of business model types. The first axis determines either a low margin or high margin product or service. Low margin products have relatively high costs as a percent of sales, meaning that you may need to sell a lot more of them to generate profits (commodities such as toilet paper are high cost, low margin products). High margin, low cost products or services mean that you don't have to sell as many to make more profits. Software is an example of low cost, since it costs almost nothing to produce, but can be sold at almost any price (depending on the value it creates). Repeatability versus one time sales is another axis. Having customers who repeatedly buy your products or services (such as in a monthly subscription) is a very different business than selling something to them only once (like a house). The third business model axis is sales complexity. More complex sales require more time and often require specialized sales skills (like home or boat sales). Less complex sales can be done online or in an app in about one second (like an in app purchase for a game token). Not every business model maps perfectly to these axes, but it is a useful task to see where you lie on each. Are you a high margin, complex sale that happens only once? That's a home sale. Are you a low margin, repeated sale that happens over and over? That's an in app game purchase. Are you a home electronics product? That's a low complex, low margin sale that happens semi annually. Wherever you fall, it will drive how you create your business model and how you build your financial plan.

Table 7.2: Business Models

Type	Description	Example
Disintermediation / Reselling	Buy finished products low from wholesale, resell for higher (simple sales)	Woot.com
Subscription	Pay monthly for service (often with a free trial)	Netflix.com
Freemium / Micro transactions	Free for basic, pay for premium service or extras	Farmville
Leasing	Pay as subscription, rather than full price up front	Rent A Center
Razor & Razor Blades Type	Pay less for the product (razor/printer) than it's worth, but refills (razor blades/ink) cost more	Gillette, Lexmark Printers
Manufacturing	Buy raw materials and have it manufactured into your finished product	Toshiba, Sony
Licensing	Earn royalties by licensing your technology to another company	Dolby
Bundling / Box	Group similar things together in a box/group and sell the bundle together (sometimes as a subscription)	Loot Crate, Stitch Fix
Marketplace	Create a market for buyers and sellers and get paid fees for transactions	eBay.com
Advertising	Get paid to show ads	Google.com

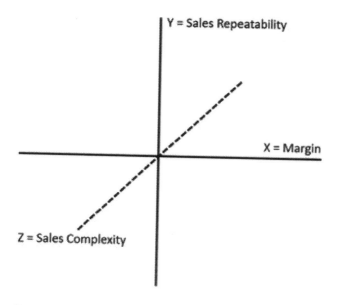

Figure 7.2: Three Axis Business Model Map

Oops, I Failed Again—Denied Funding Based on Business Model

Much later in my career after Bigfoot Networks, I was working on a new startup (Karmaback). I had gotten through several rounds of talks with one Austin venture capital (VC) firm. I was maybe one meeting away from a partner meeting and a terms sheet. I totally bombed that meeting with the managing partner.

What happened? It actually took me by surprise. Everything up until then was going so well. Everyone loved my company idea (giving rewards for people to do social actions for companies). There was one major problem. All my sales up until that point had been by direct sales (a high complexity sales model). I personally initiated and closed those sales. What's the problem, then?

The problem was that in my business model and financial forecast, I showed a low complex repeatable sale. I imagined that our website would get our sales as companies would find and use us to help them grow their social media. The reality was, that didn't work. The venture capitalists picked up on it, and told me I had to show progress on the low complexity model that I projected. It turns out that high complexity business models were not in that investor's sweet spot. The other issue was that with high complexity, you also needed high margins. My business was fairly low margin, but was supposed to make it up on volume.

That's a combination that doesn't work with a high complexity sale, because it's too costly to close the sale (requires a sales person).

I ended up continuing to do sales myself, and making money that way. I never did raise VC money for Karmaback, but it turned out I didn't need to. I simply raised the prices, continued selling our high complexity product, and got higher margins as a result. Bingo. We grew, made money, and eventually had an exit. Our failure with the VC investor actually led to our success. If that investor had given us money, we would have been stuck with the low complexity business model that they wanted, and we may have had a big uphill battle generating sales that way. This way, we kept most of the company for ourselves, and got to reap the full (if small) reward on exit.

Bottoms Up Modeling

All right, it's time to learn how to do business modeling and forecasting correctly. The bottoms up model is the preferred method for both investors and entrepreneurs. What makes it preferable is that it is built on clear growth variable assumptions, contains enough detail to actually predict multiple potential futures, and is usually more conservative than tops down modeling. Let's break each of these factors down into what they mean and why they are so useful for you.

First, what is a *growth variable assumption*? An assumption is a guess you are making about the future. By guessing using a variable (such as click to sale conversion rate) instead of an absolute number (like the percentage of SOM sold over time), it is easier to see what has to happen in order for the desired/predicted outcome to occur. A growth variable is simply a variable that causes your business to grow at a certain rate or not. Examples of growth variables are conversion rate, cost per click, time until sale, likelihood of sale, re order rate, attrition rate, and so on. Depending on your business model, you will have different growth assumptions. The more testable and actionable a growth assumption, the better—it makes it clear to you and the investor when you are making good progress on validating that assumption.

Predicting multiple potential futures is useful as well. For example, what if you are not able to secure funding? What happens to your business then? Your growth rate will probably have to slow down. For this reason, I always suggest keeping two sets of possible futures on hand as bottom up modeling cases. The first case is: What happens if you do not get funded and you continue on at your current rate? This is a very conservative planning case, but is useful to have around at all times so you can predict when you might get low or run out of cash. You do not want to fail in running completely out of cash, and knowing in advance will let you take stops to conserve cash and reduce your business size (sometimes through layoffs or salary reductions) to compensate. You can come back from a situation in which you are almost out of cash, but coming back from bankruptcy is much harder. The other case to keep on hand is your average case. It's a slightly more aggressive form of planning that you show your investors. It assumes that you are able to get the total amount you think you want for your business, and are able to put that money to work fairly quickly in growing your business. The actual variables of growth shouldn't be different between the two, but with more money from investors, you are able to put more money into growth and thus, profits that can help pay for things like salaries and further growth. In fact, growth is the major reason you should consider taking an investor's money, but more on that later.

It's hard to get into financial modeling details without the use of an example. Table 7.3 shows an example of very simple financial model. I have also provided online examples and Excel files you can download that contain simple financial models to help you get started.[5] If you are an accounting or financial professional, you may recognize these examples as being similar to an income statement. You might expect a balance sheet and cash flow statement to accompany this, but that's not forecasting—those document types are used for reporting actual results, not for making predictions. The proper term for a predictive financial statement is a pro forma. A full pro forma is not typically used by startups—instead, we use a simpler consolidated profit and loss projection (P&L projection). Profit and loss is a term that generally means the revenues, costs, and expenses of a line of business. In big companies, small departments and sometimes product lines often have their own P&L projections. The small business units also report results as compared to their quarterly and yearly projections. Managers of these kinds of departments are said to have P&L responsibility. P&L responsibility means power, and it is something that many managers want to have on their resume. It means they were responsible for the overall performance of the project, department, or product. A CEO has ultimate P&L responsibility over all departments and the whole company, and my goal for you is to be CEO of your company for as long as possible. Learning the skills of this chapter will help you stay on this path, even if you are not an expert at finance or accounting. As you will read in Chapter 12, I have had mixed success at staying the CEO. Yes, I've been fired as CEO and lived to tell the tale.

---

[5] http://fastai.com/blog/2017/07/16/financial-models-for-you

Table 7.3: Simplified P&L Financial Model (Projections)

	Jan 2018	Feb 2018	Mar 2018	Apr 2018
Units	0	1	3	5
Revenue	$0	$50	$150	$250
Cost of Goods Sold	$0	$20	$60	$100
Gross Margin	$0	$30	$90	$150
Expenses				
Marketing	$100	$200	$400	$600
Employees	$0	$0	$500	$500
Other (rent, supplies)	$50	$50	$250	$250
Total Expenses (SG&A)	$150	$250	$1,150	$1,350
Net Income	$150	$220	$1,060	$1,200
Accumulated Cash	$150	$370	$1,430	$2,630

Taking a closer look at Table 7.3, a P&L projection has four major sections. The first section, revenue, contains not just projected revenues, but also projected unit sales. Breaking it down in this way is important because it shows how many units you will sell, and the pricing of the various products you are selling. If you are selling three products or services, you should even break it down further into three unit types and three revenues that add up to total revenue. The next section is costs. Costs are those dollars that go out that you have to pay for the production or fulfillment of a sale. Think of it as the variable costs of production. Not included in costs are expenses, which is the next part. An expense is anything that you cannot directly attribute to the cost of producing a unit. Costs versus expenses is a key concept in financial modeling because costs will scale based on units sold, and expenses will scale only when you, the manager, think you might need more people, tools, or other things to support the ongoing growth of your business. An example of a cost is a blank white t shirt. An example of an expense is a t shirt printing machine. The machine can print on many t shirts, and you won't need to buy more than one for quite a while (certainly not one per t shirt), so it's an expense. The t shirt itself is a cost because you buy one blank t shirt to print on for every printed t shirt you sell. Other expenses are the marketing expense (which also varies by sale, but conventionally is considered an expense), employees (again, only one employee needs to run the machine, not one per t shirt sold), and utilities (like rent, and electricity and so on). Managers have some leeway in deciding what is a cost versus what is an expense. It is usually best to err on the side of expense. Costs are usually obvious things that actually go into the product, where expenses are less certain. Most online software companies have a $0 cost, because they produce no DVDs or CDs with their software anymore. It's all $0 cost. They don't even put network bandwidth as a cost, because it is usually a fixed amount per month, and not variable based on kilobytes or anything else.

The final section of the P&L projection is the cash projection component. This will almost never be seen on an actual income statement, but it is useful here to keep track of what you believe your cash balance will be at any point in the future. The net income line will show you if you made profit or loss in that given period (usually monthly). If you have a positive net income, that's profit, and you can keep it for future periods or maybe even pay it out as dividends. If you have a negative net income, that's a loss, and you will need to dip into your cash reserves in order to keep up with that shortfall. The accumulated cash line is exactly that—how much cash you have accumulated as a reserve to get you through any net income losses. If your accumulated cash line goes negative at any point, this is a sign that you may need to make an adjustment to your plan or consider taking an investment. How much investment will you need? At least enough to cover your lowest cash point in your accumulated cash flow. I advise a three month cash burn cushion, as well, to account for bumps in the road.

Now that we've looked at the parts of the P&L projection, it's time to put it all together to make your forecast. The first step is to think about your business model and what will drive customers to buy. Are they being exposed to ads and then eventually buying? Or do you have a sales team out there calling folks and making deals? It could be any of these or other models too. Start from your model and find the variables that will impact unit sales. In the case of advertising, the variables are how much you spend, how many will click or show interest (cost per click, or CPC), and how many of those you will convert into a sale (conversion rate). These variables should be labeled at the top of your projection and ideally used as formulas in your model. Using spreadsheet formulas will allow you and your potential investors to see which variables are most important for your ultimate success and how they work together. In the example of a sales team, the key variables are number of salespeople (which also affects employee expense), number of leads generated per month, time between a lead and a sale, and lead to sale conversion (conversion rate). If you are selling subscriptions in either model, you also have an attrition rate to account for, as your sales will compound monthly, but not indefinitely because you will lose some customers every month. These variables (at the top of your forecast) will drive unit sales. Sometimes unit sales are linked to other parts of the P&L as well—for example, marketing spending, which is listed under expenses often drives unit sales. You might see this formula in the case of sales through advertising:

$$Units\_that\_Month = Ad\_Spend\_that\_Month / CPC * Conversion\_Rate$$

Once you have a unit projection working, the rest of the P&L is pretty straightforward to build. To build revenue, simply multiply unit sales by unit price(s). Costs are unit sales multiplied by unit costs. I like to keep prices and costs as variables in their own right (at the top) so that I can see what happens to my profitability if I lower the price or cost, or both. You can now calculate gross margins as simply revenue minus costs. Expenses are a bit more difficult because they are not scaled on units, but instead, based on your thinking about what you will need to get those units sold. Will you need an engineer or a salesperson? Will you need an office or retail location? All of that makes up your expense line, and the general rule that investors like to see is that you are not over investing in expenses, except with marketing or customer acquisition (sales). Instead, growing your expenses as slow as possible (when they are not directly related to growth) is good management practice. Lean and fit is good. It's way harder to fire someone than never to have hired them at all.

Once you have your expenses put in (and kept low), you can calculate your net income (your profit or loss) for that month or period as gross margins (revenue—costs) minus your expenses. What's left over is profit or loss. Now, accumulate that profit or loss into your ending cash from the last period to get your new accumulated cash.

Remember that we were making two projections here? Now is the time to do that. In the first projection (for your own use), you will consider how you will run the business if no money can come in from investors. You will have to run your business even leaner, with lower expenses, and will need to slow your growth down so that your accumulated cash never goes negative.

To make the other forecast for investors, you should try to grow as aggressively as you think makes sense, expanding expenses when you think they are needed (such as hiring more people, or buying more equipment or office space). Try to grow to a good market share size, and build out five years of projection. Now, look at your accumulated cash, and figure out the lowest cash point(s). Now, add a line called "funding" right above accumulated cash, and put in some funding dollars whenever you go negative. The total amount you will need is the lowest accumulated cash point, but you will need some funding to come in the very first month that your accumulated cash goes negative. Figure 7.3 shows an example of accumulated cash going negative. Notice that the arrow points to the month when you will need some funding, and the total amount you will need is the lowest accumulated cash point (plus some buffer, maybe). Remember, for this or any financial model to come true, almost all of your assumptions have to be exact. That's rare. Reality is different—it's how we manage reality that is the ultimate judge of our success or failure. For now, your financial projections are done. You simply add your investment to your accumulated cash, never let it go negative, and now you have a financial model that is, if everything goes right, somewhat believable.

Investors want to understand your business, its model, and the potential upside for them if they invest. Just as much, however, they want to know, "Is this person going to be a good manager of my investment, or not?" The next sections will cover ways to convince them that you are the right business, and the right person, to invest in.

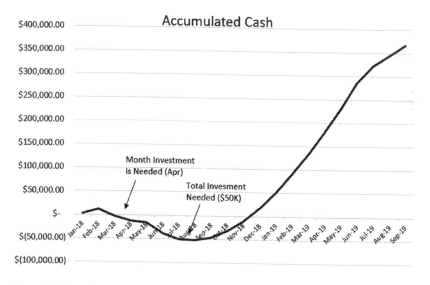

Figure 7.3: Example Accumulated Cash Chart Showing Investment Needs

How Much Funding

The lowest point in your accumulated cash flow projection is certainly one way to give you an idea of how much money you will need. Adding three months of cash burn onto that as a cushion is also a good idea. However, when speaking to investors, understanding the timing of investments, the investor's capacity to invest, their preferred means of investing, and the common types of investment will ultimately help you figure out how much to ask for a raise. Let's face it—surely you believe you could put a billion dollar investment to work, right? Well, no, it would be hard for you or anyone else to spend that much money in a few years, let alone a few months. It's all about the right amount at the right time.

Timing is critical to investment for a number of reasons. First, if you take too much money too early, you end up giving away more of your company to investors than you otherwise could have. Generally, the earlier you take money, the more stock you have to give up for it. Prudent entrepreneurs understand this and configure their fundraising plan around key events. This kind of planning is called *traunching*. Instead of taking all the investment you think you will need at the first sign of a negative accumulated cash flow, you take less at first and plan to take more at a later time (i.e. a second *traunch*). You take only enough to get you to a critical milestone, such as first unit shipped, first major deal, or validated conversion rates. This event should cause your company to be less risky, and thus, more valuable. The more valuable your company becomes the less stock you give up for the same amount of investment.

Some companies even plan two or three *rounds of funding* in order to further optimize their stock price. It is so common to traunch investments, that investors have given common names to these funding rounds. A seed round is the first amount of money contributed from a non founder investor. This can be an individual or an institution, and is often friends and family. Because it is so early in the company's history to put an accurate price on the stock, often the seed round is not even priced (the actual price of the stock is unknown until the next round, then this round converts to a discount at the next round). This is called a convertible note, and is very common during the seed round. The next round of funding after the seed round is often called Series A. It's usually the point at which a startup takes money in order to either prove out scalability or expand to some given point. Series B, C, D, and so on, simply continue scaling the business and theoretically improving operational efficiency and thus overall profits of the company. In reality, often times, all this growth is still unprofitable even up until the acquisition or IPO. Why? A fast growing company is a company with great potential profits in the future. The assumption is that the company will see tremendous profits later, once it starts to harvest all those customer relationships and stop spending on growth. Once the company stops spending on growth, the profitability of the company naturally goes up as long as customers stick around. A high growth low profit stock is often one to watch for—if they are funneling their profits into growth, that is.

Typical amounts for a seed round would be $50,000 to $500,000. This money is often used to build product, prototypes, and get to initial market, not generally to scale yet. A Series A funding is typically in the millions ($2 million to $10 million), and Series B in the $10+ millions, and so on. All these series only happen, however, if you are actually growing like you predict, and if investors see that value is getting created and their stock price is going up. The reality is also that most investors only invest at a certain time—some only seed, some seed and A, some only B, and so on. Understanding this and the amount that an investor actually has to invest is important to consider before talking to any specific investors.

Types of Funding

To understand the kind of investors to approach, how much they like to invest, and when they like to invest, it is critical to understand the common types of investments and how they work. The first type is a loan. Loans are often provided by banks, institutions, or individuals who expect to be paid back, even if everything fails. It is almost impossible to get a loan without having some type of collateral that can be sold to repay the loan in the case of bankruptcy. Once a business is established and has inventory, a cash balance, and some capital equipment, getting a bank loan is entirely possible. The bank will insist on first lien on those assets, meaning that they get them in case you go under. If you do not have enough assets to cover a loan, then the bank still might loan you money (at a higher interest rate, no doubt), but you will have to add a personal guarantee. This means that if you default, the bank owns your personal assets, including your house, your trust fund, and your savings. I almost always advise entrepreneurs (students or otherwise) to not use loans or credit cards for their startup if it will require a personal guarantee. RUN AWAY. Do not get a loan with a personal guarantee! Startups are just too risky, and you are already putting your personal time and money into it—you don't want to lose your retirement or home too. There has to be another way. As it turns out, there are many.

Grants are federal, state, institution, or even individual monies that you get to have and use without giving up stock or having to repay them. The catch? You have to apply, compete with others looking for the grant, and use the money only according to what the grant specified, and nothing else. You'll also have to keep really good records and provide regular reports to the granter. Most grants are available only for specific things, such as medical or military research on a specific topic. You can get grants, for example, to investigate new missile guidance systems, various types of cancer research, and even ecological impact studies. You probably won't be able to get a grant to hire salespeople to go out and sell boats. We have enough of those without the need for government or philanthropic sponsorship.

Angel investors are individuals who have a high net worth. In the United States, to be considered a qualified angel investor, the individual has to have a liquid net worth of $1 million or more, excluding their home. In addition, an angel investor also has to want to invest in small startups that are not on the public business markets (like the Nasdaq Stock Market). Small startups are risky, and many people do not invest in them because of the high risk of failure. Most angel investors do it not just for a chance at a risky return, but also as a means of giving back to the entrepreneurial community. They have often made their money in big business or entrepreneurial endeavors of their own, and now have enough money that they are willing to make a few (five or ten) small investments in startups. The key word is "small." Most angel investors do not invest more than $10,000 to $100,000 in any single startup. $10K is probably the most common amount invested by angels into one startup. If you are looking to raise a seed round of, say, $350,000 (the most common amount for a seed), then you will likely need between five and ten angel investors. Angel investors most commonly invest only in the seed round, and often get left behind during the Series A. Be kind to your angels, and try to get them a return or at least some good positioning during your Series A.

Asking a single angel for the full $350,000 would show your naiveté, and possibly turn the angel off. Nothing turns an investor away more than asking for a non disclosure agreement (NDA), by the way. NEVER DO THAT! Investors do not sign them, and will be offended if you ask. Just don't disclose your secret formula, patent it first. Investors won't ask *how* your thing works, necessarily, just what it's supposed to do or be and how far along you are. Later on, during diligence phase (discussed later in this chapter) you can ask for an NDA to share internal documents, but not at the initial stage. Asking for an NDA is a way to make sure you get no meetings.

Recent United States regulations have allowed for a new form of investment from any type of investor (accredited or not accredited). This law allows people who do not have $1 million in liquid net worth to potentially invest in startups as well. They are limited to between $2,000 and $10,000 (depending on the individual's income level), and must use a qualified intermediary to make the investment.[6] These kids of intermediaries are called crowd financing services, and should not be confused with crowdfunding services. Crowd financing is when individuals invest in a startup or cause through some online portal that aggregates all these investments for the company (for a fee). Individuals get stock or other consideration (such as royalties, etc.) in exchange for their small investment, which are all aggregated to make a meaningful investment into the company. Crowdfunding, on the other hand is the term that describes the preorder websites with perks that were created in the 2010's, such as Kickstarter and Indiegogo. Investments from individuals in a crowdfunding campaign lead to physical or digital perks (such as the product itself) rather than stock or royalty payments. In short, crowdfunding is not an investment at all; it's really a *presale* of some perk item. It doesn't mean crowdfunding should not be explored, it should, but it should be explored using the ideas from Chapters 4 and 5, not from this chapter. This chapter is about actual funding, not customer preorders (traction). They are related, however. Having a lot of customer traction (sales) definitely helps when it comes time to raise money. In many cases, it's essential to getting funded. Crowdfunding is one way to demonstrate traction before you even have a product. In fact, if you are fully customer funded and never need to get investors, that's called *bootstrapping*. Crowd financing, in contrast, is a way to become exposed to many more possible angel investors who aren't necessarily very wealthy, but see the value in what you are doing. It's a whole new world!

The old world is still here as well. *Venture capital* (VC) is the term for institutions that make investments in startups, professionally. In other words, unlike angel investors, who also have a personal motivation, venture capitalists are usually investing with capital gains as the primary, if not singular, motivation. Because startups are so risky, venture capital firms have to make many (twenty or more) investments in different startups to increase the chances that a few of their investments will pay off big. These one or two (of the twenty) investments that pay off are sometimes referred to as unicorns. They are mythical and hard to see until they are there. For this reason, most venture capital firms prefer to invest in startups with a lot of growth potential (big markets, low competition environments). Venture capital firms also have more money available and are usually happy to invest at the seed stage, the Series A stage, and sometimes also later stages. In fact, when they make a seed stage investment, they often allocate a portion of their cash for a future Series A that might be necessary. They do this because they don't want to get diluted out of an investment that is starting to

---

[6] https://www.sec.gov/news/pressrelease/2015-249.html

show promise and is worthy of the Series A. Typical seed investments from venture capital firms are in the $200K to $2 million range. Why would they be higher for a VC over an angel? One reason is that they have more money available than angels. A more nefarious possible reason is that VCs would like to put more money into your company than you might need. They would do that at a seed stage because it would get them more stock proportionally than if they were investing the extra amount at a later stage. If you are smart, you know how much you need to hit that next milestone (with a little extra just in case), and insist on the lower amount. Say it's in their best interest; you are limiting their risk. Just never take more money than you need, that's a failure of a different kind that can have disastrous consequences, as we will see later in Chapter 12. Series A investments from VCs range from $500K to $10 million, as mentioned before. The amount of Series A investment usually relates more to how much the firm trusts you and the amount they would like to put in at this stage, than to your actual financial plan. It's fairly easy to make a financial plan to match almost any amount invested by just raising marketing spending. The trick to good management here is to plan for the amount of growth you think is right to reach the next milestone (at which point you might consider a Series B), and insist on no more money than this. Remember, VCs are in this for the highest return they can get. This means they want a higher percentage of your company while your company continues to grow. For this reason, VC relationships with entrepreneurs are often very contentious. As your company reaches towards overall profitability, net incomes are consistently positive. With profitability, a new set of growth challenges will present themselves, as VCs are often going to try to push you to go for the home run and invest even more into growth, and sacrifice profitability. Should you? We'll examine that in Chapter 9.

Once you get past the Series A stage and consider taking investments for more rapid growth and expansion, the challenge of finding investors with enough money starts to pop up. Many VC investors are not set up to invest more than $10 million in any single company—doing so puts them at too large a risk profile for their fund. Other types of funds, on the other hand, are expressly set up to make these kinds of larger investments. Growth funds, hedge funds, and IPO (public funds) are three such types of later stage investors interested in later series of usually much bigger investments. At this point, it's important to distinguish the differences between normal growth investments, where the *series* terminology applies, and abnormal investments. If, for example, you take a Series A investment of, say, $8 million, and then your company does not grow as expected or stagnates, can you really say that next round of money you get is a Series B? You can, because the terms of the deal will say that, and technically it is, but in any round of funding where the price of the stock goes down, it is considered a *down round*, which is very bad. It means your company lost value. Investors will be unhappy, and you'll lose sizable chunks of your business. Enough about down rounds, let's get back to happy times. Growth funding in the form of Series B, C, D, and so on is usually a good thing and a sign of an ever growing company. At some point during one of these series, you may, as a founder, have an opportunity to take money off the table. That is, you may be able to get some returns for your hard work in the form of cash into your pocket, in advance of an actual sale or IPO of your company. It is a good idea to seriously consider doing this, but always keep some stock in the company too. The biggest payoffs for founders usually come at the *initial public offering* (IPO) investment. An IPO is an investment into your company by the public, like in a stock exchange such as the Nasdaq Stock Market or the New York Stock Exchange. In the case of an IPO, your company will get an infusion of capital, and fluidity in its stock. That means you, as a stockholder, will be able to sell your stock in small chunks on the open stock market at a daily price. IPOs are a very good thing—they are the home run that investors really seek. But they are not the only method of getting a positive return on an investment in a startup.

Speaking of returns, startups give investor returns under three scenarios. First, if a startup becomes profitable, it may decide to pay investor dividends. This is the cash from the year's leftover profits that goes to investors based on stock percentages. Investors could also get returns when there is a sale of the company or its assets. The *return on the investment* (ROI) is proportional to the amount of cash returned compared to the investment. A 2x return then means the investor got twice their money back that they invested—for example, if they invested $200,000, they got back $400,000 in their 2x return. In an IPO, investors also get liquid stock that they can sell on the open markets. They sell this slowly over time, but if the company holds strong, the sale of that stock can yield 100x or even more in returns on investment. IPO is the golden goose.

Investors do not all expect or even want the same return profiles. Some investors—angels, for example—will be perfectly happy with a 1x ROI. Don't get me wrong, angels would love to have 2x or 10x ROI, but many would be happy if they just saw their money back. Remember, their motivation is to help you succeed. Similarly, smaller VCs are often happy with a 5x return. Part of the reason for this is that they don't have enough investor money to take a company all the way to IPO, and they know it. As a result, they would rather exit a little bit earlier, rather than take the extra risk of getting diluted later by bigger investors and then having a smaller return than they would have had earlier. The timing of exit is one of the things that investors and entrepreneurs will fight over. These fights can sometimes come down to contractual obligations and shareholder votes. It's best to pick investors who align with your own goals, when you can.

Finding Investors: The "Laser Beam Shotgun" Approach

Enough talk about types of investors and all that. It's time to get to the business of finding the investor or investors who are willing to put money into your company. Notice that I said "company," and not "idea." Investors are not in the habit of funding ideas—grants do that. Investors invest in companies, and although this book doesn't cover this in detail, you will need to create a corporate entity at some point in order to accept any decent sized investment. There are many other reasons to incorporate, and for more on that, I would direct you to my blog.[7]

I have a reliable—not quite patentable, but my own unique approach—to finding and landing investors. It's called the "laser beam shotgun" approach to getting funded. It will sound a little strange, as a laser beam being used to guide a shotgun is pretty silly when you think about how a shotgun works. A laser is used on firearms to have precise targeting at a single target downrange. A shotgun, on the other hand, is typically used to imprecisely pepper an entire general area with pellets, with the hope that one or two pellets will land and hit vital areas. Who would put the two together? Well, I would, of course.

The laser beam portion of finding investors involves research. Just like lighting up your target with the laser before you fire, you're going to use research techniques to find investors who meet three criteria. First, you want investors who have money. It sounds silly, but many investors (VCs and angels alike) will take meetings and appear to be investing, even if they have no actual funds to invest at the present time. They are doing this to stay plugged in to the community and to keep abreast of any deals in case they do get more funds. It does nothing for you, though, except potentially networking, and there are plenty of other ways to do that. To find out if an investor has money, check their website, check when their fund closed, check any news for recent investments, or if all else fails, just ask. Second, you want to find investors who have some experience investing in companies of your type. Ideally, these are investors who have similar companies (think B2B or B2C), or individuals who have some personal experience in your field. Again, checking recent news, websites, or just asking are ways to get this done. Lastly, you want to find investors who are

---

[7] http://fastai.com/blog/2017/07/16/how-to-incorporate

entrepreneur friendly. This means avoiding investors who have a reputation of firing founders, or have heavy handed tactics. You won't read this in online news articles, but asking around your startup community for the *bad investors* will give you some investors to avoid. Every city has a few you should probably try to avoid. Now you've got your list—it should hopefully be 20 to 30 angel investors and/or 5 to 10 venture capital firms. What? Your list isn't that long? I bet I know why. You are having trouble finding angel investors, and you don't think there are that many VC firms in your town.

I should mention that finding lists of angels will be hard. Finding lists of VCs, on the other hand, is surprisingly easy. A quick online search for VCs in a given city will yield plenty of results. Don't limit yourself to just your city, either. You should also consider major cities in your state, in your country, or even in the world. Investors in Austin do sometimes invest in companies all over the world. Silicon Valley (the San Francisco Bay Area) often invests globally. You're going to have to travel to make pitches all over the country, but it can pay off big, especially if you are looking for a big VC.

There is no such thing as a comprehensive list of angel investors—they would not want that! They would be bombarded with calls and e mails. Instead, you are going to have to compile one on your own. Start by trying to find angel groups or networks in your area. Angels do prefer to invest locally, so staying within your state is probably wise, unless you know the angel some other way. Angel groups are formal or informal groups of angels that meet regularly to compare notes and occasionally make investments as a group. Sometimes, it can cost $100 or $200 to apply to speak at an angel group. It's not that much money and I encourage you to try it once or twice. Two rejections, though, indicate that you should find a different path. Looking at companies that are similar to yours on sites like AngelList is another way to find angels who might fit your profile.[8] As a last resort, you can search LinkedIn and look for board members of companies that are similar to yours. Sometimes, people will even put "investor" in their title on LinkedIn! Cool! It's going to take time, but getting a list is an important step. The harder part is actually meeting them!

Getting an investor to take a pitch meeting can be almost impossible. This is where our shotgun comes into play. Your laser identified 10, 20, or even 30 targets, right? Shoot them all. Not literally, of course, but you need to try to approach all of them in order for the chance for one or two to say yes. That means you'll likely get over 90% rejections to your first meeting, but it's not you or your idea,

---

[8] http://angel.co

trust me—it's just so hard for investors to see gems in the cloud of startup dust that surrounds them. There are ways to make you shine brighter, and I'll discuss those next, but nothing substitutes the shotgun approach. You need to get to all of them, and fast!

So, how do you get them to notice you and agree to that first meeting? You've got to look like you are one of those shiny gems that they want to find. The absolute best way to do that is to already have a relationship with the investor. This is easy with uncles and friends, but also possible if you are playing the long game with investors. Go to events where they are speaking, trade business cards, meet for lunch, and develop a relationship before you start or even need to pitch. Serial entrepreneurs often have prior relationships with investors, which gives them an advantage. New entrepreneurs can also get this leg up if they take the time to network before they actually need funding. Another tip about networking is to befriend the associates and other folks at the investment firms, not just the partners. Even junior associates at a firm can help you secure that important meeting once it is actually time to raise funds. You can even help them look good if your deal ends up getting taken, so it's in their best interest to maintain these relationships. Try a coffee meeting just to learn about them and their role.

If you don't know the person, and you are in the middle of fundraising, another way to stand out and be a gem is to get a very warm introduction. The best way is to be introduced by a current investor. This will make you seem even more desirable, and angels and VCs both will gladly do this if they are trying to help you get fully funded. This common approach is called *syndication*. Some VCs will only invest if another VC also invests with them. It's a way of making sure they are picking a winner. If you know someone who knows the investor, you can simply ask them for an introduction, but ask for a warm one. That is, ask your friend to introduce you and your company and to say how much they like the idea of your company.

If you don't know someone and can't find time to network your way to an introduction, you can try to reach out to them directly. While you can sometimes apply to an e mail address or website (for VC funds), and you should, it will almost certainly not get you a meeting. Remember, you are using a shotgun, so shoot at everything. You should fill out the application, do the networking, have the coffee with the junior associate, get a warm introduction to a partner, AND try to contact them via e mail, phone, LinkedIn, and Twitter. Twitter is an especially great way to contact investors because many partners use it for their own personal brand and often welcome a direct message or tweet. Twitter also works for angel investors, but remember, warm introductions are always best, so try for that first.

All right, you got your pitch meeting. Whether it was by applying to an angel group and getting accepted, cold calling an angel, or getting that warm introduction, your meeting is set. First and foremost, be there early. Five minutes early. Being late is a guaranteed way to not get funded. If it's a phone meeting, e mail the slides about ten minutes before the call (that way they can't cancel on you). Be prepared with your electronic slide deck and be ready with printed out backup slides as well. These days, investors of all types expect pitches to be in the form of a slide deck.

The Perfect Ten Slide Presentation Deck

If you have more than ten slides, you'll bore them. Less than ten, and they won't understand. Go with ten. Trust me.

Table 7.4 below outlines the content of the perfect ten slide presentation deck. There are four things that are absolutely critical to get right and do well. First, the problem slide. This slide needs to clearly state what the problem is for your target customer and why it is a burning need to be solved. Using an example or illustration is often helpful. I like to start all of my examples with the word "imagine," and make the problem seem really big to my audience. It's the hook that will lead the investors to think the right way. Obviously, it leads well into your solution, which, honestly, doesn't even have to be fully figured out. In other words, your solution does not have to be as detailed as you might think. Remember, you did not get any NDAs signed (because asking for an NDA would be a rookie mistake), so on the solution slide, you don't disclose exactly how you do what you do. Just describe what it generally does, and, of course, the business model.

Table 7.4: The Perfect Ten Slide Presentation Outline

Slide Number	Headline	Validation Content w/Citations
1	The Burning Need	Interviews, Surveys
2	The Problem	Interviews, Articles
3	The Solution	Customer Feedback, Sales, LOI
4	The Team	Resumes, Work History
5	The Early Adopters	Market Research / Articles
6	The Market Size	Market Research / Articles
7	The Competition	Pricing from Competition
8	The Sales Channel / Model	Sales, LOIs, Preorders
9	The Revenue Projections	Your Financial Projection Model
10	The Ask	Your Financial Model and Use of Funds

The business model, described previously in this chapter, is the second piece of critical information to convey concisely and accurately. It is important that you describe how you get sales (direct sales, online, etc.), and how they pay (lump sum, monthly recurring, razor and blade, or some combination). It's helpful to show pricing too, even if it's preliminary pricing—it makes the model clearer to the investors. As with all sections of your business plan, any evidence to support the validity of your business model, problem, or solution should always be shared clearly and cited. Evidence is critical to eventually getting the deal. Just remember that any claims you make will be tested during diligence (see "Closing the Deal" later in this chapter). Evidence to support a business plan is often called *market validation*, and is described in detail in the book *If You Build It Will They Come?* by Rob Adams.[9] Market validation for your business model would be best done by actual sales, but could also be done by customer interviews or surveys. Anything helps.

The third thing that you have to get right, and that investors care a lot about, is your market sizing. Online searching can help you find sizes that make sense, as described earlier in the chapter. You need to show your TAM, SAM, and SOM with as much supporting evidence (citations) as possible to back up your size claims.

Finally, you need to show a hockey stick revenue projection and have a clear ask. A hockey stick is shaped like a backwards L, and it represents how you should expect your revenue to grow. It will grow slowly up (the bottom of the stick) until you get some funding, and then you will quickly *turn the corner* and sales will grow dramatically. This is because your financial model is putting the investors' money to work by growing customers quickly, as described in the previous section of this chapter. Your engine of growth (marketing, salespeople, etc.) gets fuel from the investors, which causes your sales to skyrocket. This hockey stick is a monthly revenue chart derived directly from the financial model you made in the prior section. For the last slide, you simply need their money to make it happen. You are on the cusp of turning that corner, if only you had the investment to put into growth. If you do not believe you can put the investors' money to work quickly for growth, you are probably raising money too early. Remember, investors want to put money into companies that will grow quickly and offer a decent return. They don't want to invest in your science project. Having some early traction, market validation, and support will get you the credibility to get funded. In today's market, these factors are a must.

---

[9] Adams, Rob. *If You Build It Will They Come? Three Steps to Test and Validate Any Market Opportunity.* John Wiley and Sons, 2010.

On my website, I've provided an example of one of my company's business plans.[10] It's set up in the perfect ten slide format, and it was successful. Granted, it was successful in 2004, but little pieces of evidence, such as letters of intent from customers, all lead to our eventual success. Bigfoot Networks won the 2005 Texas Moot Corp competition at the University of Texas with this plan. We then raised $4 million from Austin investors. We built our product and launched it with that money, and then went on to raise another $16 million from large venture investors based in Boston—all with this plan. Feel free to use this as a starting point for your own plan. Bear in mind, however, that Bigfoot raised money before the 2008 financial crisis. Since 2008, investors are shyer about investing in companies that are pre revenue. I always advise companies today to try to get sales first, even if the sales are only preorders. Sales or presales will dramatically increase your chances with investors.

Term Sheets

One of the most common questions I get from students and entrepreneurs alike is how much of the company they should offer to investors in their ask slide. It's actually a deeper question about how much of the company they should give up. There are no easy answers here, but it's important to understand that, ultimately, it will be the investor, not you, who makes an offer. That offer will come in the form of a verbal or written term sheet, and then you'll have to decide to take it, negotiate, or politely decline. The trick is to get the investor to make you an offer (term sheet) that is close to something you will consider accepting, but it's a game of cat and mouse; you want to be the cat, at first.

As you will see in a later chapter, it is important to try to keep control of your company. That means you need to try to keep 51% of your voting stock. All stock is not created equal, except when it comes time to vote—then it doesn't matter what kind of stock someone has, they vote based on their common stock equivalent. For your ask slide, then, you need to think about all the possible future rounds of funding, and how much you think you will need before you are profitable. Then, make a plan such that at the end of your fundraising, you and your co founders still retain 51% of voting stock. To actually make your ask slide, I like to show investors my total expected funds that I think I will need to raise, where I currently am in the fundraising process (for example, at seed round or Series A),

---

[10] http://fastai.com/blog/2017/07/16/perfect-10-slide-business-plan

and the percent on offer for the current round. Since I don't know your plan, I can't really say how much of a percent to offer at the round you are at, but it's usually best to ask for less than you think you should. This way, when they become the cat and make an offer, it might be close to what you really wanted. The reality is that investors will do their own math and come up with an offer. Make sure you let the investors know that you are willing to be the mouse. I do this by clearly calling it an *ask* during my pitch. I often say, "Of course, this is just our *ask*, and we will be glad to entertain any offers."

Speaking of offers, if you get one, congrats—you are halfway there! Okay, maybe a little more than half. You'll now have to decrypt that offer, get a corporate attorney, and get ready to reply. I recommend a corporate attorney who specializes in startups. Most cities have firms that specialize as corporate attorneys. Ideally, you want a firm that has done the legal work for a startup investment before, so they know the norms for term sheets and investor documents.

Some of the terms you may see are preferred stock, pre money valuation, post money valuation, board seats, voting rights, multiple liquidation preference, and pro rata rights. *Preferred stock* is simply saying that the investors get their money returned to them in the event of the sale or IPO of the company. Sometimes, the preferred stock also has a preference multiple, and it means that the investor gets 1x, 2x, or even 3x their money back before you or anyone else sees a penny in a sale or IPO. A 1x preference is normal, but if any more than that, you should consult your lawyer. It may be a negotiation point, and having 1x can mean the difference between you and your founders seeing a penny or not when your company eventually has a successful (or unsuccessful) exit. An exit should be a happy time, but a 2x liquidation preference can kill a potential good exit for everyone and make founders very upset when they get nothing and their investors make a 100% return on their investment.

Board seats are important because the board can hire and fire the CEO. Board seats should follow percent ownership of each party as closely as possible, or else important decisions may have to go to a shareholder vote too often. As the founder, you want to keep as many board seats for you and your co founders as possible. For a venture capital investor, they will insist on at least one board seat. Voting rights are also very important. They allow preferred stockholders to potentially block the sale of a company. You'll have to give up some voting rights, but be careful here, and get a lawyer to make sure you are giving up a normal voting right. Finally, *pro rata rights* are rights for investors to get to buy stock first and keep their percentage if you ever sell stock again. Sometimes, they will even have pay to play provisions that mean if any investor fails to invest their percentage, they lose their stock preference. Pay to play provisions are bad for your angel investors and should be avoided if possible. Pro rata rights are normal.

Pre money valuation is the value that the investor assigns to your company before they make their investment. *Post money valuation* must be their investment plus the pre money amount. To calculate the ownership percentage that they will have of your company (the key thing you want to know), you must divide their investment amount by the post money valuation. This will be the percent that the new investor will own, if you go ahead with the deal.

If you get a verbal offer, you should put it on paper or ask the investor to do so. You need it in writing before you can hire a lawyer to review it. Once your lawyer has reviewed it, it's decision time. Most offers come with a time limit to prevent you from shopping around and looking for a better deal. Your choice is to accept, decline, or negotiate. It's okay to negotiate one more time, but not many more. Make your full list of changes and requests before you negotiate with your counter offer.

It is also possible that you will get an offer for a convertible note. All the same math above applies, except that you will need to consider the valuation cap as the pre money valuation. A convertible note converts at the price of the next round, minus a discount. However, the valuation cap is what happens if there never is a next round, so it should be considered now when thinking about the offer. A convertible note is very common for seed rounds, but especially from angel investors because it ensures that the angel gets preferred stock at a price that a professional investor thinks is fair, minus their discount for investing early.

Closing the Deal

Your work is not over once you accept a term sheet. Now, your lawyer and the investor's lawyer will spring into action. It's usually best to have their lawyer draft the investment paperwork, and then pay your lawyer to review their documents and compare the term sheet for accuracy. There will always be little things that come up with the final paperwork that need to be discussed. It's a good idea to understand what is happening, what you want to happen, and then let your lawyer do the dirty work of getting it for you. Remember, you already agreed to the term sheet, so don't change that aspect, but other little things will come up.

Speaking of little things, your offer letter was most likely contingent upon due diligence. *Due diligence* is the process in which you open all of your actual financials and business details, including your IP, customer lists, and legal documents. It is normal and customary to require an NDA at this point before you enter due diligence of your IP. The investor will want all your financial statements to date, as well as your financial projection models. They will want any piece of legal documentation you have, including sales contracts, letters of intent, and anything you referenced in your business plan presentation. They want to check it all, and they will. The due diligence phase usually happens in conjunction with the document drafting phase. You will also be asked to disclose and make personal representations that you are not holding anything back. My advice is to not withhold anything and to disclose everything you know, even if it's a possible lawsuit or problem. It probably won't kill the deal, and you'll be glad later that you mentioned it in your disclosure if something does happen.

Once all the documents are drafted and agreed upon, and the due diligence is complete, it's signing time. There will be stacks and stacks of papers to sign. Once it is over, have a small party with your team. You're nearly done! There is one last thing to wait for: the check. Once the check is in the bank or the wire transfer is complete, you can now have the real party, and of course, get to work growing your company.

BeatBox Beverages

"What I want to do is make you an offer," Mark said. It was on national television, and the hearts of the three founders of BeatBox Beverages were beating like mad. The popular television show *Shark Tank* was recording, and the founders were about to hear if they would get an offer they could stomach, or not. The investors—or the "sharks," as they are called on the show—are known for low balling and often getting a much better deal than what the founders want. Sometimes, though, that was okay, because the sharks have huge networks of contacts that could make or break a company. Mark Cuban had those networks, as well as relationships with distributors, bottlers, and more. The co founders of BeatBox Beverages—Justin Fenchel, Jason Schieck, Brad Schultz, Dan Singer and Aimy Steadman—knew that having Mark or any of the other sharks as an investor would be at least as valuable as the cash itself.

BeatBox Beverages had to make a lot of progress before getting invited to be part of the television show. They started with their idea for a boxed wine like cocktail drink while attending the University of Texas and studying entrepreneurship. The founders took every startup class they could and leveraged all the resources that the university had to offer. One of the key resources was their fellow students. They interviewed and tested their products on students whenever they could. They made batches of their product (not yet for sale) in their garage, brought it to parties, and got feedback on flavors and branding. Their product hinged on the idea that young people, like college students, wanted alcohol options that were different from beer. They also knew that packaging and branding styles were nearly as important as taste in the beverage business. With their own $55K in self funding, they built prototypes of packaging and logos. They had a good start on branding and product well before they ever applied to be on the television show or really sought funding at all.

BeatBox Beverages then did what many other founders do—they looked to friends and family. They knew that they would need to get some early sales in order to attract big time investors. Using a convertible note structure, they raised $100K from friends and family in a seed round funding. With those dollars and their own investment, they were able to get the proper licenses as a Texas winery and start self distributing. After generating over $230,000 in sales, they finally decided to raise professional investor money. They needed the funding to grow to the next level, land a national distributor, and expand their sales across the United States.

When the team heard that the Shark Tank show was interviewing people in Austin to potentially be on the show, the team was ready. They had their financial models, their market validation, their early sales and deals, and their business plan ready to go. They printed t shirts and more boxes, and headed to the casting call. They were delighted to be selected, and knew this was a big opportunity to land an investor few others could: someone like Mark Cuban. Needless to say, the show was a big hit for BeatBox Beverages.[11]

The BeatBox team's ask of $200K for a 10% stake was not at all what they expected to be offered, but they wanted to start their offer low so that the sharks wouldn't bid too high. Barbara offered them $400K for 20%, and that was a very exciting moment—getting an offer at all is incredibly rare! Next, Kevin offered them $200K for 20%, which was certainly a low ball offer. When Mark Cuban offered them $600K for a 33% stake, they were surprised, but excited. Because they had three offers, they thought that they could negotiate a little and get an even better deal. The team had talked about potential offers before the show, and on the show Justin knew that he could counter for what they had discussed earlier. "Would you do a million for a third?" he asked, unabashedly. Deal. Deal.

The show was over, and they got their deal... but did they? A verbal offer is not necessarily binding, especially when there are so many other terms to consider. Would Mark get common stock, or preferred stock? What about voting rights and board seats? Mark would also surely want to perform due diligence, and all the lawyers would need to review everything too. There was a long road to go from the

---

[11] https://www.youtube.com/watch?v=NbNaTNX-1DU&t=239s

verbal offer to a closed deal, but for the BeatBox Beverages team, it was a win. Several months later, they closed the deal and the check came in. They celebrated with some tasty beverages of their own creation. BeatBox Beverages continues to grow today.

Chapter 8
I Got Sued—It can happen to you

"It's a letter," said Mike.

"I can see that, dude. What does it say?" I asked in reply.

"Well, it's registered mail," he said, with a shocked look in his eye.

"And?" I prompted.

"Dude, they are threatening to sue us," he said, looking up from the letter.

"Okay, about what?" I asked, thinking we had caused somebody's computer to catch fire, or worse.

"Well, apparently the trademark we filed is something that this other company already uses," he said.

"Oh, which trademark?" I asked. We had filed about a dozen of them in a plan to beef up our IP portfolio. We knew early on that our company, Bigfoot Networks would most likely be acquired for our IP. We were a technology company at our heart and a brand on top, a double whammy in favor of being acquired for our IP.

"Well, you won't believe this, but they are complaining about PingThrottle," Mike said.

"What? Who is complaining about that? Intel? They don't do that," I said, and I should know. I was one of the lead designers for Intel's networking group. I had recently been promoted to chip architect when I left Intel the previous year to start Bigfoot Networks.

"No, no, that's the funny part," Mike said, smiling. "It's Ping, the golf company!"

Mike was an avid golfer, so I'm sure he did think this was funny. I did not. I knew that Ping had a lot, and I mean a lot, of money. They could drown us in motions and legal proceedings and kill our company by a thousand cuts. I also knew that companies with lawsuits pending didn't get funded or acquired. We had a big problem on our hands.

"So, wait, are we getting sued, or what is this, exactly?" I asked. Neither Mike nor I knew, but we did know that we needed to act fast. The letter mentioned ten days to "remedy," and I wanted to do that if I could.

Three hours later, our lawyer handed us a drafted official response for us to sign. It stated that we apologized, that we would withdraw our trademark application, and asked if we could humbly sell the remainder of our current stack of 5,000 boxes that had the PingThrottle name listed as a feature. The cost to us? $1,200 for three hours of the lawyer's time. Ping accepted the letter in a written response, and the entire company breathed an incredible sigh of relief.

DOI 10.1515/9781501507083-008

Our lawyer explained that technically, we were in different markets than Ping and thus they didn't really have a leg to stand on to challenge our trademark. The trademark likely would not cause any confusion in the market, and a judge would possibly throw the case out. He did say, though, that case preparation, a trial lawyer, and likely many motions would cost us upwards of $100K to try to fight back. Even then, Ping might go after our other terminology or even appeal or worse. Having the lawsuit pending would definitely spoil any forthcoming investments we had, and either winning or losing a lawsuit would not look good to investors.

We made the smart decision by choosing not to fight and settling for essentially zero dollars. It was the best legal decision we ever made. As you will read at the end of this chapter, some of my other friends were not so lucky.

Who Can Sue Whom

First, I must make a short disclaimer. I am not a lawyer and this chapter, nor any of the contents of this book, should be considered legal advice. If you want legal advice, hire a lawyer—that's what they are paid to do and they have insurance to cover their butts if they get it wrong. I don't have such insurance or training, hence this disclaimer. That said, I do understand and have experience with many legal aspects of running a business, and I believe this chapter can really help you understand your risks, how to avoid mistakes, how to optimize your legal budget (costs), and how to stay calm! There are risks, but they are small ones, and the entire system of American corporate law is designed to protect you and your personal assets. Read on to understand what I mean.

One of the most important lessons of law in the United States is understanding that anyone can sue another person or company at any time for any reason. In order to sue someone, all you have to do is go to a courthouse and file a piece of paper. Granted, some of these lawsuits are thrown out at that stage as "frivolous" or "lacking documentation." But you can do it, and so can your enemies. Before you go freaking out, however, bear in mind, getting sued in business is actually pretty rare, and is usually a last resort.

Why is it rare? To win a lawsuit, you have to show a judge or jury that you have enough evidence to support your claim. Getting that evidence is difficult. Unless there is a signed and dated agreement on file, and you have evidence that the agreement was broken, it will be hard to win a lawsuit against a business. Taking a lawsuit to court is costly for the American taxpayer (who pays for the courthouse, judge, bailiff, etc.), for the person who is bringing the lawsuit (the plaintiff), and the person who is getting sued (the defendant). What costs? Lawsuits cost time, money for lawyers, damages to your reputation (as plaintiff or defendant), and the potential for a countersuit. For this reason, suing someone is rare. Suing someone who has little to no money (like a startup) is very rare. Even if you win, you aren't likely to get much, if anything. You may not even win enough to be able to pay your own lawyer in the event you win.

A countersuit is when someone you are suing sues you back! It happens all the time, and is actually a smart play. If the person or company suing you believes you are doing something wrong to them, often, you will probably have reason to believe they are doing something wrong to you as well. If it gets too nasty, though, it may never settle, and it will have to go to court. Having it go to court or even arbitration (explained next) is not a good outcome for you.

One final thing to be aware of is that there are some companies that have a business model of suing other companies. Patent trolls are one such type of company. Your best defense against patent trolls and other kinds of predatory legal actions is to have a great IP portfolio. I will share more on IP strategy later in this chapter.

Types of Lawsuits (and Arbitration)

What does it actually mean to get *sued*? There are two kinds of lawsuits—civil and criminal. When we say "sue," we mean a civil lawsuit. A *civil lawsuit* is when one party feels that they were wronged by another party and seeks monetary compensation or other damages. Sometimes, this means that they are seeking money. Other times, this means the judge compels someone to take action or face worsening consequences, including contempt of court or jail time. For example, if you got sued for using someone else's trademark and lost, you might be compelled to give up the trademark and stop using that name. If you didn't do that, you might get a fine from the court. If you still didn't do it, you might spend some time in jail for contempt. You might also have to pay the company that sued you money to pay for their legal fees, damages (if customers went to you instead of them, for example), or even punitive damages (like a big fee to discourage you from doing this again). All of this (except the jail time) is moot, however, if you have no money, the company goes bankrupt, or if it ceases to be an operating company (shuts down). In fact, lawsuits against a company do not affect the individual owners of the company (you) except in certain situations. Specifically, if you broke the law, you can be sued personally. The other situation is if you mingled your money with the company's money, then all your money is tainted and subject to confiscation to pay for a lost lawsuit. Don't do either of those things!

A *criminal lawsuit* is when you broke the law, got caught, and a prosecutor (someone from the county, state, or federal government) decided to pursue you as a criminal. In business, you can face criminal prosecution only if you break a law. Things like falsifying documents, lying to investors, or lying to customers are considered fraud, and you could be criminally charged. In addition, since you were charged, you could also be sued personally (not just your company). There are other laws that you could break in business too, but they are mostly obvious. You could go to jail for embezzlement, sexual harassment, killing someone—you know, the obvious stuff. I can't think of any *non obvious laws* that you can be prosecuted for breaking while running a business. Even stuff like selling alcohol without having a license to sell liquor (a pretty serious crime) is usually first delivered as a warning or cease order, rather than criminal prosecution. Don't break obvious laws, and you will almost certainly be fine. And yes, every state requires you to have a license to sell alcohol, so don't screw that one up either.

Most lawsuits are first processed by a judge to determine validity and to set a court date. After that, both kinds of lawsuits are eventually heard in front of a jury, just like on TV. That is, if they are not first settled in a civil case, or resolved through a plea bargain in a criminal case. Most lawsuits do get settled or have a plea bargain, though, because it's cheaper, faster, and usually less punitive than taking it all the way to a jury trial.

Sometimes, both parties sign a legal document that says that they will accept binding arbitration in the event of a dispute. In these cases, a professional—usually a former or current judge—hears the case and issues a decision. The decision is binding because of the contract you signed. This can be appealed and eventually taken to civil court, but the costs will go up. Arbitration is usually faster and cheaper than a jury trial, anyway. It's kind of like a forced way to try to settle before going to full court.

Avoiding Lawsuits

As scary as lawsuits sound, they really are quite rare. In fact, there are at least three ways you can be sure to avoid lawsuits. None of these ways involve actually hiring a lawyer, by the way. If you have to hire a lawyer, you are already in deep trouble. In my experience, many lawyers tend to tilt toward proceeding with a lawsuit, or at least pushing the envelope. Unless you have the money to do that, I usually suggest that people try their very best to avoid hiring a lawyer unless a lawsuit really is pending. It is better to try to avoid lawsuits.

First, avoid lawsuits by limiting the number of documents that you sign to the bare minimum. Every document you sign is a contract that could potentially get you into trouble. It might be tempting to sign everyone's NDA or lots of contracts, but it would be better to only sign those that you really need. When you do sign them, be sure to read them and understand clearly what the contract is. When I sign a contract or NDA, I always check three important things. First, am I signing on behalf of my company, or myself? Never sign on behalf of yourself; be sure you are signing only as a representative (such as a CEO) of the company. Second, is there a term of the contract, and is it three years or less? Don't sign NDAs, contracts, or any other documents that don't have a term, and the term should usually be for one year. I might sign a three year NDA if I really wanted to have the meeting or get the information, but it would be rare. The longer the contract, the longer your exposure, and the longer you are obligated to fulfill the contract. Finally, I read the entire contract and make sure that I understand the terms of the contract and that they match the business intent that I want to have. If possible, I also make sure that the governing laws are for Texas, Travis County, or at least the United States. The closer to me, the better, in case I have to defend a lawsuit in another state. If you are going to do business with someone, it is better to have a contract than not. Try to get one. Just be sure that you understand the contract and that you really do need to do business with them.

The second tip to avoid lawsuits is to try to be aboveboard. If you need to do or change something that might involve the other party with whom you have a contract or even a verbal agreement, try to at least inform them ahead of time or get their consent. If, for example, you have a contract with a supplier—say, someone who supplies you t shirts—and you need to cancel an order, try to ask them (instead of demanding them) to cancel the order, and explain why. If they agree to cancel it, even in an e mail, they can't come after you later for damages or any breach of contract—they agreed to the cancellation. You didn't force it on them. This principle holds true as good business partner practice, but can also help you avoid lawsuits. If they complain, remind them that they agreed. If they say that you own them some money anyway, read the next section.

The final tip to avoid lawsuits is to settle early and settle often. Sometimes, you can settle a potential lawsuit even before it comes to anything. In the previous example, you canceled an order of t shirts at the last minute. The supplier agreed to it, but now you get a bill for 10% restocking fee for the canceled order. You don't see that in the contract, per se, but you do know that you canceled the order last minute. Should you pay, or should you challenge? There is actually a bit of quick math you can do to determine if you should just pay or not. Remember, paying up avoids a potential lawsuit, keeps the partner happy, and might just save you money. Table 8.1 below shows how the simple math works. The basic idea is that if the amount being asked for is less than what you would likely pay in legal costs (win or lose), you should just pay!

If there is no money being requested at all, the math gets really simple: pay the zero dollars! In many potential lawsuits, there is no money being asked of you at all, you are just being asked to *do something* (like remove a picture from your website), and it may not even cost you anything. Avoid the lawsuit, and just do it. These kinds of actions are often cease and desist requests. You might get an e mail or a letter that asks you to cease using, say, a photograph on your website (which has happened to me many times). Why fight that? If you do, you are likely going to lose, despite whether you win or not, because of legal fees. The same goes for trademark disputes, such as the one with Ping golf in my personal example at the start of this chapter. That decision was easy. *Don't fight it, it's silly. We don't really need that trademark, anyway.* In most cases, the legal costs are just not worth it. Avoid the lawsuit by settling, paying up, or doing the action requested. Only if it is central to your business or if your math works out with the table below should you consider fighting it. If you are a really good negotiator, you may even be able to negotiate the amount owed to be a little lower. If they accept your lower offer of payment, you are good to go. Well done!

Table 8.1: To Pay or Not to Pay: Avoiding Lawsuits

Item	Value	Your Calculation
What is the total dollar amount that the other party is asking you to pay them?	$ Owed	
How clear is the contract (or case law) that you owe it to them?	% Clear	
How likely is it that you would lose if it came before a jury?	% Likely Lose	
How much would you have to pay your attorney if it went to a jury trial?	Your lawyer's hourly rate (or use $400, whichever is greater) * 200 hours	
Should you pay them or not?	If $ Owed < ([% Clear] + [% Likely Lose]) * ([Legal Fees] + [$ Owed]), then Pay.	

Importance and Types of Intellectual Property

Intellectual property (IP) is something that your company owns that is not necessarily a physical thing, but an intangible thing that is important to the company.

Everything from a customer list to a secret formula to a patented design can be considered intellectual property. IP is important to a company for at least three distinct reasons. First, it's important to the operation of your business. If you don't have customer lists, you don't have customers. If you don't know your own formulas or processes for making your products or services, you can't make or deliver them. IP is the know how to do what you do, and you need that!

The second reason IP is important is that companies are bought at a premium of their value because of growth potential, most of which is tied up with their IP. In other words, companies get bought in large part because of their IP. Would you want to buy a company that didn't have customer lists, formulas, or anything at all unique and special about them? Probably not. IP doesn't have to be a patent, as you will see, but companies buy other companies for technology/patents, brand, customer access, revenue, and many other reasons. Each reason you give them to buy increases both your chances of being bought and the final purchase price. These are all good things to you (as a founder) and your shareholders (your investors). The IP is the reason that your company will likely be bought.

Finally, IP is important in defending your company's uniqueness against other companies attacking you. Imagine that you open a store called "Happiness in a Bottle" on the main street of your town. You sell liquor and beer (with the proper licenses, mind you), and you provide little snippets of advice like fortune cookies in each bag that you sell. A new store opens up three blocks away that is also called "Happiness in a Bottle," and they sell liquor too. Are you going to be happy about that? I sure hope not, and I also hope that you at least filed the name of your business with your state, if not already secured a full on trademark. Without IP such as a state filing or trademark to protect your name, you will have a hard (read: costly!) time defending your name. Now customers are confused and you are losing customers to the other store. Worse, imagine that you invented a new way to send data over the Internet that speeds up the web by 85%. You get it all working, and launch your business. A few weeks later, Cisco, the world leader in internet switches, starts using it and selling it inside their routers, included for free. What used to be a paid download from your site is now free with most routers and switches. Now, a free app comes out that does it too, and you are screwed. Your sales drop to zero. If you had patented your new technology and remembered to include a use case where the technology is embedded into a device, you would have a strong chance to pull through this. If you had a patent, you could shut down Cisco, make them pay you or buy your company, and cause that free app to shut down too. You would also likely get awarded damages in a civil lawsuit. Unfortunately, since you didn't patent it and it's been over a year, you have no recourse but to watch as your company dies. Any IP you create needs to be protected, or else if it is any good, someone else will use it, claim it, and cause your business to die.

IP that is used as a defense against other people's claims is very similar to making claims yourself. In other words, imagine if Cisco sends you a letter saying that you should stop using your 85% algorithm because they have a patent on it. Well, if you have your patent too, then you can countersue them. Alternatively, if you have a different patent on something they are doing, you can also countersue them for that. This is often how cross licensing happens. Cisco would allow you to use their first patent while you allowed them to use your second patent, and the case would be settled. Without your own IP, however, you have no defense, and you can't even cross license.

Types of Intellectual Property

There are many different types of IP. They can broadly be categorized into two categories: unregistered IP and registered IP. Unregistered IP is IP that you have not taken active steps to protect. A customer list that gets leaked onto the Internet or taken home by one of your salespeople is an example of unregistered IP.

The most common type of unregistered IP is the trade secret. A *trade secret* is internal to your company and has not been disclosed to the public. That customer list is a trade secret for as long as it is truly kept secret. So are your formulas and processes for making your products or delivering your services. Internal documents, training manuals, leads, e mails, internal prototypes, design drafts, and anything else not disclosed to the public is a trade secret. Your job as the founder is to decide what simply stays a trade secret, and what you might need to protect even more. Trade secrets can be lost or stolen, and when that happens, you often have no way to get them back; they are loose in the public, and nothing can be done about it. It is always a good idea to prevent valuable trade secrets from being lost or stolen by putting passwords on things like the customer database, limiting access to only trusted people, or keeping them in a vault (virtual or physical). Sometimes, though, it is important to protect IP even more than just keeping it under lock and key.

The words you write and the pictures and graphics you make are another form of unregistered IP. This kind of IP is protected by copyright. *Copyright* is the term used to describe original content rights that an author or artist receives because they were the first to create that content. Whenever you write, draw, paint, compose something, or generally create a work of original design, you do not need to register it to receive a copyright; you get it through the act of creation. Even software code (which falls under the writing category) gets a free copyright, no paperwork required, if you are the one to originally write it. It is part of common law of the United States and most other nations that the first artist or writer to make something gets the copyright to that content, which prevents others from claiming it as their own work or benefiting from it. In the U.S., this copyright lasts for 95 years or 70 years after the author's death, and then that work becomes part of the public domain and others can benefit from it.[1] Short phrases, however, such as "Happiness in a Bottle" will probably not be protectable under copyright, because they are not long enough to be considered unique, original, or copyrightable. In the case where something is short, like a company name, or important enough, like your logo, a good founder should consider protecting the IP further by registering it. Short things can be registered as trademarks, and longer works that are really important can be registered as "registered copyrights."[2] You don't have to register copyrightable work, but it does help in case you ever want to prosecute someone if they use it without your permission.

Registered IP falls into two general types: trademarks and patents. A *trademark* is when you register a phrase, name, or graphic (logo) and claim it for exclusive use in the United States (or other countries) for companies of your type. Trademarks generally last for ten years and can be renewed.[3] As a founder, you should absolutely consider trademarking your company name and logo (usually done together), as well as any key product or service names, feature names, or other slogans. The cost to trademark something is fairly low and having a trademark builds value in your company. You can also register your name(s) in your state in your incorporation documents, which prevents other companies in your state from having that same name. You can also file a *Doing Business As* (DBA) form in your state or other states to protect your name or names you use to describe your company in those states.

A patent is a way to protect a novel, useful invention that is not obvious. It must pass three criteria to be issued. First, it must have novelty—you must be the first one to have invented it. A bicycle chain is an example of something no longer novel, as it was invented hundreds of years ago. Second, it must be useful—it has to serve some purpose and be useful to solving a problem. A pair of glasses with antenna on top is not useful unless the antenna serves a purpose (e.g. fashion is not patentable). Finally, it should be non obvious—this just means that the invention is not so simple and trivial that it is obvious that it could or should be

---

[1] https://www.copyright.gov/circs/circ15a.pdf
[2] https://www.copyright.gov/registration
[3] https://www.uspto.gov/learning-and-resources/trademark-faqs

done. Watching streaming movies on a TV instead of just watching live TV shows is an example of something obvious, not patentable.

There are four kinds of patents to be aware of: *provisional patents, utility patents, design patents,* and *international patents.*[4] A *provisional patent* is the cheapest to file and simply sets the priority date of when you filed the invention. You have one year of time to file the full utility or design patent, or else the patent goes away. During the time at which you file a provisional patent all the way until the patent issues with its unique number, you can say, "patent pending." Investors and companies that buy other companies love patents. Even provisional patents have value when a company gets invested in or acquired. A *utility patent* is the most common kind of real patent. It is the kind that protects your invention, how it works, and its use for twenty years, after which it becomes public domain. A *design patent* is different in that it only protects the shape or look of something, not necessarily how it works. Design patents last for fifteen years. Finally, an international patent is a patent that gets submitted to other countries, usually through the Patent Cooperation Treaty (PCT).[5] The duration of these patents can vary by country. Bear in mind, however, that disclosing your invention at a trade show, conference, or in a published paper sets a one year clock for you to file the patent in the US, and may prevent you from filing a PCT (international rules differ regarding discloser). Be sure to talk to an attorney before you disclose anything to the public about something you might patent.

Corporate Innovation

Most corporations have legal teams or specific law firms that they use commonly for various tasks, such as filing patents. In a corporate setting, you will probably not be filing patents or trademarks on your own. Your corporation where you work will own your IP regardless of how you go about filing or reporting it. It is usually best to document your innovation well, date it, and keep it handy for when your project gets a green light. Figure out who at your organization manages intellectual property and get them on board with your vision. They will help you figure out the right time to file things.

The key thing to remember is to never make something public that hasn't been disclosed and discussed first with your internal legal or IP teams. The timing of making something public can prevent you from getting certain kinds of IP protection.

In the event that your corporate innovation does not get the green light from your management team, many corporations will want to file the patent for the innovation anyways. Lucky for you, filing patents inside your corporation often gets you a nice bonus too!

---

[4] https://www.uspto.gov/web/offices/ac/ido/oeip/taf/patdesc.htm
[5] http://www.wipo.int/pct/en

Filing Patents and Trademarks

Do you need a lawyer to file a patent or trademark? How much does it cost? When should I do it? What if I don't have very much money? What are the risks of doing it or not doing it? How do I file the patent or trademark?

These questions and many more would probably be best answered by an IP lawyer. They will usually answer these kinds of questions for free as part of an initial consultation, because they are interested in winning the bigger business of actually doing the work. That said, in my experience as CEO of four different startups, I can lend you my business advice as to how to go about this. Every business has limited funds—even more so for startups. Read on, and I'll share with you some of the tips I've used to optimize my legal dollars for the most and best IP possible. I should mention that my name is on more than twenty one patents, and I have also filed countless trademarks, not to mention written a ton of articles (copyright) and code (copyright). My experiences are that as a business owner (founder), not as a lawyer, so ask a professional for true advice. For tips on how to be cheap, read on.

Filing a provisional patent can be cheap and easy. For me, I do this myself and I do it often. The cost benefit analysis of filing a provisional patent is very favorable—low cost, high benefit. The cost is as low as $65 for a micro entity.[6] That is incredibly inexpensive for the value received. With a provisional patent filed, you get to claim a patent is pending when describing your solution. You can share the provisional under NDA with investors, who see patents as important to protecting a company's advantage. You can prove without a doubt that you were first to file based on the provisional date. The best thing about it is that it's super easy too. You can do it in about an hour.

In order to file a provisional patent, you can either hire a lawyer (including possibly a virtual lawyer through LegalZoom.com or RocketLawyer.com), or you can file it yourself. I usually file provisional patents myself, because it is so easy. I simply write up what my invention does, make a very simple black and white drawing, and then go to USPTO.gov and do what is called an EFS Web e filing.[7] E filing is an online submission form, no stamps involved, where you submit the two items together in PDF format. You will have to save your files as PDFs to be able to upload them to the USPTO. Once you have done this and paid your very small fee, you are done. Save the unique number and filing records for your reference. The hard part

---

[6] https://www.uspto.gov/learning-and-resources/fees-and-payment/uspto-fee-schedule
[7] https://www.uspto.gov/patents-application-process/applying-online/about-efs-web

is writing up the invention and drawing. Lawyers write it in such a way as to make sure all your claims are there and protected. That's good, because you want those things. However, it is also not really necessary, as this is not the full patent yet. As long as you have described well how your patent works, you should be good. To help illustrate what a provisional patent looks like, I've written one here and provided it for you to see as Table 8.2 (the text) and Figure 8.1 (the drawing). The drawing must be black and white and is usually best as just lines and boxes—more than that, and it'll be too much for the patent examiners to interpret. The important part of the text, also called the *specification*, is that someone who is skilled in the art of my invention type (electrical engineering) would be able to create my invention with the details I have provided. In addition, I have described in the patent how it works, what is useful about it, and what I believe is novel about it. I've used mostly layperson's terms for this, but I do talk about a method, system, and device. The purpose for this is that in the future, I might be granted only the device, or only the system and so forth, so I want to be sure to say all of them.

Filing a full patent is quite different from filing a provisional. A full patent must have claims that are well supported in the text of the patent. Where my example provisional patent application was just a few paragraphs long, a full patent to describe this would be more than twenty pages. Why the huge difference? The full patent must use legal jargon, must describe each and every possible use case and combination, and must be even more detailed. In addition, the claims must be very precisely worded with, again, every possible combination of claims listed. Because of this complexity, I always use a patent attorney to assist with the drafting and filing of a full patent application, regardless of the type. Since a full patent will be examined to determine if it is written correctly or not, it must be done just so, or it will be rejected. Paying a patent attorney to draft the application will cost at least $5,000, and possibly as much as $15,000. In addition, the filing fees for full patents are much higher, and can run you as high as $2,000. So, is all this worth it? If you are a startup, the short answer is: maybe. If you have budgeted for this, and you believe that the patent is important enough and core to your business, then yes. However, if the patent is not core, and not really related to what you actually do, then probably not. Not unless you are creating a patent troll company, and if so, please... just don't. Patent trolls are people who file patents that they never intend to use, only to get a fee from someone who might have to use it in the future. They are not well liked.

People often ask me if they should search patents to see if someone has already patented it or not. I always advise them not to. First, you will have to disclose any results you get. Second, it might convince you not to file, when, in reality, you are probably doing something slightly different enough to go ahead and file anyway. Finally, that is the job of the patent agent—don't do their job for them!

Filing a copyright is easy and can be done on the copyright.gov website. Personally, I have never done it, because you get a copyright just by right of authorship—no paperwork required. Filing a trademark, however, is a little more complex and important. First, unlike a patent, you should search the USPTO.gov website to see if the trademark already exists. If it does, check to see if it is in your same class of goods (e.g. same or similar business type). If it does not already exist or it is in a different class of goods such that you would not be confused together, then you can proceed to file the trademark. You could file it yourself, but their paperwork is a little tricky, and mistakes can get made. It's actually really cheap to simply let LegalZoom.com or RocketLawyer.com do it for you. They don't charge more than fifty to a hundred dollars on top of the filing fee of around $275. I find they have better success than I do getting the trademark successfully. The cost benefit analysis of having a trademark for your company name or product name is quite high. You can list it as part of your IP with investors, and you get to put a ® symbol by it, which shows that it is a registered trademark. This helps lend credibility to your business and protects you from others trying to copy you.

Table 8.2: Example Provisional Patent Filing Text (Specification)

Specification Application Part
The following describes a method, system, and device that are useful for improving driver safety during an emergency situation. Drivers use their horn to alert other drivers of an important situation and to avoid collisions. A normal horn uses audible frequencies, usually by means of an electrically powered device. This patent is for a better horn, a horn disruptor, which uses both a traditional horn, as well as one or more frequency jammers to help get other drivers' attentions. What is novel about this system is the use of frequency jammers to interrupt what may be happening in the car and distracting other drivers.
The basic technique is to attach transmitters at various frequencies to the same or different switch that runs the car horn. These jammers put out a signal that interrupts frequencies that may be in use in a radius around the car. The jammer might interrupt Bluetooth, Wi Fi, AM, FM, satellite, or other signals, ideally causing a "silence" and an alert tone such as, "Watch out on the road" or other alerts. While this silence or alert is transmitted with the jammers, the normal horn may also sound to alert other drivers as well.
Frequency transmitters are common in the art of electronics, meaning that any skilled electronics expert could reduce one to practice easily. What is novel here is attaching the jammers to the same circuit as the horn, and using them to alert nearby drivers of a potential danger.
This provisional patent includes the method of horn and jamming, the system of horn and jamming, and the device of the horn jammer.

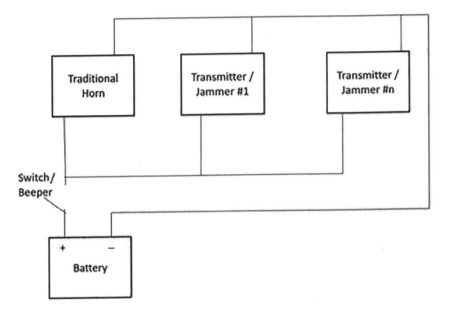

Figure 8.1: Example Provisional Patent Black and White Drawing

Incorporation and the Corporate Veil

Remember, anyone can sue another person or company at any time for any reason. While this is true, the laws in the United States are set up very specifically to encourage entrepreneurship and protect the investors who risk their fortunes. Most other countries have similar laws, because without them, the potential negatives of starting a business would curtail new businesses from ever starting. These laws are part of corporate law and the way they work in the U.S. is that a corporation, for many legal purposes, is considered a person. A person or a corporation can be sued. Both could be sued too, but in general, a person who owns a corporation (a founder or investor) cannot be sued unless the corporate veil has been pierced.

The *corporate veil* is an imaginary shield that protects owners and directors of companies (shareholders, founders, investors and managers/employees) from getting sued for things the company does or has happen (like a malfunctioning product, or even a fire caused by a product), unless the person has broken the corporate veil in one of three ways. First, if the person breaks a law, such as committing fraud, and is convicted, that conviction then breaks the veil and allows for civil suits to be brought against the individual person. Second, if the finances of the person are mixed in with the finances of the company, then all the assets of the person might be available to access if the company is sued. In this situation, the company gets sued, loses, and not only do the company's assets get taken, but also the individual's assets because they were mingled and the distinction between accounts is not kept clear. Finally, certain types of lawsuits can target or include shareholders, investors, employees or founders directly, separately from the company. In those cases, there is some specific claim and evidence of wrongdoing that will have to be proven against the individual. This last category is a catchall, because, as previously stated, anyone can be sued. If you can prove you were working on behalf of the company and the aforementioned corporate veil has not been broken, you can probably defeat any such lawsuit.

In order to create a corporate veil to protect your personal assets, a corporation must exist and all business dealings (contracts and so forth) must be done on behalf of the company, not the individual. It's not hard to incorporate, as has been described before—a quick e mail setup on RocketLawyer.com or LegalZoom.com can get you going there fast. The harder part is to be sure to keep the company separate from the individual afterward.

From then on, investments go to the company, not the individual. Checks should be written to and from the company. The best way to make sure this happens is to open up a separate bank account for the company. All moneys should flow into and out of that bank account with good documentation. This is especially true for investor moneys and your own moneys that you put in (founder investment) or take out (founder payments). It's all right to pay yourself as a contractor or an employee, depending on your time commitment. It's not all right to just take money out of your business account and spend it. Every dollar in and out needs a paper trail to protect your corporate veil.

Ways to Get Thrown in Prison

Lest you think that running a company is without risk, keep in mind that there are ways to get thrown into prison. There are two ways this can happen. First, you can be *held* for a limited time without any charges at all (just suspicion of wrongdoing). Second, you can be convicted of a crime and have to serve time. For small mistakes, like trespassing or operating without a proper license, you won't usually do hard time, but will likely be *held* overnight or at most a few nights in the county jail. Other reasons for being held are being drunk and disorderly, driving under the influence, and domestic violence. Don't do those things! They aren't related to your business. Being held for your business is more common if you get caught loitering or soliciting AND you refuse to follow the orders of the police officer. If this happens, you have probably been a bit too aggressive about trying to get sales. Following officer instructions usually gets you just a warning. As an example, you might get held, as I have, for standing outside a convention center and handing out fliers. You might get held for passing out a bunch of fliers on people's cars, or inside of other peoples' businesses. Some businesses are okay with it. Most are not, and it's considered loitering. Sometimes, though, a founder just needs a few more data points or customers. Why not hit the gym and accost people while they are exercising? Well, you might get asked to stop, if you refuse, you might get held by the police. You might even get formally charged and con-·, victed of loitering, but generally, loitering is not a big deal (not a felony).

Did an author really just tell you to get arrested? No, that's not what I mean. What I mean to say is it's not that big of a deal in the grander scheme. Misdemeanors are minor affairs. Felonies, on the other hand, are major affairs. A felony conviction probably means you won't ever be able to raise money from investors again, as they often do background checks. When in doubt, follow the law, and always comply with the police, it can save you a lot of trouble.

Insurance for Companies (Liability, D&O, Key Man)

Insurance for a company might take some math skills. Remember, as a startup operator, you are forced to make decisions with scarce resources. Having insurance won't protect you from getting sued, and it probably won't even help you much if you do get sued. How does that work?

There are many kinds of insurance, and each one serves a different purpose with its own set of limitations. The one insurance that may be worth getting as a company is called general liability insurance. This kind of insurance will cost you anywhere from a few hundred dollars to a few thousand dollars per year. It's designed to protect you in case someone gets hurt on your property or in the event of damage to your property. It's kind of like homeowner's insurance for your company. It may, depending on the details of the policy, offer some legal fees in certain cases, but generally not. It's cheap enough, though, that having it is usually worth it.

Product liability insurance protects you against your product or service causing damage to someone else or someone else's property. It is much more expensive at thousands to tens of thousands per year, and is usually not worth it until you have enough products in the market or if you do risky things. This kind of insurance still doesn't really protect you from getting sued, but it does help pay for legal costs and damages if you lose.

There are many other kinds of insurance that insurance agents will try to sell you. Your general approach should be to avoid it, unless an investor is making you do it. Directors and officers (D&O) liability insurance is one example. This kind of insurance protects directors and officers of the company personally, just in case they too get named in a lawsuit. It's expensive, and you really shouldn't need it with your corporate veil. Some investors require it, however. Key man insurance is used in case the primary inventor or founder of the company dies. I was forced to get this by my investors as part of my closing, because they were worried that all the knowledge was in my head. It wasn't, but to get the funding, we got the insurance.

As with all insurance, there is a risk of not having it. The risk is that if you don't have it, and you get sued, you could lose your company. That risk still exists even with it, though, so I try to avoid insurance for my companies, except for general liability insurance. Insurance is an expense that offers no returns on investment unless you are in deep trouble.

As your company grows, however, the risks increase. Now, losing a lawsuit could mean a much bigger loss. Plus, with more customers and business dealings comes more risk. As companies grow, they should continuously consider what kind of insurance is appropriate for their stage. Generally, the bigger the company, the more insurance they are likely to carry to protect the company, its shareholders and its key employees.

Lawsuits from Investors/Founders (CEO Power)—Key Ingredient

One of the most damaging kinds of lawsuits is when founders sue investors, or investors sue founders. This kind of lawsuit kills most companies because a fight like this turns ugly fast. Why would a founder sue his investors? There are a lot of reasons. First, a founder might get terminated (see Chapter 9), and they may not be happy about that. In this situation, the founder might sue for wrongful termination, minority shareholder abuse, or any other reasons to get back at the investors who, through board control only, fired the founder.

Investors might sue the founder for fraud (if they lied), but the criminal case would also need to be filed. Just like anyone, investors could sue anyone for any reason, but they usually don't. Investors value their personal reputation just as much as you and I do and suing people is not a good way to make friends.

Investor/founder lawsuits usually get settled. More often than not, in my experience, the founders win and get a settlement (usually cash) for their trouble. For this reason, as you will learn in Chapter 10, founders, especially CEO founders, have a lot more power than they may think. The courts like founders and dislike rich investors, so trials scare investors very much. Remember, they even made you get D&O insurance to personally protect them. That's probably because they know they would usually lose any such cases.

Suing an investor comes with consequences, however. Investors are a tight knit group, and if you sue one, they will talk. After that, it will be very hard to raise money from professional or even angel investors again. You may have to move to a different city, and even then, a bad reputation might follow you. Try to resolve problems with investors or board members on your own first. Threaten to sue, but be careful about actually doing it.

I took over a startup called Key Ingredient in 2013, and I had to help settle a lawsuit from the prior CEO against the company and the board members (investors). I was brought in as the new CEO and had this big mess to clean up. I was able to eventually help the case settle, but do you know who won out in the end? The CEO who got fired ended up winning big. He got paid a large sum of money (undisclosed, but big), and the investors had to pay (not the company). It was a win for the company (since we didn't have to pay anything), a win for the fired founder, but a loss for the investor. The consequence to the company was that from then on, that investor was a bit timid about investing in startups and became very cautious with our business dealings together. It wasn't a great outcome for the company after all, because of the unexpected side consequences. Lawsuits are bad for business.

When to Sue Someone Else

Suing someone who has no money is pointless. Why would you sue an employee? They are working for salary or wages, and probably don't have a big nest egg to pay you. Do you really want to encumber their paycheck for $50 per month for the rest of their life? It's usually not worth it. People generally don't sue people who don't have significant money—it's a waste of time.

Suing also has consequences. You can get a bad reputation. Suing suppliers, for example, can get you blackballed (or listed as a bad customer) from other suppliers. Suing investors can get you blackballed from other investors. There had better be a good reason, or you should really think twice.

In some cases, the investor or supplier already has a bad reputation. Their bad reputation (something you should have checked before going into business with them—always ask for references) can help you. If you sue someone with a bad reputation, they can't really blackball you, because others already know about their reputation. So, go ahead if they have money and you think you can win. Remember, though, you will also need money to pay for your lawyer if you lose, and sometimes even if you win.

Personally, I have never sued anyone. I wish I had occasionally threatened it more often. However, I am glad to say that I have never actually done it. My reputation is intact.

The Analytical Approach to Settling (or Not)

Paying up to prevent a lawsuit, as discussed previously in this chapter, is not the same as agreeing to settle a lawsuit. To settle a lawsuit, one has to first be filed. If you pay up, or otherwise prevent the lawsuit from getting filed in the first place, you can avoid this altogether. However, if a lawsuit does get filed, you need to think seriously about settling as early and as often as possible.

Settling a lawsuit means coming to an agreement outside of the courts or arbitration that you and the other party are happy with and agree to drop the lawsuit. This is a good thing—it signals the end of the legal fees and the headaches, and you no longer have to disclose that lawsuit to investors (except to say that it was settled out of court, if they ask). The issue of settling or not is not one of right and wrong. If you are suing or being sued because you feel unjustly treated, wronged, or want to punish someone, you are doing it for the wrong reason. You have to think: *Okay, here I am now. Should I continue?*

The math is simple. Estimate how much money it will take to go all the way through court, add on the amount of damages you might lose if you lose in court (or the winnings you might get if you win), and decide if it's worth it or not to continue (or just settle for less right now!). Note that I did not say that you should consider past amount spent—that's already done. I did not say anything about the emotional feeling of winning or losing, which should not be considered. It's purely financial—what are your odds of winning or losing when multiplying the gain or loss and the cost of paying your lawyer and your own time, compared to the cost of just settling? In my experience, settling is almost always worth it.

Coming Back from Losing a Lawsuit (Survival)

If you were able to settle the lawsuit without it going to trial, whether by arbitration or not, coming back is a lot easier than if you lost in court. When you settle a lawsuit you do not have to disclose it to anyone. In fact, it's usually best to just keep it secret (from the public) and move on quickly. Be sure to pay your lawyer or work out a payment plan, though, or you may soon have another lawsuit!

If the lawsuit went through trial, however, it becomes permanent record and you must reveal that you have lost a lawsuit, if asked. Winning a lawsuit is better, but still not great. Do you really want that reputation of someone who can't settle your disputes outside of court?

So, how do you come back from losing a lawsuit? There are at least three ways to consider making your epic comeback. First, should you start a new company or not? Starting a new company and buying the assets of the old company is a way of playing switcheroo. The new company is not burdened with the bad brand of the lawsuit. You personally, however, might still get tagged as being a bad founder (depending on the situation), but at least your new company's name is not tarnished. Remember, the new company is like a different person, even if it buys the assets of the old company (for, say $1). Personally, I think this solution to staging your epic comeback may be the best. Why keep that lawsuit saddled to the old company's name? Unless you are getting sued often, consider a rebrand.

If you choose to not start a new company, you can take another path to stage your epic comeback—terminating some employees. It sounds awful, but you see this on Wall Street all the time. The offenders, or people who made the mistake, get fired. It will often satisfy investors that the issue is behind them, and it will also help with your press issues, if you have any. Just be sure that you are firing the right person and that you are doing it somewhat tastefully. Firing someone should never be taken lightly, and the laws of termination vary greatly by state and country.

The last way to consider staging your epic comeback is to truly own the mistake and make good on your apology. Instead of hiding the lawsuit behind a name change or a termination event, you own the mistake, and explain that you've learned from it. This technique is great for companies that are nonprofits or are otherwise designed with some kind of corporate good in mind. It may not fix your problem with investors, but the public may accept this owning of your mistakes and may forgive you.

However you decide to make your epic comeback, don't give up. You can come back from losing a lawsuit, and life is not over. You can even keep your same company and everything, provided that you have enough funds to pay for your loss. If you don't, bankruptcy and starting over (even bigger than a rebrand) are in order. Remember when I told you not to mix your funds? In bankruptcy of a business, your personal assets will not be lost. Remember when I told you not to use personal assets (like your house) as collateral? In bankruptcy of your business, your house is safe, as long as you didn't use it for collateral. Smart, eh?

Story of Cutting Edge Gamer

"Holy crap, man. Can you believe that this is happening?" James asked, sweat pouring down his forehead.

"I'm surprised as hell. I thought for sure they would accept your settlement offer," I replied.

"It's probably going to cost them a ton of money to keep fighting, and I was willing to pay them," James replied.

"Yep, I think someone over there is just pissed off or something. It seems like they are suing you just because they are angry and want some kind of sick revenge," I said.

"Yeah, and I thought we were friends," James said, sadly.

We looked down together at the latest letter from the supplier's lawyer. One of James' suppliers of technology had filed a lawsuit in Travis County for breach of contract. Breach of contract is a very common thing you might get sued for, but is also usually one of the easiest to settle. In this case, James had tried to settle multiple times to make it right, even though James didn't believe he did anything wrong, all to no avail. The lawsuit was happening. Or was it?

"What's this about?" James asked, pointing to the last section.

"Arbitration clause," I said, "It means that this will go to arbitration instead of the courts."

"Was that in our original contract?" he asked.

"Yep, you signed it. Didn't you read it?" I asked.

James just looked at me. He wasn't in the mood for a lecture.

I had been serving as an advisor to Cutting Edge Gamer (CEG) for more than two years. As an advisor, I earned a percent or less of stock each year that I helped the company grow. This usually included a commitment of time giving advice on my part, as well as helping out with connections and small projects as needed. I enjoyed it because it was a way for me to help another entrepreneur be successful, and it gave me a small amount of stock if the company hit it big.

Personally, this lawsuit didn't worry me. For one, as a shareholder, I was protected because it was the company getting sued, not me. The U.S. laws protected my personal assets in these cases, so nothing except the value of my stock in the company was at risk. Furthermore, I knew the situation and agreed that James hadn't done wrong. The system wouldn't screw him over, right?

Cutting Edge Gamer is one of the only places where you can lease a computer graphics card instead of buying one. CEG targets high end gamers as well as cryptocurrency miners and graphic artists. The graphics cards can retail for over $1,000, so being able to lease one instead makes the best affordable option for some folks. More importantly, since new graphics cards come out every year, as a leaser, you can simply trade in your old card for the best every year in what James calls "Infinite Upgrades.®" Infinite Upgrades is a registered trademark for CEG, and is a linchpin of their customer value story. Gamer customers love to upgrade their computer hardware, and being able to infinitely upgrade your graphics card is a very strong and clear value to gamers for what Cutting Edge Gamer does. To date, no one has sued CEG about that trademark, and as time goes on, it becomes clear that they couldn't succeed even if they did. Infinite Upgrades is part of the CEG IP.

CEG also has several trade secrets as part of their IP portfolio. They have software that tracks and manages leases. Some of this software was developed under contract, and it's a contract like this that caused the lawsuit headache. The company that did the work claimed that James used their software wrong, and James disagreed. Regardless of how he got there, James was in for a fight. The other party wouldn't settle.

Because a contract exists between the two parties, the terms of the contract are the points where disputes can occur, and any resolution—including limitation of damages and venue, such as arbitration—must be bound. James' next step was to select an impartial arbiter (which both parties share the cost of) to try to resolve the dispute.

Tens of thousands of dollars later, James was still fighting the lawsuit. James had to pay for his lawyer and hire a trial lawyer to represent him with the arbiter, all while trying to keep his business afloat. When the arbiter finally made her decision, it was still not very clear who won or lost. In fact, both parties ended up losing.

Both parties had racked up tens of thousands of dollars in legal fees, and since the arbiter said both parties did wrong by the contract, neither side won a large award, it all sort of offset. Both parties still had to pay off the rest of their legal fees, and so neither party was happy with the results. The dispute was resolved, however, and did not go to actual trial. Nevertheless, the entire expense could have been avoided if the other party had agreed to settle earlier. In the end, James' cash offer would have been a way better outcome for everyone if the other party had accepted it. What a waste!

Chapter 9
Help, I'm Sinking—Controlling growth

"Here's the deal: anyone who works past 6:00 pm will get free dinner ordered in. If anyone wants to bring their family in for dinner at 6:00 so that they can work at least two more hours, they are welcome to do so, and we'll buy them dinner too," I said. I was standing in front of a wall full of projects and tasks in a crowded room filled with thirty engineers. Our planning board (we used a method of Kanban planning) was filled to the brim. We were behind schedule on most of the projects under way, and we had more than six major projects going at once. From the development of our new product to a massive new software product to a new mobile version and even some crazy projects like VoIP inside our card, we were swamped. Each of these projects represented a big deal, some of them six or seven figures or more in size, and each one needed constant attention and management from the founder, the CEO, and the key architect of it all: me.

I thought for days about one question: *How do I scale myself?*

The one project on time was the VoIP project. One of my employees, Ryan, was working on that one. He had flown to Germany to work onsite with the creators of TeamSpeak to put TeamSpeak 3 inside our product. It was a really cool idea, and of all the projects, the only one on schedule. In fact, it was ahead of schedule. How was that?

Actually, I thought that project was the one that didn't really need me. In fact, it was being run almost completely by Ryan. I had given him full autonomy and authority to run the project and get it done how he thought best. So, I hadn't really scaled myself in that case—I had just given it to Ryan.

Bingo. That's when it hit me. I can't scale myself—there are only so many hours per day of me. I had to get out of the *me* mode and get into the *you* mode. I needed to get more people like Ryan whom I could trust to own the project completely without me. *So, I needed more middle management,* I thought. *That's not right, Ryan's not actually a manager, he's an engineer like everyone else.* What then? He did own the project. Maybe that was the key.

Several months later, I rolled out what would become a core part of Bigfoot Networks and all of the companies I've been involved in since. I presented the first draft of the official Bigfoot Networks culture and opened the floor for discussion. The key concept was *ownership*. Everything would have an owner and that owner would be fully empowered to get the job done however they thought best. I thought, *I am going to create more Ryans—that way product development would need less of me and I could focus on other important things.* There was only one

DOI 10.1515/9781501507083-009

problem: not everyone is ready to be a fully empowered owner of a complete project. In fact, as I've come to realize, it's a difficult thing to find in people, and I had to learn to identify that capability in interviews to specifically hire for it.

That same year, Bigfoot Networks tripled in size, launched internationally, secured dozens of big partnerships, and became the networking product of the year. We had to expand our marketing efforts, sales efforts, and development efforts. We also secured $8 million in funding and had to put that money to work quickly, lest it just sit in our cashbox doing nothing. The pressure to grow was immense, and I truly felt like I was sinking. I needed help, and the ownership and empowerment idea did help, but it was not enough. I failed to control growth, which ultimately led to me leaving the company that I started. What could I have done better? A lot! I have done better since then. Read on for ideas about how you can control growth—an area where I have sometimes failed.

Failing at Growth

One of the most important steps in navigating your way to startup success is growth. In order to get success, you have to grow to the right size and attract enough attention in order to get the outcome you desire (usually acquisition). Failing at growth can happen in one of three ways. First, you might fail at growing—in other words, you might not get to the point where slowing growth is needed, and you're not growing fast enough. This chapter is not about not growing fast enough. Chapters 3 through 6 are about getting to the growth phase. This chapter is about what to do when you get there.

The second way to fail at growth is to fail to sustain growth. When you fail to sustain growth, you get a tapering off or a flattening of sales. You aren't necessarily shrinking, but you are not growing as much either. You are just sort of flat. This chapter will discuss this, what might be causing it, and how you might be able to fix it.

Finally, the main point of this chapter is about the third way to fail at growth. Growing too fast is an actual problem. Few entrepreneurs recognize it as a problem until after it has happened, but there are warning signs. Being spread too thin, not knowing everyone's names, feeling overloaded, having too many projects going at once, and generally having too many meetings are all warning signs that your growth may be too fast. Growing too fast is bad because quality suffers, focus suffers, and inevitably, some of the projects you invest in fail. It doesn't mean that your company fails, but a string of failed projects hurts moral, weakens your position with investors or board members, and causes you to use up cash that could have otherwise been used for a better purpose. Ultimately, growing too fast can mean that you also run out of resources too fast. When this happens and you have to go back to investors, that's when you can lose control of your company completely—the investors can swoop in and eat up your stock. All of this is because you grew too quickly, just like they wanted. Investors aren't the enemy, but they will seize any opportunity. More cash is not the answer. There are better ways to control growth, and often they include learning to say "no." It's harder than it seems, especially when you are saying no to your investors or your board of directors.

Metrics of Growth: Key Performance Indicators (KPIs)

What is growth, anyway? Growth is when your company gets bigger. There are several ways in which a company can get bigger, and the metrics of growth are well known. The metrics of growth are some of the *key performance indicators* (KPIs) that you as founder, CEO, leader, and manager need to pay attention to. A KPI is any metric that helps give you a quick, useful, and actionable insight as to the progress of your company. As CEO, you need to focus on the KPIs only, and not get lost in every metric you can get your fingers on. Other metrics are for your team to use to solve problems or answer questions. KPIs are for you to notice problems and see how the company is being balanced. Growing well, and not out of control, means keeping everything in balance. Keeping growth KPIs in balance can be a full time job.

The first metric of growth, or a KPI, to pay close attention to is revenue. Revenue is a key metric of the company, and probably the one that your investors and board members look at most closely. You will eventually have revenue goals to hit each quarter and each year that your board of directors has set. These goals are often tied to management bonuses (and yes, you should give yourself a bonus too, once you are handing out bonuses). The problem with revenue as a growth metric is when it becomes too much of a focus. Revenue is not profits. Too much revenue, but too little profit often means that you have to expand the company before it is time to expand. If you are generating too little revenue, investors don't believe your business can get big. To make things more complex, companies often get valued at a multiple of revenue when they get sold, so having a lot of revenue is very beneficial in that situation. While growth in revenue is generally good, it is important to watch some of the other growth metrics to keep everything aligned. Figure 9.1 shows the five metrics of growth and an example of positive and negative growth. In the event of negative growth, you grew too fast in one of the metrics and are starting to lose control as a result. You need to tighten up to fix it quickly, or a failure could be imminent.

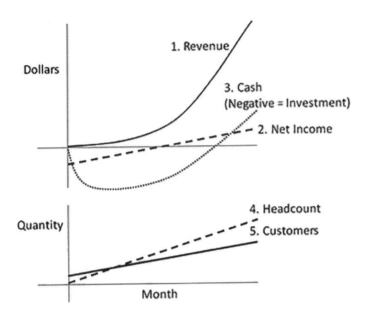

Figure 9.1: The Five Metrics of Growth

Net income is a measure of the profitability of a company. This metric can grow as fast as it wants, and you need have no worry. While you may have other troubles, at least your company is safe if the net income is growing and positive. Cumulative cash is similar. If your accumulated cash is piling up, and your net income is positive, you are in good shape. Again, you might have other growing pains, but your company is fine. The exception to this is if the cumulative cash is going up due to investment. If your net income is negative, but your cash is going up, you are getting investment dollars, and too much investment can be bad. Once your company enters the growth phase, you really need to think: *Is this investment really necessary? How risky is this investment? How fast will I put it to work, and what will I do with it?* Too much investment kills companies more than anything else during the growth phase. Founders might lose voting control and their power, thus letting the investors replace them and the company culture, and what made the company successful in the first place. The most common horror stories I hear are when the founders are replaced as CEO. It almost never works out, yet it is one of the main things investors want to do. To this day, it confuses me why investors do this.

Headcount going up at a faster rate than net income is another metric to watch out for and identify. Headcount is a KPI, and if it goes up too quickly, a company can quickly spiral out of control. A higher headcount means higher burn rates (and probably lower net income). It can often lead to unexpected expenses such as healthcare, office space, legal expenses, and intangibles. At a certain size, the CEO (you) can't meet or know everyone. As will be discussed later in this chapter, your span of control is only so big, and a headcount too large means your leadership style has to change. Many CEOs don't realize it, so they get replaced again, which leads to the failure of the company. Headcount is one of the KPIs that—if it becomes too high, regardless of net income—can cause companies to explode.

Number of customers or users is the final KPI to analyze. If this number spikes up faster than revenue and net income, you might be extending too many free trials or signing on unprofitable customers. You or your management team will have to investigate why it's happening. Like headcount, having too many customers or users can bring its own headaches. Customer support and the customer retention team may have to grow. The risk profiles of things like returns or lawsuits increases may also need to grow. Growing with the right customers at the right time and with net income is the best way to grow without failure. Having too much of any single thing without the net income or cash to support it may mean that you are growing too fast and are likely headed for a problem.

The general idea, as Figure 9.1 shows, is to keep everything growing at the same or at very similar rates. It's like spinning plates on top of sticks—the CEO has to switch focus often, and it can be dizzying. It is a crucial skill, though, and the rest of this chapter will focus on the topic of keeping everything in balance. If net income is growing as fast as everything else, you are probably in good shape.

Sustaining Growth

Before I get into the techniques that you can use to control the growth of revenue, net income, cash, headcount, and customers, it is important to know that growth is good, and stagnation is bad. Stagnation is when your growth starts to flatten or goes negative. Ironically, one of the reasons to not grow too fast is so that the company doesn't stagnate later. Saturating your market before you are ready to expand to a new market is one of the ways that stagnation occurs. This happened at Bigfoot Networks when we had saturated the early adopter market for our high end network card for gamers and needed to reach a new, mainstream market. Some people call this "crossing the chasm," from the popular book of the same title. Because our growth through the early adopter market was so fast, we sold out of product. Our growth stagnated while I pushed and prodded and did all I could (including dinner at the office with employees' families) to try to get the more mainstream version out. In the end, we got clever and simply removed the heatsink on the expensive version, and sold a version of our Killer NIC called the K1 at half the price. This helped us cross the chasm and sustain growth, but at a huge profitability penalty. Suddenly, we were not making profits on those cards, and then the real trouble started. Regardless of the situation, stagnation is something that needs to be avoided. Controlling growth can help, but there can be many reasons why your growth stagnates.

The first reason your growth may be stagnating is the same as the problem we had at Bigfoot Networks: a failure to cross the chasm. The chasm is the final tweak to your product or service that causes it to become adopted by the mainstream. Often, this tweak is simply a cost reduction that leads to a price reduction, thus making the product or service more available to the broader public. Sometimes, it's adding a key feature that makes the solution more complete and thus, more desirable. Frequently, the product or service needs to be further simplified, especially for ease of use. Sometimes, the world just needs to catch up, and more people begin to encounter the problem or become comfortable with the technology. Whatever the reason, if you fail to cross the chasm, your market will remain those early adopters and you may soon find that you have run out of them, which can cause stagnation and even a sudden drop (worse than a flattening) of sales.

Stagnation can also occur even after you have crossed the chasm with your market. Sales will naturally start to flatten once you start to get decent (10%+) market penetration. In other words, the more you sell, the fewer customers you have in the market you started with. No product or service is built for everyone. In fact, as discussed in Chapter 1 and 2, the more generic the product, the less interesting it is. The more targeted the product, the faster early adopters will try it out. This balance between focused and generic can sometimes be a struggle for startups. Instead of compromising to break out of the stagnation caused by capturing too much of your first market, launch a new version of your product or service and target it toward a new market. This might even mean a new or slightly different brand. Fitness buffs don't want a Coke after a hard workout. Vitamin Water, though, or a drink with acai berries—now that is different. Coke controls hundreds of brands, each one targeting a different market segment. You, too, can break stagnation of growth by launching in a new market, sometimes with a new brand.

Stagnation is a slowing or flattening of growth. One of the best ways to avoid it is to try to keep your growth constant—not increasing growth, but not decreasing, either. A flat pace of growth is unsurprising to investors and is one of the main goals of controlling growth.

Controlling Growth

As the startup matures, it will slowly look more and more like a *real* company. Real companies have departments, managers, middle management, and boards of directors. With your first professional investor, you will create a board of directors. The board's purpose is to ensure that the managers of the company (or the CEO) are constantly working for the benefit of the shareholders. The board hires and fires the CEO, and influences all other aspects of the company. The board members have rights to see the books of the company, and based on this, they make their suggestions to the CEO and retain the right to hire or fire the CEO. Of course, as a CEO with more than 50% of the voting stock, you can't be fired, except for some extreme cause like breaking the law. That said, the board can and does apply pressure—they are your future funders and your colleagues, and they can sometimes even block the funding or sale of your company. It is best to keep them happy. Boards of directors expect you to have a financial model and to create an annual plan for them. This plan is your statement of what you believe will happen over the course of the year, regarding growth, revenue, expenses, and so on. These become your targets for the year, and your goal is to get them to be as low as the board will accept: at a constant growth rate.

To keep the board of directors happy, it is really simple—hit your targets. The best part is that you get to set your targets. One of the keys to controlling growth, then, is to set targets that show revenue growth at a constant pace, not at any divergent or super fast pace. Everything should grow at the slow, consistent pace that you had in your financial model, and not faster. This way, you don't run out of growth too quickly, and you don't get fired (or disciplined) if your growth doesn't match your plan. You should show the board of directors the slowest growth plan they will accept, and then control growth to make sure you grow at that rate and not much higher than that. Is this lunacy? Maybe... but many founders and CEOs have been fired for failing to sustain the high growth that was unrealistic to begin with (see Chapter 10).

Okay, so how do you artificially constrain growth? First, controlling inventory is an easy way to control growth. Too many dollars in inventory is risky, anyway. To control growth, simply create a lean company that keeps as little inventory on hand as possible, and build products based upon orders or from your quarterly or annual plan. If you are building to order, control growth by controlling capacity of production, again, to that low level that you have in your plan and no higher. The temptation to grow faster just because you can will be immense. If you do ramp up for faster growth but the sales then stop materializing, you are left with employees you have to fire, equipment you have to sell, and a frustrated board of directors who may lose patience. If you had only grown at the slower, more controlled pace, you would not have over invested in inventory or production capability. Service companies control growth by controlling head-count, but it is the same thing. Because people are usually the product in service companies, growing people no faster than your planned growth rate can control growth to keep it linear and targeted to your plan.

Customers are always correct, right? Well, yes and no. Sometimes, in order to control growth, you have to say "no" to a customer. You may not be ready for that big enterprise deployment yet. Having many customers can cause your company to shift its focus to the problems of the large customer by investing in features that meet their needs, and sometimes attracting more people than it can accommodate. Customers that ask for features, big or small, should not drive the pace of your product development or evolution. Even in a service business, customers asking for different kinds or levels of service can cause you to attempt doing so, even before you are ready for growth in that direction. While this might lead to even more revenue and profits than what you had in your plan, exceeding your plan changes the expectations of the board and can cause stagnation through market penetration problems. The goal here is to restrain R&D and product or service offering expansion to the plan that you set for yourself. To do otherwise means to grow too fast in both sales and expenses. Sure, those new sales offset the expenses now, but what happens if the expansion or new features don't work out? You are left with a higher burn rate, and, even at the same revenue level, lower or negative profitability.

Controlling expenses is perhaps even more important than artificially constraining sales growth. If you grow faster than your plan, sure, you may be at risk of higher board expectations and market saturation problems, but the board won't be unhappy with you. If your expenses outpace your revenue growth, however, your board will almost certainly be unhappy, your cash will start to dwindle, and doom may be upon you. Resist the urge to over invest past what you had planned. Even unexpected cash outlays should be offset by reductions in other areas, even if it means sacrificing some sales. The worst thing you can do as a CEO of a startup is run out of cash. The best way you can prevent this is to become and stay profitable. This means growing to plan while controlling expenses to plan. Getting to $10 million in revenue is not nearly as beneficial as getting to $10 million in revenue AND becoming profitable.

Controlling expenses means not going above your plan and reducing expenses if gross margin (revenue—cost of goods) doesn't meet that plan. "Controlling expenses" is such a pedantic term for something that can be so cruel. Remember, employees are expenses, so controlling expenses can sometimes mean letting people go. This may be the hardest thing to ever do as a manager, but it is essential if you want to keep expenses under control. To reduce the need to cut people, just don't hire them. In other words, hire only when you absolutely have to and when you are sure that you won't have to cut them. Remember, the one aspect of growth you NEVER have to limit is profit or net income growth. So, if your revenues are growing at a steady rate and you delay hiring someone even just a quarter, your profit and net income will be higher, which is not a bad thing. You don't want to delay too much, though, because not hiring that person could be a factor limiting your next phase of growth. It's a constant balancing act, but it's also the reason you get to be called CEO.

There are other expenses besides just employees to control. New equipment, office space, travel, and entertainment are all expenses. These ones may be even easier to control than headcount. Marketing, in fact, is an expense. You can over invest in marketing. Most marketing falls into two categories—marketing that works, and marketing that you are not certain works. If you are in a pinch and need to cut expenses quickly, cutting out marketing you are not sure works (such as trade shows) can help. Just be sure to note whether sales drop—if so, you have evidence that the thing you cut might have been working, after all, so you'd better try it again. The uncertainty of marketing effectiveness is why I always build in analytics to my marketing efforts. If I don't know what my marketing dollars do (or don't do), then I will have trouble controlling expenses. Every marketing dollar should bring revenue ROI, especially for startups. In *lean months* when you don't hit your gross margin target, trimming experimental marketing can save the month or quarter. Skip that business trip, too—have those meetings by Skype, instead (if the quarter isn't going well).

The final aspect of controlling growth is to keep yourself in control. A CEO needs to be able to understand the mechanisms that make the company money and cause the company to spend money. Cash is king. In order to keep tabs on this cash, you need to set up good KPIs, good dash boarding, and, as you grow, good and open lines of communication with your employees. Slowly, the role of the CEO will shift from leadership toward management. While this is happening, however, you have to maintain the culture and vision that got you here in the first place. The next sections will focus on building and maintaining a winning culture while growing and expanding. The CEOs who can master this skill will last longer in the role, which, as a founder, might mean not being replaced as CEO—a goal I believe all founders should have.

Leadership vs. Management

Dr. Stephen Covey put it best with his description of leadership versus management as a road being built through the trees.[1] In that story, management is sharpening tools, handing out hard hats and cheering from the back. Leadership, in that story, is when one of the workers climbs the tree and says, "We're going the wrong way!" Whether that makes sense to you or not probably depends on if you had a good manager or a bad one. The key idea is still valid, though—a leader is someone with a vision and passion and is willing to get their hands dirty. A manager is someone with the ability to organize and plan, but who may sometimes forget to align well with the vision. As CEO, you have to balance these two roles of your life, initially being the leader that everyone needs, and then evolving later into the manager that is essential to move a larger organization forward. Failing to manage when the time comes for that is one of the ways that founder CEOs get overwhelmed and fail to grow. Growth is not just about revenue, it's also about you as a person, and your team as an effective group to keep the growth sustained.

Leadership in the context of a startup starts with the founder CEO and flows to the rest of the team. The best form of leadership is called *transformational leadership*, which stems from having a clear vision of the future, understanding the tasks and changes that need to happen, and empowering your team to see it through to success.[2] Good transformational leaders focus on ensuring that the whole team works with the common goal in mind, and providing a sense of identity, meaning, and value to achieving the goal.

Transactional leadership, by comparison, focuses on hitting the milestones and goals set out in a clear plan. Rewards align with meeting goals and maintaining the status quo. The goal of transactional leaders isn't necessarily to grow, but to grow at the same rate as always (even if that rate is zero). What does that sound like? The boards of directors of most companies manage their CEO with transactional leadership. Your board approved financial plan and how you maintain and meet it are how you are rewarded (with keeping your job or bonuses). One of your challenges as founding CEO is to be the bridge between the team (your company) and the board of directors (shareholders), and translate the transactional style of board members into the visionary style of transformational leadership to the

[1] http://www.rickety.us/2011/01/epic-excerpts-stephen-covey-on-management
[2] Bass, Bernard M. "From Transactional to Transformational Leadership: Learning to Share the Vision." *Organizational Dynamics*, vol. 18, no. 3, Dec. 1990, pp. 19–31. ScienceDirect, doi:10.1016/0090-2616(90)90061-S.

team. This gap can create an *us versus them* mentality between management and the board of directors, but I think that is a healthy thing. You, as the leader, are part of the team, and letting your team be the *us* is a good thing for team morale as long as it doesn't impact your performance evaluation when you are with *them*.

A final form of leadership should be avoided at all costs. *Laissez faire leadership* is short for lazy leadership. A lazy leadership style means that leaders sit back and observe, then jump in and discipline only when there is a problem. This kind of tyranny simply doesn't work in the 21ˢᵗ century. Not being involved or ignoring your employees and their problems, as well as lashing out are bad things to do as a leader. Who wants to follow the person who never speaks up or has an opinion? Who wants to follow the person who lashes out when something doesn't go right, despite their complete lack of involvement until that point? Leadership is about teamwork. Teamwork means that the leader has to stay involved, but not too involved, which is the big challenge. As you (the founding CEO) grow, you have to be less involved in the day to day activities of the various parts of the organization. Transformational leaders solve this by meeting regularly with the team to espouse the vision and direct the team toward the changes necessary for continual growth.

Leadership and management go hand in hand. As founder and CEO, you have to strike the balance between management—planning, measuring, rewarding—and leadership—envisioning, motivating, and empowering. As your company grows, the need for management increases, because you just can't have your hands in everything. *Dash boarding* is one way to make the measurement part of your management job easy, letting you spend more time on leadership. To dashboard, you create a set of KPIs and have your team report them daily or weekly, sometimes in a visual dashboard for all to see. It can be both a management and a leadership tool if it can be used to show the team that you are making progress toward the vision. Planning is a skill that is both technical and political. As the founder/CEO, you have to plan effectively, both to support the vision of what you are trying to do, but also to not overpromise to the board of directors; it's a political game that you have to learn quickly. Remember, they already invested. Now, during planning, it's time to set goals you think will be easily achievable, as low as possible, but that the board will accept.

Company Culture

One of the tools available to leaders and managers is the company culture. A company culture is a formal or informal set of values or statements that are there to set expectations of the entire team. It should establish in writing what the company values, and why. Each value statement of a company culture should be designed to help your team answer prioritization questions and solve dilemmas. In short, it should be there to help your team make the decisions that you, as the founder/CEO, will almost always agree with. With a well constructed company culture, you will no longer have to be personally involved in every decision. You will not limit your growth any longer, because when everyone is aligned with the same culture, *you* don't have to make all the decisions. What's more, the core of what made your team successful can spread to new people as you hire, fire, reward, and train based upon the culture.

Which kind of culture works? There are three things to consider when choosing a winning culture. First, consider what has worked for you so far. Codifying the positive aspects of the culture you have now that is already working can be a great foundation to a written culture. These things might be, for example: "We win as a team," "We like to have fun at work," and "We are passionate about our cause." The trick is to be sure not to codify the things that either don't really work, or are not legally or politically sound. For example, you don't want to make it a part of your culture that you only hire men or white people—that's sexism and racism, and it will get you into big trouble. In fact, if by chance that's whom you have hired so far, you should start actively looking for candidates of diverse genders and races to join the team. You want to hire them not for legal reasons, but because diversity has been shown to increase creativity and positively impact team performance.[3]

Next, consider the things that you want to have happen, and integrate these into your culture. In a way, it's visionary leadership through culture. These visionary culture statements might be things such as, "We believe in diversity," "We treat each other with respect," and the all important statement, "Everything has an owner." While these statements may not match the kind of culture you have today, these visionary statements can build the backbone of the company culture you ultimately aspire to.

Finally, consider the decisions that your team will be faced with, and decide how you would make those decisions in most cases. There is almost always a trade off between time and quality, for example. To help your team make the right decisions when there is a question about doing something fast or doing it with high quality, your value statements should make it clear which one to pick. For example, your value statement will be either "we care about quality" or "time to

---

[3]Herring, Cedric. "Does Diversity Pay?: Race, Gender, and the Business Case for Diversity." *American Sociological Review*, vol. 74, no. 2, Apr. 2009, pp. 208–24. SAGE Journals, doi:10.1177/000312240907400203.

market is essential", but should not be both. If you have both as your culture then managers won't know which one to pick when faced with difficult tradeoffs between time and quality. Other decision assisting culture statements include statements about price, service, competition, scale, and professionalism. The following three types of culture statements should make up the core of your written company culture: actual, aspirational, and decision making. There is no correct number of cultural statements—Intel had nine, Key Ingredient had six. I think somewhere in between is probably just about right. The key is to capture high level concepts that convey a lot of meaning. It's not enough to just use words, though; you have to explain what you mean by them too.

In my four times being a CEO, I have come to believe that a specific set of value statements best capture what I believe makes my team have a winning culture. This winning culture is an example of my values and my vision for what works, but yours may be different. None of my companies, for example, are surf shops, where I would expect the culture to be very different. None of my companies are factories, either—again; I would expect factory culture to be very different. My companies tend to be heavily loaded with professional workers, software, and marketing. Table 9.1 lists the culture from my first company, Bigfoot Networks, where I established the culture formally in 2005. Table 9.2 lists the culture from my most recent big company, Key Ingredient, where I established the formal culture in 2013 and revised it every year until 2016. You can see that ownership is one of the main themes; this is the key theme for me, and one that I think every good culture needs to have. Ownership is really just another way to say empowerment. Empowerment is one of the keys to scaling up, to transformational leadership, and to making that transition from pure leader to leader manager. This has to happen because once the team hits a certain size you cannot manage the team with leadership alone. You have to learn management and leadership skills and apply them both at the right time. Later in my career, as you can see by the differences in the culture statements, the importance of teamwork became more important to me. Both teamwork and respect for one another are becoming more important in the workplace as it gets more diverse and younger employees' values shift towards work life balance. I have found that adding teamwork and "win win" to the culture allowed everyone to be a part of the team, and not just the engineers who I was used to leading. Win win or no deal refers to the concept that both parties in a negotiation or conflict resolve not as a compromise, but as a superior idea that makes everyone happy. There is no deal until such a win win resolution is found. This combined with teamwork means that we are going to work together to be creative to find solutions that take into account everyone's point of view.

Table 9.1: Bigfoot Networks Culture (2005)

Value	Definition
Ownership	I COMPLETELY OWN the work I am assigned. Everything that matters has an owner. Ownership means driving those around me for the things I need to be successful, even the CEO.
Passion	I am passionate about what I do. I continue to learn new things in and out of the office, and I share my knowledge when I can.
Flexibility & Redemption	Flexibility is my weapon—I don't let momentum make me do the wrong things correctly. If I make a mistake, I announce it. I know redemption is possible, and flexibility means sometimes being wrong.
Directness	I am direct with feedback and ideas. I never hold back, even when it's painful. I never punish or squash ideas, feedback, or directness. I don't keep secrets or practice politics.

Table 9.2: Key Ingredient Culture (2016)

Value	Definition
Owner-ship	Everyone at the company shares common goals and knows their role in achieving success. We proactively empower ownership and responsibility. We respect each other and our roles, and trust each other to deliver results.
Passion	We love what we do, and always strive to learn more and improve. We leverage our passion with a focus on goals and desired results. We know that the work we do matters.
Customer Oriented	We strive to understand and satisfy our customers' true needs. We celebrate happy customers and reviews. We actively listen to customer feedback to improve.
Teamwork	We proactively seek to do whatever is needed to help the team win. We celebrate shipping and getting stuff done. We encourage cross functional collaboration.
Win win	We believe in win win or no deal. A positive vibe and being happy at work is an essential part of win win. We don't discriminate, keep secrets, or play politics. Respect is required.

Management Span of Control

One of the limiting factors of managing through leadership alone is that your span of control can only go so far. Once you have about 50 employees, you will simply not be able to meet with each one and know what they are doing daily.

The most common limit of span of control for direct leadership is about 14.[4] Beyond this, and your ability to lead them directly may be limited. I've had success up to 50, but it takes a dedication to meeting regularly with each person, and even then, I have to rely on structural management skills to ultimately put in the right reward and control structure.

Span of control actually has two meanings. First, the meaning applies to you and the world around you, regardless of whether you are a manager or not. Figure 9.2 illustrates the span of control of your personal world. Every person has things over which they have direct control. Your car, house, chair, hair, clothes, and what you say are all in your direct control. Beyond the things you can directly control are the things you can influence. You can influence your spouse, pets, boss, friends, and politicians. Then, there are the things you cannot control or influence. Some of these things you could eventually influence or control if you spent a lot of time and energy, but most will never be in your span of control. Your president's decisions, the weather, the laws of society, world politics, war, and the physical laws of the universe are out of your span of control—you have no direct control, and really no influence either. As a form of personal leadership, it is important to understand the things you can directly control, and focus on managing those aspects of your life. It is also important to understand that the things you can influence and apply influence and deal with their decisions only instead of thinking you can control them. Finally, it's not worth stressing at all over those things you cannot control, at least not until it's time to vote again.

---

[4] Fleet, David D. Van, and Arthur G. Bedeian. "A History of the Span of Management." *Academy of Management Review*, vol. 2, no. 3, July 1977, pp. 356–72. amr.aom.org, doi:10.5465/AMR.1977.4281795.

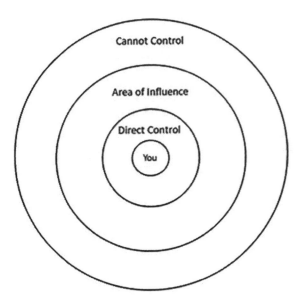

Figure 9.2: Personal Span of Control

The span of control in management is a little different. The idea here is that at some point, you simply will have trouble influencing—let alone directly controlling—subordinates when you have too many. The reason is because there are limits in time and space to how many people you can see each day. There are also limits to how many things you can remember, and how many things you can really be good at or be able to help resolve when problems arise. As a manager, then, you will no longer be able to sharpen the tools of your workers, help them resolve issues, and help them make decisions, because you simply won't have enough hours. Recognizing the point at which you are losing touch and control is the moment of truth for a founder/CEO. Do you want to develop the skills to be an effective leader manager? Or do you want to turn over the company to someone else so that you can stay focused on your small area of expertise?

I hope that you decide to stay CEO. Although I have not seen scientific/statistical evidence of this, I believe that founder CEOs make better CEOs. Just consider Jeff Bezos, Bill Gates, Mark Zuckerberg, and the late Steve Jobs. While these are one off examples, they all represent extreme success stories of the founder CEO growing the company into a huge success. In comparison, when the founder is replaced as CEO, all too often, the end of that company is very near.

In order to stay CEO, you have to develop this leadership management skill that combines both into what you do every day. Dash boarding to track and reward employee behavior is as important as holding full company meetings or video presentations to evangelize your company vision. Being both a visionary leader and a good manager can seem daunting at times, but it is totally doable. You just have to realize that you wear two hats now: leader and manager. Put on the right hat at the right time. On stage, you are the charismatic leader with the vision and the passion to see it through. Off stage in your one on one meetings with employees, you are the objective, goals driven manager who wants to help sharpen your employees' tools so they can be great.

As a manager, you should be having one on one meetings with every one of your direct reports (people who report directly to you) and, when possible, as many indirect reports as possible. One on ones are important because they give people direct access to you, allow for a good flow of feedback in both directions, and are a means of helping the employee understand their role and their importance. My one on one process is to break it into a 30 minute section with ten minutes for each section. First, I ask what problems the employee is having. This section is about sharpening their tools, helping them solve problems, and making sure they have all the means necessary for being successful. Second, I provide feedback on my assessment of their performance so far. I give them quantitative feedback on their results (when possible, from the dashboard). I then give them my assessment on a one to ten scale for each value from the company's value statements, and let them know which areas they could improve. During this section, I might inform an underperforming employee that they need to shape up in certain areas, or else there could be a problem. When I say a "problem," in that context, I usually mean that I will have to fire them within 30 days if the issue is not corrected. Firing people is difficult when you have to do so because of downsizing or not meeting goals. Firing people because they are not performing is almost equally hard, and that's why I have monthly one on ones and give employees 30 days to correct any performance issues (in most cases, except in cases of serious problems). The last part of the one on one is career development. This is often the most fun part for the employee, because I work with them to map out what their next job will be and the one after that. Then, we talk about ways to help them get the experience they need to get to that next level in their career even if it's not necessarily going to be in this company. I've had many employees go on to be high level executives, CEOs, and founders in their own right. I enjoy the employee development part so much that I now teach full time at UT Austin to make it the core of what I do every day! It's also the reason that so many successful entrepreneurs decide to become mentors and angel investors—we want to give back and see our protégés succeed.

Corporate Innovation

One of the reasons that corporate innovation is necessary is because the culture of big companies is often not suited to the kind of leadership or management that it takes to create something new. Empowerment in particular is often lacking in large organizations where centralized decision making is more the norm. Use the opportunity of your new initiative to build a new subculture where empowerment and making mistakes is okay. It's essential, and the theme of this book, to make mistakes in order to learn. Be sure to tie your culture in with your corporate owners though, with dotted lines from their culture to yours, showing clearly that your culture is a subculture.

Having this subculture will even be an attractor to potential employees both from inside your parent company and also from without. Many folks will be attracted to a more empowered, mission driven business. During your one on one meetings, reinforce this by being sure everyone in your new mini organization knows their role and how what they do connects to the mission.

Hiring Right

Speaking of protégés, hiring the right people is the first step in not having to fire poor performers. If you can develop a methodology of hiring those who will align well with all three aspects of your culture (actual, aspirational, and decision making), then you won't have to fire someone for not performing well or not aligning with your culture.

About half of the people I have had to let go were because they didn't perform well. They either did not work fast enough, did not care enough, or were not able to learn on their feet. As a result of those experiences, I now try hard to test for those three things during every interview. I don't care too much what you can remember or may know. What predicts good performance for me is how much you care about what you do. If you are a product tester, I want you to love product testing and demonstrate that during the interview. You can't fake love. I can tell by asking what you read, what forums you are on, and who you socialize with. After this, the technical and performance part of the interview is just that—performance. I want to see you in action to assess how fast you work, and how you learn and think on your feet. I want to see that you are able to get answers yourself and feel empowered to do so. I want to see that you are quick and don't delay things. This one may seem strange, but I also want to see how fast you talk. In my experience, people who talk too slowly are not going to do well at my companies. It's strange, I know, but for me, it has been a very accurate prediction of performance. This means that I probably hire too many Type A people who are extroverted, but so be it. Table 9.3 below lists the types of performance questions and tasks I might have an interviewee answer and complete.

Table 9.3: Example Performance Interview Questions

Goal to Understand	Questions
Is passionate about the role	What websites do you read every day, and why? What do you like and dislike about the kind of work you do? What tools do you prefer to use in your job, and why?
Is diligent and highly conscientious	Give me an example of when you had to work overtime. How do you achieve a work/life balance? What do you love about your role?
Thinks and works fast	Using this pad of paper, sketch your daily work routine. Now, sketch an outline of how people in your role can be most efficient. Write some [code/copy/e mail, etc.] for a [problem related to your field].
Listens well and responds quickly	I'm going to ask you a series of opinion questions about our company and products. Please answer them as quickly as truthfully as you can. What do you like about our website? What feature of our product is the most interesting? Do you enjoy reading? What have you read lately?

Testing for culture during an interview is as important as testing for performance. I have found that I can best test for cultural alignment with a series of scenario questions that do not have intuitive or obvious answers. I want to see if your personal values align with the company's values, but without just asking you directly. If I asked directly, most people would just say "yes." By using scenario questions, like my ever popular skunk question, I am able to gain more understanding about how you tick, and thus, how you align naturally with our cultural values. Table 9.4 below lists the types of scenario questions I might ask that match up to the cultural values of, in this case, Key Ingredient.

Table 9.4: Example Culture Scenario Questions

Goal to Understand	Questions
Amount of passion	What do you love most in the universe, and why? What do you hate most, and why?
Can take ownership	You smell something in the kitchen and find a dead skunk. You are alone and it is late. What do you do?
Customer orientation	In a team meeting, we are discussing adding more advertisements to the website, specifically pop up ads. What concerns would you have about that, and why?
Teamwork/Team identity	You are at a trade show and are called onstage to receive an award for your role in the success of a product that you and your team worked on. The award includes a trophy and $100. What do you do with the money?
Level of directness/ Aversion to politics	You walk by my desk and see a past due rent notice for our office space. Next to that is another stack of late notices. What do you do or say?

A good match for one of my companies is someone who has previously held the job or was one level below the position level I'm hiring. For example, if I'm hiring a software engineer, I'd like you to have previously worked as one. If I'm hiring a VP of Marketing, I'd like you to at least have previously been a Director of Marketing (one level below VP). Once I've got that set, I want you to demonstrate that you are and will be a high performer. Sometimes, this even means "homework" for people I interview with. I always promise (and keep that promise) that I will not use the work at all unless you are hired. I usually let my team handle the first interviews, including the performance interviews. Finally, the last interview, which I prefer to do personally when I can, is the cultural alignment interview. Since the culture comes from me as founder/CEO, I want to make sure that I get that part right. For you, especially if your company has fewer than 50 employees, I encourage you to take an active role in everyone you hire. It will set the tone right, give you a chance to train your hiring managers better, and allow you to hire for something that matters a great deal: cultural alignment.

Investing in Growth vs. Investing in Ideas

You've got the people. You've got the money. You've got time. Now, what do you do with those? One of the failures in navigating to success that I keep on making is investing in ideas instead of growth. This is a personal failing, I think, because I just love new things. I love to build new things, and I love to brainstorm and try new ideas. It's perhaps the thing that has kept all my companies below the $20 million exit mark. It's common for entrepreneurs to reach a limit on the size of companies they can grow. For me, it's not so much a span of control issue as it is a *bright, shiny object* issue.

I like bright, shiny things too much to really stick it out past $20 million in revenue. Instead of making smart investment decisions in continued growth and expansion of the core business, I tend to want to kick off side projects, new technology development, and new products. This failing is common, and truthfully, one I've been working to personally improve. If my past mistakes can help you, hey, that's what this whole book is about!

At Bigfoot Networks, I was CEO and founder, and CTO, as well. I was in charge of many different aspects of the company, but I spent most of my time on sales and new technology. We hit several million in revenue through our first generation of products (the Killer NIC and Killer K1). Instead of focusing solely on the next generation of Killer, I kicked off three projects (with our $8 million in funding), one of which was the new Killer, but the other two were completely crazy. One of them was the VoIP project that Ryan led. The technology was a great idea—run the VoIP software in our network card to reduce latency and control network lag. The problem was, I skipped right past Chapters 2 through 4 in this book, and went right to development, which was not smart. The other was a technology that would work with game servers to speed them up, but it was completely outside our core competency, and an entire new team had to be hired to get this done. In the end, both products shipped, and neither one was anywhere near a hit. The next Killer NIC, the Killer M1, was a success. A lack of focus and an over investment in things that were not core to our growth strategy were some of the main reasons that Bigfoot Networks ran out of money again. It's a lesson learned through dwindling ownership percentages and higher liquidation preferences, which will be discussed more in Chapter 12.

As the founder/CEO, your job is to find a good product or market fit for your solution. Once you've found it, your next job is to push it all the way to the end. Focusing on the growth of your core product or solution should be your main focus. Learning to say no to bright, shiny ideas is a hard thing to do, but if you want to grow, you have to learn this lesson quickly. Instead, invest in things such as new product variations, market expansion, marketing, sales, and scale. If you run out of those, invest in cost reductions, operational efficiency, and then—and only then—a new series or line of products. As Colgate learned when it tried to launch frozen meals (yes, this was a real thing), you need to stay as close to your core as possible, or you may find yourself over invested in an idea at the expense of your growth.

Agile Development

In 2001, a group of dedicated programmers and passionate visionaries released the Manifesto for Agile Software Development.[5] This short declaration voiced the desires of almost every software developer in existence: shipping was more important than planning. Since then, the concept of agile development has grown to encompass the entire software industry and has permeated into nearly every other industry in the world. Agile (sometimes called "lean") is not a new idea—in fact, Toyota got its lead in car manufacturing by installing it into their car plants in the 1980s. However, what was once an idea mostly for manufacturing has now swept the world and is part of nearly every job.

---

[5] http://agilemanifesto.org

Why has agile taken off? The short answer is that it cuts to the quick. It focuses on shipping and results over process and efficiency. Running an expensive machine for 24 hours a day, just because it was an expensive machine to buy, is a huge waste if you can't use all that it produces. Inventory piles up and you end up with products or work in process inventory you can't sell. Similarly, building a massive software product all at once, and then shipping it only when it's completely done is also a waste. It will likely be riddled with bugs and filled with stuff customers don't want (waste).

The modern trend of agile is something that you, as the founder/CEO, will need to learn and understand. Even if you are a hardware company or a service business, there are aspects of lean that apply to how you think and what you do. There are three basic tenants that I think everyone should clearly understand. First, focus on output, not process. Establishing a results based culture with KPIs on the outputs of production can help you avoid micro optimizing parts of your process, whether you are a hardware, software, or service business. In a service business, for example, a dry cleaning operation, it's important to measure how many customers you can service, not how many clothes you can dry. Doing this allows you to realize that your front office may be overloaded (hire more help) or that marketing is ineffective (you can dry 10,000 suits, but you only get 1,000 suits per day in sales). By focusing on the output, you can then turn your attention only to those things that are restricting the output.

The second tenant of lean/agile that every CEO should know is the idea of the minimum viable product. This book has already covered this in detail in Chapter 4, but it bears reiterating. Shipping sooner with less will allow you to have valuable insight into what customers really want. This should be a part of the mantra of every product or service that you create.

Finally, agile teaches us that planning beyond a certain point is not only useless, but it can also be harmful. It's okay to have a plan for the year, but beyond a year is a long time. The popular military saying is that no plan survives contact with the enemy. Now imagine every day, a different enemy (the reality of the world), and now consider that you still want to follow the year's plan you laid out without that knowledge. Most agile processes like Scrum and Kanban are designed with two week planning cycles.[6] They also happen to line up with two week release cycles of MVPs and software versions. Regardless of whether you are hardware or software, you must be free as a manager to take new knowledge (from customers, from competitors, and so on) and adjust in at least two week

---

[6] http://fastai.com/blog/2014/06/17/3-planning-techniques-to-save-your-job

increments based on the new knowledge. Over planning and worse, sticking blindly to bad plans MUST be avoided if you want to grow.

Power of Profitability

This chapter has focused on growth. One of the key ideas was to control growth such that you don't outpace yourself, outgrow your market, or get out of control with expenses. As mentioned at the beginning of the chapter, the one thing you can feel totally safe about is if your net income is growing too fast. When net income flips from negative to positive and stays positive, you have achieved profitability. Being profitable comes with the incredible power of controlling your own destiny.

With profitability, you do not need to raise more money unless you want to. You don't have to sell the company unless you want to. You can slow growth and keep the company at its current size. You can also expand more and invest all your profits into future growth.

If you (or you and your cofounders) were able to keep 51% ownership of your company, you truly are now masters of your own destiny. Board members can want you to raise more money, they can want you to invest more into growth, they can want you to sell your company, but because you are profitable and hold 51%, they cannot force you. They cannot force you to give up more of your company because you need funding, they cannot force you to sell the company, and they cannot fire you as CEO, ever. That's power that, as you will learn in the next chapter, many entrepreneurs have always dreamed of, but have rarely had. If you want to truly *work for yourself* as one of your goals from Chapter 1, then this is how you get it. If you can become profitable and maintain 51%+ ownership, you win.

Story of Spacetime Studios

In 2007, the release of the iPhone changed the world as we once knew it. Smartphones became ubiquitous and more than just a silly gadget. Fast forward to 2011, when, as Gary Gattis, founder of Spacetime Studios explained, gaming on mobile phones had become "like the wild, wild West."[7] It was a gold rush to see who could launch games for the new phone market faster, better, and with higher

---

[7] http://www.computerworld.com/article/2470750/mobile-apps/android-now-more-profitable-than-ios-for-well-known-game-developer.html

monetization. Spacetime Studios entered that gold rush in 2010 with their launch of *Pocket Legends*, and for several years, led the pack in user adoption and revenue.

Pocket Legends was one of, if not the, very first *massively multiplayer online role playing games* (MMORPGs) for mobile phones. Unlike other phone apps that were massive in players but with asynchronous game play, *Pocket Legends* was played in real time (synchronous) with other players in a virtual world. The third person top down 3D graphics were cutting edge and immersed the player in the world with other players. Its uniqueness, graphics, gameplay, and monetization scheme caused the game to be a big hit and grow to nearly five million players.

The monetization scheme of *Pocket Legends* was common for MMORPGs, but somewhat new to mobile phones. The game was free to play, but made money based on a virtual currency called Platinum. Platinum could be purchased only with money, and could be used for in game buffs, new maps or worlds, and vanity items. Like most games of this type, players get hooked on the free version, and end up spending money once they really get into the game. The problem with games like this, however, is that they can quickly outgrow their own audience, making it difficult to reach new players. *Pocket Legends*, like so many others, started shrinking after just two years in the market.

Gary and the team at Spacetime Studios had decisions to make. They had built technology that would allow them to build mobile MMO games quickly. They had also made a hit game, but it was dwindling due to the free to play model and general games market. Gary decided to shift the team towards a new game, *Star Legends*. *Star Legends* was a moderate success, but did not surpass *Pocket Legends*. The revenue the company was generating simply could not sustain the same team size and cuts had to be made. Although they got through it, Spacetime, at one point, had grown too large, focused on too many things, and struggled to sustain the early success that *Pocket Legends* had shown them. What could Gary have done better?

Understanding that games are a hit driven business means predicting that your hit today does not mean your next game will also be a hit. Games, like all pop culture and entertainment, have to evolve with the times. Gary could have done a few things to ease this problem. First, don't staff up beyond what today's revenue is bringing. Hiring a new team to work on a new game while the first game was dying meant Gary had to later do the hard task of downsizing. Second, Gary could have actually tried to slow the growth of *Pocket Legends* when it was growing. Instead of focusing on acquiring new players, Gary could have invested in better monetization, more content, and a more meaningful user experience for his current players. This way, *Pocket Legends* may have had more players left who had not yet played it when the game was improved. I don't know if these would have been the right strategies, and I'm sure Gary took some of these actions as well, but controlling growth is always important to consider—especially when things are going right. Save some gas for later on when you need it, and you might just avoid downsizing and giving up more of your company to those ever present investors who are ready to capitalize on your struggles.

Chapter 10
The Press Hates Me—Bad reviews

"Snake oil," I said, with frustration. "That's what some of them are calling us—snake oil. As in, it doesn't do anything."

"Okay, hold on. Who is saying this? Specifically, I mean," Aaron replied.

"The forums.[1] I mean, almost every gaming forum out there has people saying this or something similar. Aaron, this is bad, really bad," I say, worried and frustrated. Aaron was our press guy. We hired his PR firm, one of the biggest in the country, and they sent us Aaron. Aaron was probably the perfect guy because he was a gamer, understood the gaming business, had good connections to hardware reviewers, and was generally a great guy. The problem was that our PR strategy didn't seem to be working.

"Forums? Come on, those don't matter," Aaron said.

"What? Are you crazy? Of course they matter! Gamers are big forum users. They are all over the forums—they get more news from there than they do from the articles!" I screamed.

"Calm down! The product isn't even out yet. Just wait for some real reviews to come out, okay?" Aaron said, still sure of his strategy.

"Hey look at this," Sean said, one of the members of the PR team. "Some other forum members are actually defending you and saying that it could actually work."

"I want to post something," I said.

"You shouldn't..." Aaron said.

"You don't have to..." Sean started.

"I'm gonna..." I said.

I did, and it didn't really help. I spent hours and hours debating people in forums and explaining how the card worked. I published white papers, built a lag and latency measurement tool (the Lag Meter), and even tried to convince people based on my prior products that I had built at Intel. It did nothing to stem the haters and doubters. What it did do, though, was give my supporters facts to fight back against the haters with. The white papers were particularly helpful as tools for our fans to explain things to our haters.

...

A few weeks later, Aaron called me on the phone.

---

[1] https://slashdot.org/story/06/08/08/193237/network-card-for-gamers---uses-linux-to-reduce-lag

DOI 10.1515/9781501507083-010

...

"Dude, everyone wants to review the card, and I mean everyone. *Tom's Hardware*, *AnandTech*, and *HotHardware*. Even *CNET* wants to do a review," he said excitedly. "I think the controversy is what got them interested. They all want to see for themselves if it is snake oil or not."

"That's good, I guess, right?" I asked, confused.

"Well, as they say in the business, any news is good news," Aaron replied, half jokingly.

"It'll be good news, Aaron. The cards work," I explained.

"Well, we better explain how to test it well, then. What is your recommended testing procedure to show that it works?" he asked.

"Just load it on two identical PCs and play *World of Warcraft* side by side. The difference is obvious when you press the spacebar to jump," I explained.

"Okay, anything else?" Aaron asked.

"If you don't play simultaneously on two identical PCs, it's not a great test. If they have to do it that way, at least make sure they connect to the same server in, say, *Counter Strike*. The should see 1 to 10ms lower ping," I answered.

"Okay, I'll write something up as a testing procedure. We'll see," Aaron said, doubtful.

...

A few weeks after that, I had another phone chat with Aaron.

...

"So?" I asked.

"*AnandTech* launched their review.[2] It's bad—they couldn't find a difference, and they are calling it snake oil," Aaron replied.

"Snake oil, really, again?" I said, exasperated.

"Well, the good news is that some of the other reviewers are trying harder to get the card to work for them. The problem is, most of the reviewers are having trouble. It turns out that having two identical PCs is not easy, and the testing procedure is very complex," Aaron said.

"Okay, so we need to help them! Let's lend them PCs, get them on the phone, fly them here, or we go there—anything," I replied, knowing that reviews would make or break the product's success.

"On it." Aaron said.

...

A week later, we are face to face with Aaron.

---

[2] http://www.anandtech.com/show/2111

...

"All the controversy has gotten us a lot of press," Aaron started, handing me his monthly coverage sheet. "We've got major articles in *Forbes, CNET, IGN, GameSpot*, really all the major press outlets are covering us at some level," he continues, pointing to the section on press coverage.

"Okay, okay, but the reviews, Aaron. Come on, you're killing me!" I said, knowing half the answer, since I'd read a few reviews that morning.

"Right, so, aside from *AnandTech* and *Tom's Hardware*, which both were kind of neutral..." Aaron started out.

"Come on, they hated us, dude," I replied.

"Well, the comments from your defenders and some customers on those forums certainly create a different story. They defended you well on those sites, and I think other reviews might be posted," Aaron said. "Especially when they start to read some of the other sites' reviews." Aaron smiled, perhaps for the first time in months.

"We got great reviews on *HardOCP*, and it even got picked up on *Wired*, and they are kingmakers," Aaron said. "Flying them here to do testing worked well."[3]

"I know, they said it was great!"

"Yep, and *HotHardware*[4] and about a dozen others all were able to do the tests on side by side computers and see the results you claimed. Harlan, you have a hit on your hands," he said, holding his hand out to shake it.

I smiled for the first time in months and shook his hand back.

"How in the hell did we pull this off?" I asked rhetorically to myself, knowing the answer already.

"Honestly, I think the controversy actually helped us. It got us way more media attention than we expected, and it put people in corners. It's hard to get the press to agree on anything, and when one bad review came out, others raced to be the ones to find the good in it. We got lucky," Aaron said.

"It wasn't luck," I said, smiling.

Failing at Reviews and Press

Whether you are B2B or B2C, reviews and press are an important part of navigating your way to startup success. There is no such thing as a free lunch, nor is

---

[3] https://www.wired.com/2006/12/hardocp_reviews
[4] https://hothardware.com/reviews/bigfoot-networks-killer-network-interface-card?page=5

there such a thing as free marketing and PR. Sure, getting press is supposed to be free, but it usually takes at least three things to get noticed—all of which cost you something, even if the cost is only your time. First, you have to have a story worth telling, which means making your product remarkable (see Chapter 2 of this book). Second, you need to reach out to the press, which takes a lot of time and sometimes even money. Finding e mail addresses and phone numbers, calling, following up, and tracking all take time and money. Lastly, if the product or service is going to be reviewed, you almost always have to provide free copies or versions. While the cost may not be high, again, it takes time. If you don't have all three, you are probably not going to get much coverage, if any. Not getting coverage is one of the two ways to fail at reviews and press. The second way, as in Bigfoot Networks' case, is to get bad reviews. I believe and have demonstrated that bad press can sometimes lead to good press.

Failing to get press attention is the most common failure. You have to understand that the press is bombarded by requests for reviews, interviews, stories, and more. You are just one more noisemaker asking for a story in their pile of thousands. You will know that you failed to get a story when none have come out. Early indicators of your failure will be unreturned e mails, no return calls, and general apathy. There are ways to fight this failure, as will be discussed in the next section, but in the end, what the press writes about you is out of your direct span of control.

Getting bad press or bad reviews is the other way to fail at press. But what is press? Press is most commonly referred to as media outlets that do not accept money for their story. If someone accepts money to write a story, they are a writer, not part of the press. So, does that mean that forum users are press? You didn't pay them, so I think so. What about bloggers? Usually, they are also press members, since you don't pay them (although you can). Social media? Yep, press. Managing the situation of bad press, getting press (and social media), and all things that you can't directly control are the subjects of this chapter. Read on to learn how to get some of that marketing "for free"! Free lunch, anyone? (Hint: It's going to cost you!)

Building a Press Plan

You do not have to pay anyone to build a press plan. In fact, I've outlined one for you here in Table 10.1. The next section will talk about when you should consider hiring a PR agency or social media agency to help you, but for now, assume you should start out doing it yourself. Hey, at least you'll learn along the way!

A good press plan has three elements. First, it has the goals of the plan clearly laid out in terms that are measurable. If you can't measure success, you'll never know whether all the effort was worth it or not. Second, you should create a list of target press outlets. The list should be as long as possible, but sorted by the most important press first. Finally, include a few story angles that you think the press may find *remarkable*. It may even be beneficial to write part of your own story that the press can use in their review. Helping to write part of the story makes it just that much easier for the press to cover you. This is why press releases are made. A press release is simply a story written by the company who wants their story out there, and it often gets posted word for word. Press releases don't necessarily mean that you'll get press, but they do help. Getting someone to simply repost a press release you wrote, however, is not the goal at all. It will almost certainly get you nothing. What you want is a story written by the press, themselves. You want their angle, their spin, and their voice. That's what will drive the results you are hoping to get, not simply a repost of your self aggrandized press release.

Table 10.1: Example Press/PR Plan

Item		Example
1.	Goal	Clicks to our site and sales
2.	List	*CNET, AnandTech, Tom's Hardware, TechCrunch, Mashable*, etc.
3.	Story	Gamers hate lag. It has been listed as the number one most frustrating thing about online gaming. Competitive gamers do everything they can to have the lowest lag possible.
		The Killer NIC doesn't solve lag, but it does help. It reduces lag through lower latency and higher frame rates. It also speeds up the game overall by offloading the network functions to the card. Gamers can expect 5 to 10% lower ping and 5 to 10% higher FPS, on average.

Following Table 10.1's example, a good goal is always a measurable goal. A few things that are measurable and simple to track would be the number of stories written, press releases reposted, people who read the articles that get written about you (yes, this is something you can measure, called "impressions"). The problem with these metrics is that they do not easily connect to what you really want: sales. Wouldn't it be better if you could measure clicks to your site, or sales as a result of stories? Those goals are much better, even if they are somewhat harder to track. Track the other things too—they are not meaningless, but having the goal to track clicks or sales is better.

Once you have that goal, now you have to build in plans to make it measurable. It is harder to track clicks and sales, especially in PR, but not impossible. Sometimes, tracking clicks means creating one or more vanity URLs. What I like to do is register a new domain name, something short and silly, like "endlag.org," then use that in my press releases and during interviews or stories. This vanity URL simply redirects to our main site, but I can keep a counter as to the number of people who visited the vanity URL, thus knowing clicks. Sometimes, using a service like Bit.ly to make a series of traceable URLs (one for each press outlet you reach out to) can let you figure out which press got you more clicks than others! Tracking clicks is even possible just by using Google Analytics and looking at referrals. Referrals from press sites are clicks that were driven by press. Tracking clicks is totally doable.

Tracking sales is a bit harder. First, you could track referral all the way to a Google Analytics sales event. This is good if you are doing sales online on your own site, but not as easy if you sell other places too. One thing to consider is a survey as part of the software install or onboarding, or even product registration. The survey can be two questions long: "How did you find out about us?" and "Did you read any press about us before purchasing?" They may have found you from an ad, but you would be surprised at how many people read reviews before purchasing. Customer reviews are sometimes even more important than press reviews, but more on that later in this chapter.

Creating a media list is the next part of a good plan. A good way to start is to find reviews and stories about your competitors or other companies in your market. What magazines, TV shows, websites, newspapers, and so on are reporting on them? Did they get on *Oprah*? That goes on the list. Did they get on *The Today Show*? On the list. How about *CNET*, *Wired*, *Forbes*, or *TechCrunch*? On the list. Once you have your list, now think of where you read for news like this, and add those to the list. Now go through the list and find each outlet's Alexa ranking. Alexa.com is an online web ranking tool that ranks sites based on their web traffic. Now that they are ranked, use your own judgment and Alexa rankings to sort the list from most important to least. A final step is to find contact information for as many as you can. That's the hard part, but many sites actually list their writer's e mail addresses. You want a writer's e mail address or phone, not just a simple submission form. Good luck!

Now, about that story... The last part of your PR plan is to draft all or part of a story. You can do this in press release form, but really, I like to put it into e mail form better. Get to the point of why the story is important to their readers, and what is unique or special about it. If you can connect it to human interests, something society wants or needs, even better! You've helped them position their story about your product or service in terms that popular press wants, and readers want to read. It should be about your customers, not you. It's about what you do for them, not what you do. Just a few paragraphs, one on the human interest and one with some facts, a traceable URL, and you are done. Now, customize it for each media target. Once you are ready to execute, start sending out those e mails and phone calls, and see what happens!

At some point, you are going to realize, hey, this is taking a lot of work, and I don't even have a single article to show for it yet. At this point, you might consider hiring a PR agency. They are going to build a plan just like yours, but having yours to show them will give them a great place to start. Of course, a PR agency is not all it is set up to be...

When and How to Hire a PR Agency

Sometimes I hire a PR agency, sometimes I don't—it really just depends on the situation. A mistake I have made, and one that gets made often, is hiring one too soon, or with the wrong expectations. Another mistake is paying for more than you really need. If you wonder if you need to hire a PR agency, read on.

To know when to hire a PR agency or not, you first must understand what they really do. They won't tell you this—they are trying to sell you the dream, after all—but the reality is that even the best PR agents in the world can only do so much. PR agencies do three things really well. They offer a lot of other services, but they actually can deliver on these three things. First, they do have contacts and e mail addresses and phone numbers of tons of writers and press. This doesn't mean they can get anyone to actually answer the phone or e mail, but they do have the contacts. They keep massive databases and have fields of interns that try to keep it all up to date. Second, they can and will reach out to them for you. Again, no guarantee that any of the media they know will be able to answer, but they will try, again, usually using their fields of interns and junior staff. Finally, they can track stuff really well: from how many people answered the phone to how many stories got written and their reach and everything in between. That's it. If you are expecting more from your PR agency, your mileage may vary greatly.

Most PR agencies also do the following *standard* things as part of their retainer. It's free, so take it, right? Not so fast—PR agencies are actually NOT good at these things, and in my experience, it is cheaper and better for you and your staff to do them instead. Writing press releases is one of the most common things PR agencies do. Sure, they can do it, but they can't craft your story, they don't know you well enough and they typically forget to make the story about humans. PR agencies are also very cautious with their wording. It is better to not have a press release, but to have a short, two paragraph story instead that you use to try to get writers to write a story about you. You can come up with that! Second, PR agencies will offer to give you PR training. Let me save you the trouble. Here is the PR training in three bullet points in Table 10.2. See, was that worth $500? PR agencies are also very expensive if all you want to do is file a press release. You can do that yourself for much cheaper, just do some online research and many results will come up showing you how to do it. Finally, they will help you with a PR plan. They'll do one for you, but hey, I just taught you that. By the way, you should make a new plan every time something big happens, such as funding, a product launch, a big customer, and so on. Also, don't forget reviews!

Table 10.2: Free PR Training (For the cost of this book, and your time, that is)

Item	Example
1. Focus on conveying the main points only, and never more than three. Memorize those three points and keep coming back to them.	"I want to share three things with you today. First, our new product is launching and will help millions of [customers] do [thing]. Second, we're very proud of [unique feature], because [customer reasons]. Third, I'd really love it if you [wrote a story or review]."
2. Do not answer just anything. Be prepared to just say "I can't talk about that" or "No comment" if it's anything off of your main three points.	"No comment."
3. Don't be an idiot and say things that are racist, sexist, supremacist, or derogatory in any way, or anything to do with politics or religion. Just stick to your three main points.	DON'T SAY: "I hate [insert political/religious group]."

I know I sound cynical, and that is partly because I have been burned. In order to learn when and how to use a PR agency, I had to do it the hard way: by trial and error. Another thing to know is that PR agencies will try to sell you on more things that you also don't need. They are not even the experts in much of what they are trying to sell you, so just politely say no. If you need help in these areas, hire a relevant expert. Just say no to a PR agency's offers to do social media marketing, trade shows, blogger outreach, and writing services. You want them for their list and their willingness to call for you—that's it, really.

In summary, when to hire a PR agency is when you need one. If you don't have time to make a list of media, find contact information, and do outreach for your story, hire some help, and a PR agency (or a freelance agent) can be a big help! Hire only for those things you need, such as media lists, outreach, and tracking, and nothing else. How much will that cost you? It varies, but you should expect to spend around $3,000 to $5,000 per month for at least three months. They will want to sign a longer contract with you, but I advise keeping it as short as possible and automatically renewing. Parting ways with a PR agency can be hard, and ending it at the end of a contract makes it easy. These people will become your friends, so keep it contractual and avoid the pain of firing them.

Corporate Innovation

In the case of corporations, you may be stuck with using some of your parent companies' resources such as marketing and PR. In this case, it is important to not alienate those people or let them work alone. The key to getting the most out of internal resources, such as an internal PR department, is to be involved as much as possible in the process. Sometimes they may try to shut you out and keep what they do a mystery. Don't let them. Show up in person and ask questions. Ask about their plan, ask to see it, provide input to it, and buy them this book even! Oh, bring cookies or snacks too, why not? The worst thing you can do is leave PR, marketing, or any other function to chance. Whether you know it or not, your career is probably on the line here, not theirs.

Customer Reviews (Good and Bad)

You can fire a PR agency (usually with a one month penalty), but you can't fire a customer—they already bought your product or service. So, what do you do when a customer, or someone who you think is a customer, writes a bad review? For that matter, how can you get the customers who love the product to write a review? Customer reviews in both B2C and B2B are becoming ever important to the success of a product or service. In a B2B context, they call it a testimonial or reference customer. Either way, you want it, because people make their purchase decisions based on their peers and other real users or customers more than they do from actual media reviews. Spending time harvesting good consumer or B2B testimonials and reviews is well worth the investment. Dealing with bad ones is an imperative.

There are four techniques I have used to help foster good reviews and testimonials. These techniques have all shown good results, depending on the situation. First, for online services, such as online games and online apps, as well as mobile apps, I have used the common pop up. After the user uses the app or game for a period of time, I offer them some minor reward (in game item, extra time, etc.) if they take the time to write a review on their platform. That might be PC, Android, or iPhone or whatever, but asking them to write a review after they have used it for a while has worked wonders to get lots of reviews. There is even a plug in software for apps that does this for you, it's called Appirater.[5]

Second, for products I sell online, such as on Amazon or my own website, I reach out by e mail to customers a week or so after they get their product. I ask them if they are having any trouble, and if so, to reply and we'll help. I then say, "If everything is working well, would you mind writing us a positive review? It can really help small businesses like us be more successful and bring you even more innovative products." What I'm trying to do is prevent a bad review (by offering a solution if they are having trouble) while encouraging a good one (if they are happy). It has worked very well, and most online retailers, Amazon included, allow you as a retailer or manufacturer to contact their customers (usually through the retailer's e mail systems).

Third, for products or software sold in stores, you do not usually get any e mail address or customer contact information. If the product has a software installation, however, you can require a registration to use the product (e mail address). I always do this because it allows me to send an e mail about two weeks after they installed it, just like for online sales. Sometimes, though, there is no software or way to do that, so you must incentivize people to register their product. Adding an insert card for a free gift if they register online or a chance to win money if they register with their e mail is a good way to do this. Even in service businesses, businesses like fast food restaurants incentivize their customers to take surveys for a small reward like free French fries. Why? Because they want to make you a happy, loyal customer who doesn't complain publicly, but instead complains to them so that they can fix it. While you are there, if you are happy, why not share your positive experience for the world to see. That's the name of the game, and it's a vital one.

Finally, in big B2B sales (products or services), you may not have that many total possible customers. With so few potential customers, you probably do not want to chance even a single relationship. It becomes ever so vital to please each customer and turn them into a reference customer. A reference customer is a customer who is so delighted that they are willing to become a reference for you with future prospective customers. Why would they do that? Well, you could offer them an incentive, but the best reason they would do that is because they like you that much and want to see you succeed. If you succeed, they know that they will get to keep using your products and services. Once you sense a customer is happy enough, ask them, "Would you consider being a reference customer from

---

[5] https://github.com/arashpayan/appirater

time to time?" If they say no, you can always say, "No problem, I know you are busy. How about writing a quick testimonial for our website?" A testimonial is almost as good as a reference customer. It's a sentence or two about how it helps your customer succeed that you can share publicly. If they really like you, you can ask for both a reference and a testimonial. However, once you get one or the other, wait a few months before you ask for the other one—you don't want to smother them!

Positive reviews are important, but not as important as not getting negative ones! That may sound counter intuitive until you realize that sites like Amazon usually display a high rating and review as well as a low rating and review. People who shop often read the one and two star ratings of products before they buy, even if the average is 4.5 stars. Why? Customers are wary and want to know the hidden secrets behind a product before they buy it. They want to know if it will actually break after three weeks or if the company is miserable to work with. Just a few bad customer reviews can really hurt a product or company if steps aren't taken to remedy it quickly.

There is no way to avoid bad reviews. You will get some bad reviews no matter how hard you try. However, many could be avoided if you follow these three steps. First, have a customer support phone number and e mail address, and make sure you respond to it at least daily. Giving customers a place where they can contact you with any problems can often give you the chance to remedy an issue before it turns into a bad review. In fact, it can sometimes lead to a good review if you are able to fix the problem quickly, calmly, and completely. In every one of my companies, I have always offered a full money back guarantee if we can't solve the problem. I also offer free cross ship exchanges for broken products. These two policies, as well as a commitment to solving any problem even if I have to ship a new one or give some money back have saved me from bad reviews. Second, being proactive about making sure customers are happy can also help. A money back guarantee is great, but you have to reach out and ask the customer if everything is going okay. That's why I try so hard to get customer e mail addresses. I don't just want the customers to write a good review, but I want to prevent bad reviews from getting written in the first place if the customer isn't happy. In my outreach when I ask for a review, I always start it with "If you are unhappy or are having any problems, please let us try to remedy the issue or offer a refund by calling xxx or e mailing us at yyy."

Eventually, the inevitable will happen, and someone will write a bad review. When this happens, you have to decide, are you going to just let it happen, or do you care? I care. I try to understand if we have a systemic issue, or some error in production or testing that can be fixed. More than that, when a customer writes a bad review, anything less than four stars, it's an opportunity for me to reach out and try to help rectify the problem. Most review systems, like Amazon, allow you to either write a comment on the review or contact the reviewer or both. I do both when I can, with a message such as, "We are so sorry you are having trouble or are not satisfied. We offer a 100% money back guarantee and a dedication to making our customers happy. Please reach out to us and let us try to rectify the issue at xxx or by e mail at yyy."

This is it. Doing more or getting specific doesn't usually help much, and can turn nasty. Saying this, even if the customer doesn't reach out, shows other customers that you tried to help, which often negates the bad review. If you are contacted, for goodness' sake, give the person their money back and ask them to change the review to four stars because of your great customer support. Never ask for five stars from a previously disgruntled customer. Never ask for any stars if you can't get the customer to be happy again. Making customers happy is the key to good reviews; dedicate yourself and your team to it, and you will find that good reviews and good sales will follow. In some cases, however, a series of bad reviews might mean you need to consider a product reboot (see later in this chapter).

Dealing with Forums

There are two kinds of forums, yours and not yours. Each one deserves its own strategy. Companies sometimes use forums that are not yours to drum up leads and sales. Reddit is the biggest online forum these days, and companies will often post links, stories, or questions to Reddit in order to garner attention from a specific and very loyal set of hardcore customers. Bear in mind though, these customers are vocal on Reddit, so you better be ready to make sure they are made happy. Eventually, the inevitable will happen—someone will post a negative review or a bad comment on a public forum. How you handle a negative review is very important, because future customers will read this when they search about you or your product. You have to avoid the trolls, or the people who just want to make you mad. You have to prevent or avoid flame wars: back and forth attacks with escalating negativity. The following strategies will help you do it right.

There are two strategies to consider when someone writes a bad review or a negative comment on a public forum. First, since it's a public forum, you are not really expected to respond. Most companies don't watch every public forum, and responding, especially responding late, can do more harm than good. In most forum systems, the thread will eventually be buried, but responding to it will make it jump back to the top and remind everyone. Also, responding wrong can backfire badly. What you don't want to do ever is start a flame war or a bunch of back and forth commenting on a public forum. It makes you look unprofessional and lets the trolls win. The best strategy, but one I can never bring myself to do, is to say nothing at all. Just let it lie there, it will die out eventually, and sometimes other users will jump to your defense for you, and that's way better than you responding.

Personally, I have a hard time saying nothing. Especially if I started the thread for marketing purposes, or if I notice the forum post fairly quickly, I can't keep my mouth shut. The reason is that I have dedicated myself to making happy customers. I don't know if the forum troll is a real customer or not, but others might read it and get the wrong idea. The best response (if, like me, you must respond) is to provide facts or offer customer support. Use the same message you used in a review, saying you are sorry and offering your support line and even a refund. If it is an issue of incorrect facts, simply state the facts, and leave it at that. The one thing you should never do is comment more than twice in a single thread. Once you've offered facts and then support, you are done, leave it lie. You are not expected to keep interacting in a forum—again, it makes you look unprofessional. Keep your head high, take the high ground, offer support, and move on with your life.

Internal forums, or forums that you have on your own site, however, are a different matter. If you are going to have forums on your site (for a game for example), you better have someone who is at least half time responsible for managing those forums. Managing forums means locking threads, responding professionally with facts at all times, and generally making sure the forums are kept free of trolls and flame wars. Banning bad users, deleting posts, and removing spammers and bots are all also necessary. It's a near full time job, so forums are to be taken on with care only. Remember that a forum is not where customer support should happen. Many of your responses will have to be "I'm sorry, please contact our support team," as it would on a public forum. It's just so much more difficult on your own forum, because the option to say nothing is no longer there—you must respond, it's your own forum!

Dealing with Social Media

Speaking of your own forum, your social media channels are like your own forum. Getting a review, comment, or question on social media not only happens, but it is becoming more common. How you handle it on your social media is like managing your own forum—you must respond, and you must respond quickly. To not do so shows customers that you don't care and you are probably some tiny, untrustworthy company that is too small to bother to read comments on their social media, which is not good. The worst part, your social media is a public forum too—the world can see it, and they do.

Fortunately, you already have a commitment to making customers happy, and that, just like a review or public forum, is something you know how to do. If you do it the same way on your social media, forums, and reviews, you suddenly look like a professional company that cares. You already know what to do. First, respond quickly, at least daily. Not responding is not an option, because it's your social media! If you don't have an account on that social media, say, Snapchat, then you don't have to respond. If you do, you must do it quickly. Second, respond with facts (if questions) or offers of customer support and money back (if a negative review or a problem). Avoid flame wars and trolls like you would on any forum by only responding once or twice (first with facts and then offering support). You don't have to do more, other customers and readers will see that you tried to help, and if the other person tries to start a flame war with you, simply take the high ground and shut up. You've already tried to help and the world saw it.

Some companies have tried to solve customer issues directly in their social media in a public way. They do this, perhaps, to avoid future people having the same issue. I think it's a bad idea. If you want to prevent future issues, the company should fix the problems customers are having in the product itself and make it so that customers simply don't have that same problem, not show customers how to fix it themselves in a public setting. Things in social media can turn bad so quickly that it's just not worth the trouble. Do you really want to have a product where customers routinely have the same issue that they need to be shown how to solve their problems on social media? Maybe you should improve the product instead!

Besides marketing and customer interaction, social media can have other uses too. For example, it can be used to get people to take surveys for you, or to inspire greater brand loyalty. An unconventional use of social media, however, is using it in the event of scandal or major product issues.

Dealing with Scandal

A scandal can be anything that hurts you, your employees, your products or services, or your company's reputation. Handling a customer poorly is an example of a light scandal. Getting sued for sexual harassment is a big scandal. There is everything in between too. Having your product injure or kill someone or start a fire is the worst kind of scandal, and may even require a product reboot (more on that later). How you choose to handle the scandal is not unlike how you choose to handle a real lawsuit—try to settle and keep the lawyers out of it whenever possible.

The first step of handling a scandal is to acknowledge the facts. Do not admit fault or try to root cause or publish any details (save that for the court). Do, however, admit that someone has a complaint and that it is your wish to help that person or company and resolve it as fast as possible. As always, provide that customer support and e mail address for them to reach out to you directly. Similar to a bad review, other people who read this and who have heard about the scandal will see how professional you are being about it, which will help roll back some of the negativity from the scandal.

Lie low until the scandal is resolved. Do not feel like you have to defend every comment or answer any questions about it. "It is an ongoing investigation and we are working hard to resolve any possible issues," is a perfectly acceptable answer. Under no circumstances should you leak information about the issue or confirm any facts about anything—all of that can only hurt you. Take the high road, and stick to your mantra: you want every customer to be happy and will work diligently to make that happen, even if there *may* have been a scandal. "May" is the key word until the scandal is resolved.

Once the scandal gets resolved (privately!), it is time to decide if there is anything else to say about it. It's perfectly fine to simply state that the issue has been resolved. It's better if you can get the customer or other party who had the problem or scandal to allow you to explain what happened and how it was resolved. Keep it brief and stick to what you both agreed you would say about the scandal.

If the scandal was about a product, and it was bad, a product reboot may be in order.

Product Reboot

A product reboot is what happens when a problem so bad happens that the product's reputation is permanently ruined. A series of one star reviews is a very hard thing to overcome. A major scandal, like a fire or serious injury, can also mean it's too big of a risk to keep moving forward with the product as it is. A product reboot involves taking three clear and calm steps.

First, stop selling the current product. Simply let it go "out of stock" and if necessary, you can even move product from warehouses back to your headquarters (or home, whichever the case may be). In extreme cases, like phones setting people's houses on fire, or cars losing their braking ability, a product recall is in order. Most recalls are for repair, but as a startup, a recall with refund may be a better, if more costly, option. Once the product is out of stock, it is effectively the end of its life for now. You will never sell that product again, and it's time for the reboot.

The second step in the product reboot is to fix the issue. This might mean scrapping inventory or it could mean a simple rework. I've had to do this and all it took was one wire soldered onto the back of a card. It fixed the issue and meant I didn't have to scrap the entire product. Regardless of how you do the rework, be sure you are addressing the core issue that caused the scandal or series of bad reviews. You are not done, though. You also need to think about your rebrand, and that probably means new packaging as well.

Finally, relaunch the product under a new name. It's not enough to call it 2.0. You need a new name to distance this version as far from the bad one as possible. For this reason, new packaging or even new plastics might be in order. Certainly, new marketing, a new logo, new product listings, and new messaging are all in order. Create a new item in your store, the Amazon store, or wherever it is being sold. The old one will never be in stock, so it's now all about this one.

Some customers, and maybe even some channel partners, will pick up on the fact that this one is very similar to the last one. If necessary, throw in an extra accessory or feature to make sure it's different enough. You don't have to hide the fact that it's similar to the old one—just make sure it's clear that this one doesn't have the same problems, that you've learned, and that this ultimate version has fixed the problem AND MORE. It's now time to seek new reviews, new reference customers, and get new PR for this version. Consider it a new launch.

Managing Bloggers and Influencers

Bloggers and influencers are similar to press in that they are considered media. They are also different in that they usually do not make much (if any) money with their blog, and are sometimes willing to accept free products or even cash for a good review. Bloggers run a website where they post their own stories and content for others to read. Influencers are the same as bloggers, but may not do so with a website, but with other media, like YouTube, Snapchat, Instagram, or other social media or video platforms. Regardless of the media, however, bloggers and influencers are growing in importance, as the next generation of consumers has learned to regard sources like professional YouTubers as the new forms of social media. These influencers and bloggers cannot be ignored.

The first step in managing bloggers and influencers is to include them in your PR plan. To do this, identify the top bloggers and influencers in your field or company type and be sure to try to get some Alexa (or number of YouTube subscribers/Snapchat followers/etc.) so you can understand the reach of the influencer. Keep in mind that, depending on the influencer, the reach may be small, but extremely focused—it may be worth more than, say, a *Forbes* article where only some of the readers will care. Once you have your list sorted, create a plan to reach out to them and try to get them to write or video about you "as media." Don't offer to pay or send product, just ask them for a review or video about your product. You don't have to offer anything, trust me, they will ask.

Handling requests from bloggers or influencers is the same regardless of if you asked them for a review or if they reached out to you directly. In both cases, you have to justify if it is worth it to send them one or more free products or even pay them (professional YouTubers, for example). The calculation is just like any other you would do for marketing spend: consider the reach (CPM), the potential clicks (CPC), and any potential sales (CPA), and compare that to the cost of your product (plus shipping) or any money they are asking for. Compare all that to other ways you could spend the same dollars and make your decision. Don't go with your gut—it will usually say, "Sure, do it." Go with the numbers instead. If the CPM of the influencer is higher than the CPM of, for example Facebook ads, don't do it. If the potential CPA or CPC is going to be higher than other methods, don't do it unless you can't spend enough in the other marketing channel. Only do it if you think the sales will be worth it.

Personally, I have had the best results working with bloggers by providing them with two free products. You offer one for them to try (and keep), and the other for them to give away as a prize to their readers. For influencers, I've had good success getting them to write a review by offering them one free copy (of the game) or a bunch of free in game currency (to experience the game more fully). I have also paid influencers with a very large and targeted audience from time to time, including Kim Kardashian for her Twitter (which temporarily shut down my website with the amount of clicks we got, by the way). More recently, paying YouTubers to play your game on their YouTube channel, to perform an unboxing, or to make a video review has been very effective. Remember, bloggers and influencers are not media because they can be paid, and they will almost always note only positive things (because they got paid). Use accordingly, and do not feel bad that this is their model. The world knows that the review is not impartial, and yet, it works anyway.

Dealing with Media Hate

At some time or another, you will eventually have someone from the media—or maybe a reviewer, a blogger, or a YouTuber—who hates you. They may even go out of their way to attack you in a public way. They write bad things about your products, your company, and sometimes, even bad things about you. No matter how nice you are or want to be, you will still have that person in the media who hates you regardless. It's very hard not to take it personally. However, realize that this is normal. In fact, if someone in the media doesn't hate you, it probably means nobody cares at all. In order to be remarkable in the first place, you must be different. Different means that somewhere, some other status quo is getting upturned. To get the press to remark at all, you have to be interesting enough that camps will form. Getting camps to form is a good thing, and you must embrace both sides. They fuel each other and get you more press cycles than you probably really deserve.

Camps are formed when one group loves what you are doing and some other group hates it. Why would this happen? Usually this happens because there is something controversial or remarkable about what you are doing. In order to get attention in the media, inevitably, one reviewer or writer will take the opposite viewpoint, even if they don't really believe it. Why? If their story is negative in a field of positive, then the entire positive camp will run to read why it was negative and post on social media to defend it. See? The negative stance caused the media outlet to get more eyeballs. It may sound personal, but it probably isn't. If it is personal, go back and read the part about scandal, because you are dealing with one. Most likely, it's just a writer trying to get views on a story that they may not even believe in.

How do you deal with media hate, then? Ignore it. Embrace it. Outright be glad it exists, because if nobody hated you, nobody would love you either. Be glad that you are getting press, and step back and let your fans defend you. If your fans aren't defending you, take an even lower road and share the bad review on your social media with a call to action to your fans. Say something like, "If you agree with this review, please let us know. If you don't, please let the reviewer know on their comments section and let the world know." Usually encouraging the controversy will work in your favor!

The Story of Psyko Audio Labs

Psyko Audio Labs was created by James Hildebrandt in Alberta, Canada. James was an acoustic engineer who had a mad scientist idea: why not build a pair of headphones that actually used 5.1 speakers, just like a home theater surround sound setup? The problem was that putting five speakers into a pair of headphones would be strange—after all, which side gets the extra speaker? For those not familiar with 5.1 audio, there are two front speakers, two rear speakers, a middle speaker, and a subwoofer (the .1 is the subwoofer). James' brilliant idea was to put the speakers above the head in a little room made of plastic, and to pipe the sound from the room to the ears in the right proportion to make it seem as though the person was in a room. The awesome part of the technology and the idea was that it worked!

The Psyko Audio 5.1 PC Gaming headphones were launched in 2010 to great applause and reviewer appeal. In fact, media reviewers loved the technology and loved the sound, saying how the technology actually worked well.[6] The company amped up its marketing efforts and opened in online and retail stores across the U.S. and Canada. Sales were strong, as gamers and movie buffs flocked to the new technology and the radically unique audio experience.

But disaster struck. Within a few months after launch, returns started to spike up. A few weeks later, bad reviews started showing up on Amazon and other online sites.[7] What was going on? The media loved the product, but the public hated it. It turns out that there were two problems with the headphones. First, the amplification was just a bit less than gamers were used to. Gamers like to listen at high volumes, and the Psyko 5.1 had built the amplification at a lower volume than other headphones. This led some gamers to be unsatisfied with the speakers, thinking that they were too soft. The second problem, a much bigger one, was that the plastic didn't last as long as expected. After a few months of heavy use, the earphones formed a crack and then a hole. On a normal pair of headphones, it would be purely cosmetic, but on the Psyko 5.1 headphones, this meant a hole in the sound pipe, essentially ruining the headphones from getting sound to your ears. This meant James and Psyko Audio Labs had to deal with customer reviews, complaints, returns, social media, forums, and more, all at the same time. There was a real problem with the plastics as well, and James had to decide what to do about it. Should he issue a recall? Should he offer full refunds? What about his channel partners like Fry's and Newegg? What would he tell them?

A product reboot was in order. James decided to relaunch the Psyko 5.1 with improved plastics, improved cabling, and more amplification. He did this under a new name as well, the Psyko Audio Labs Carbon. The Psyko Carbon was able to garner the same great reviews, but unhindered by the negative reviews from consumers about returns and weak speakers.[8] Eventually, Psyko would phase out the old Psyko 5.1 in favor of the Carbon and other editions. The plastics problem behind them, Psyko moved forward and did quite well with the new product.

---

[6] https://techcrunch.com/2010/01/10/hands-on-psyko-audio-labs-5-1-headphones
[7] https://www.amazon.com/PSYKO-AUDIO-Gaming-Headphones-Retail/product-reviews/B003BWAZB8/ref=cm_cr_arp_d_viewpnt_rgt?filterByStar=critical&pageNumber=1
[8] http://www.pcgamer.com/hard-stuff-psyko-audio-labs-carbon-review/#

Chapter 11
I'm Bankrupt—Saving costs and finding profits

"We aren't going to be able to pay everyone," Mike said, staring at his spreadsheet.

"What? We're not bankrupt—what do you mean?" I asked, knowing we still had cash in the bank.

"No, we are not bankrupt, but I've already been slow paying our suppliers," he started.

"Slow paying?" I asked interrupting, never having heard that term before.

"Yeah. I basically don't pay anything until I get a past due notice, pretending to have lost the original bill," he said sheepishly, but also with a bit of pride in his eyes. The technique is common, and many CFOs like Mike have used it to conserve cash when it's really needed.

It was 2007, and Bigfoot Networks had been going great. Our product, the Killer NIC, had won the networking product of the year from *CPU Magazine*, and since then, we had been accelerating our marketing efforts, our R&D efforts, and expanding inventory. We were just about to sign a big deal with Dell that would mean thousands more units sold per month, and the future was looking great. There was a problem, though. Apparently, Bigfoot Networks was nearly out of cash.

"So, what? I mean, we're not bankrupt, I know we have money coming in. What's the deal?" I asked.

"Well, we're technically insolvent," he said in his CFO speak. "You'll need to let the board know, like today."

"What? What do you mean 'insolvent'?" I asked.

"Well, insolvent is now, the moment when our debts are bigger than our ability to pay them. We're not bankrupt because nobody has filed anything yet. I'm trying to avoid bankruptcy—that's why I started slow paying our suppliers," he said.

"You saw this coming?" I asked, frustrated.

"Well, it's not really that big of a surprise. We never expected this first four million investment to take us all the way," he said.

"True, I guess, I just didn't realize that it was already happening," I said. "We've been looking to raise our next round for a while, but I thought we had more time." In fact, Mike and I had spent days and days traveling to California and Boston meeting with investors, sharing a hotel room, and eating cheap diner food. We hadn't yet had our big partner meeting in Boston to secure our next round. Although we believed that day was coming soon, it hadn't even been scheduled yet.

DOI 10.1515/9781501507083-011

"So, what are our options?" I asked.

"We need cash, and I have a lead to a bridge loan," he said.

"What about our team?" I asked. "I promised to give them at least a month's notice if we were ever in trouble," I explained. I made this promise biweekly to our team as I gave them our business update. I hadn't mentioned it in the last meeting, which was barely a week ago.

"Well, we could pay them for a month more," Mike said, "but if we do, we'll be bankrupt with several of our suppliers, and that would be bad."

"I'll say. So, crap, how long until we can get this bridge loan?" I asked.

"Probably more than a month," Mike said, weirdly calmly.

I just looked at him stunned, like a deer in headlights. "Why are you so calm?" I asked.

"I have an idea," he said, and then hatched his plan to me.

...

A few days later, I stood in our conference room in front of my team of over twenty engineers, testers, and managers. I had just given them the surprise business update, and explained our situation. We were doing well, but cash was a problem. We had a lead on the bridge loan, but that was for suppliers. We had a lead on our next round—several, actually—but it was probably months away.

"So, here's what I'm asking. I don't want to have to downsize and slow down our progress. Instead, I am instituting a voluntary pay deferral program. It is completely optional. Everyone who opts in will get extra stock options and their paycheck will be deferred until we raise our next full round, not the bridge round. You don't have to opt in 100%, you can defer 50%, 25%, or even 0%, if you can't manage it. If I have to pay everyone here, we'll survive one more month, the suppliers be damned. Personally, I'm going on 25% pay until we get funded."

That was my speech. To my surprise, delight, and to this day proudest moment, 100% of the company opted in to take the deferred salary. Most people also took 25%, extending our runway by three additional months. We secured a small bridge loan within the month, raised our next round of $8 million within three months, and closed the Dell deal too. There was still a problem though. How did we get into this mess in the first place?

The answer was obvious. We weren't even trying for profitability. In hindsight, we should have been. I just didn't realize yet how important *being my own boss* really was.

Going Bankrupt or Insolvent

Bankruptcy is when you have debts beyond your means, and paperwork is filed to put you into the legal status of bankrupt, often called Chapter 11 in the United States. There are different types of bankruptcy, each defined as a chapter. Chapter 7 means liquidation of assets, and Chapters 11 and 13 mean the reorganization of the company in an effort to ultimately come out of bankruptcy. To be bankrupt, paperwork is filed in federal bankruptcy court, and evidence is gathered and provided. Having the legal status of bankruptcy carries a lot of very specific meanings to your creditors. Most importantly, it means that they will be paid back under the reorganization plan, or they will not be paid back and must accept the bankruptcy court's liquidation decisions. Although Chapter 11 or 13 is often a slower pay back period, allowing for the company to reorganize and pay them back according to a plan, it is usually preferable to Chapter 7, where the creditors may not get nearly the full amount due paid back. In Chapter 7, creditors line up in order of their liens.

Insolvency is the state right before bankruptcy. It's that moment when, if no actions are taken, you run the risk of upsetting a creditor and them filing bankruptcy on you, potentially laying claim to your assets. Insolvency is an internal state that others may not yet know about. Bankruptcy is a public status with legal paperwork associated with it. It's better to be insolvent and create a plan than to be bankrupt on a federally mandated plan.

Up until this chapter, I have focused on managing cash as your most important metric of survival. Cash is critical, but so is cash flow. Just because you don't have a zero or negative cash balance, it doesn't mean you are solvent. You can have cash in the bank and still be insolvent. If your earnings (profits) are not sufficient to pay for your debts and expenses, and if you don't have enough cash to cover the difference, you are in trouble. That trouble may be coming this month, next month, or some time down the line, but it's coming if you don't take action. If that trouble is this month, you are insolvent, despite having cash in your bank. It's just not enough cash.

To understand this better, Figure 11.1 shows what I call the scales of solvency. On the left side of the scale are things that negatively impact your solvency, and on the right side, positive effects. Notice that the middle of the scale includes things that don't directly impact your solvency, but absolutely do have an indirect effect. Each month, your expenses impact your scale of solvency. Expenses are things like employees and office spaces that are not part of your costs for your product. Presuming that you are selling your products at a profit, gross margin is the difference between your revenue and costs, such that selling product actually generates margin. The big question is: Is that gross margin enough to offset your expenses? It's not the only question, though! You may have other obligations that make your gross margin goal much higher than you thought to achieve profitability, or even solvency. If you have debt, then those debts will have to be paid, either as payment plus interest, or at some later time as a lump sum. In either case, you need to be paying off or saving up to pay off the debt each month and accounting for interest. You may also have deferred some costs or expenses—in effect, delaying payment and artificially boosting gross margins one month (increasing your cash temporarily), but those payments come due in future periods. It's also possible that you extended credit to someone else (a reseller, for example), and they owe you money, leading to expected deferred payments. Those delayed payments come into consideration when figuring out your solvency. This is part of why companies have CFOs and accountants—it can get complex.

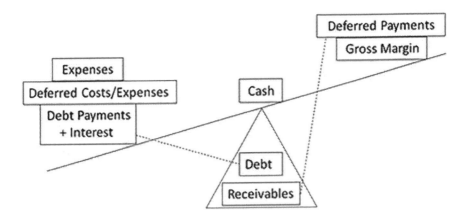

Figure 11.1: The Scales of Solvency

It's the inability to pay (from your cash or assets) your expenses, deferred cost and debt payments, and interest, even after the positive effects of gross margin and deferred payments that make you insolvent. If paying what you owe that month would take you to a negative cash balance, you are insolvent, or soon will be (later that month). It's not an uncommon state to have happen in the future. That's why companies, like Bigfoot Networks, plan several rounds of funding. The problem is, if you don't get funding before that time, you are in a pickle. You will have to take action, and investors will sense your weakness and pounce. You want to avoid being even three months away from insolvency, at all costs. Taking action may be necessary well in advance of the actual month when insolvency would occur.

Corporate Innovation

If you are a corporate innovator, leader of a skunkworks, or manager of a new project/product initiative, you may think that you are immune to bankruptcy and insolvency. You are wrong. Whether you have profit and loss (P&L) responsibility or not, it is all too possible that you will get the dreadful news that your idea is going to get shut down. This chapter is about how to deal with that moment if it comes, but more importantly, how to possibly prevent it.

Insolvency (rather than bankruptcy) is your primary concern when it comes to corporate innovation. Bankruptcy is unlikely because you are a small part of a big company. Unfortunately, you must worry about a few different kinds of insolvency that normal startups don't. First, like a normal startup, you should worry about eventually generating enough profits to sustain your group/division/department/project. Second, running out of budget is somewhat unique to corporate innovation because without budget, you'll have to get more internal funding or start your wind down process. Finally, truly unique to corporate innovation, you must eventually reach a profit margin that is above some threshold that your corporation probably doesn't even tell you about. This undocumented goal is how corporations decide to continue having a product/service as part of their core offering or if they should spin it out or wind it down.

Taking Action on Potential Insolvency

If according to your financial plan and status, insolvency is coming, there are several actions that can be taken to either delay it, or possibly even avoid it altogether. First, you can stop the bleeding and make cuts in expenses, costs, or both. Second, you can make efforts to renegotiate your debts and deferrals. Third, you can raise prices and improve gross margins. Fourth, you can call in receivables and stop offering lines of credit, or reduce the lines of credit. Finally, you can raise additional money, including taking on additional debt. Each technique has its pros and cons, and part of your job as the founder and CEO is knowing when to apply which technique and why. Hopefully, you have a good sense of finance, or have a great teammate, as I had with Mike, to help you figure it out.

Cutting Expenses

The difference between an expense and a cost cannot be understated. A cost is any cash spent in the production of a single unit of your product or service. In order for cash expenditures to be considered a cost, they must vary directly based on the number of units produced or served. An expense does not vary with production and is a fixed or semi fixed amount. I say semi fixed because, contrary to what you may think, cutting expenses is actually a lot easier than cutting costs. In fact, cutting costs may even increase your expenses. Here's why.

Common expenses are rent, payroll (employees), marketing, and miscellaneous (such as paper, travel, entertainment, etc.). Expenses are semi fixed—rent, for example, is often under contract and you have to pay your rent, right? Wrong. You *can* get out of those contracts: you can sublease, break the lease, or simply be evicted for non payment. All of these options make your lease semi fixed. One way to cut expenses is to downsize your rent. Maybe everyone can work from home. Maybe co working or working at an incubator would save money. Don't be afraid to break a lease if you need to cut expenses.

While we are at it, it's pretty easy to go paperless, cut all travel, and eliminate entertainment expense. Should you do it? If insolvency is months away, then yes, you should cut all of that. The only travel you should be doing is the absolutely essential, such as closing a funding round.

Employees are also semi fixed. While you can technically, according to the laws of your state or country, fire your entire team in a day, you will still likely have to pay them through that day, if not through the end of the week or month. So, employees are a semi fixed cost. However, employees can be laid off (fired) or have their salary cut (and they can quit if they want) with one or two months of notice. It's no different than breaking your lease. You may not be able to do it in a day, but a company can go to zero paid employees within a month in almost all cases. Should you, though? That question is a little bit harder, because there are three pressures that are keeping you from downsizing your employees.

First, cutting employees is hard on the soul. The good news is that the best CEOs have no soul. That's kind of a joke, but also not. If the only thing stopping you from downsizing your employees is that you would feel bad, consider that if you don't downsize (or do something), then the entire company goes under and you can't save anyone's job. In my experience, having laid off people and downsized many times, it never gets easier. The best I can do, and hope you can do, is to give employees at least a few weeks of notice or severance. This allows them at least some time to save up and start looking. I always encourage people to look for work while still working for me during their two weeks of notice.

The second reason cutting employees is hard is that it may impact your ability to sell. For this reason, you have to choose whom to cut very carefully. Culling your lowest performers and keeping your top performers is probably the best tactic you can make. Sometimes, it doesn't make sense to fire everyone, because you need employees to keep the sales and production moving. However, if they are not bringing in sales or are not critical to the delivery of product, do you really need them? Maybe not. Even if you do, in times of near insolvency, you have to cut down to the bare minimum. Keeping only your very top performers is common and smart business.

Finally, cutting non essential employees may be difficult for another reason: strategy. It is possible that your strategy is to eventually be acquired. You don't plan to be acquired for your great profits, but rather, for your innovation and team. It's possible that you need to release that new product and it will cause a windfall of revenue. It's possible that you are close to a new software release or a new funding round and need the team to stay focused. It's possible that you need your staff to work on cost savings (see the next section) and need them to stay focused. There are a lot of very strategic reasons to not downsize, or to minimize the downsizing. In these cases, you can always do what I did, and ask people to defer salaries. It's a way to cut your payroll expense in order to remain solvent for just those few more months that you need for the next good thing to happen.

Cutting marketing expense can also help, provided that it doesn't impact sales too much. For this reason, having great analytics and understanding which marketing tactics work and which do not is critical to the successful management of your company. Certainly, cutting all marketing experiments is necessary when insolvency is near. Cutting wasteful marketing or marketing that you are not sure is working is also useful. Ultimately, marketing is probably the easiest expense to cut, but also the last one to consider, provided that it is generating profitable results in sales.

Cutting Costs: Prototyping vs. Scaling Up

Cutting costs is entirely different than cutting expenses. First, costs are the variable costs of production, so they theoretically vary based on how many units you produce. When I say "cutting costs," I mean somehow producing your product or service in a cheaper way. Second, although costs seem variable, and they do vary based on units, they are sometimes also semi fixed. How is that? Costs of production are often tied to contracts, like rent. You agreed to produce at a certain price from your supplier and have a contract that says so. Just like rent, however, every contract is subject to renegotiation. Unlike rent, you probably have more contract options, including simply finding a different supplier or manufacturer. Who's to say you *have* to spend money with the supplier who won't help you reduce costs and wants to stick to their contract? Let them have their contract, and simply don't do business with them anymore. Hopefully you were smart and didn't negotiate anything exclusive, but even if you did, you can always break the contract or take the easy way out and do a product reboot.

It's easy to say, "Sure, reduce costs, make stuff cheaper, and that would be great." More gross margins should mean you can pay off your debts faster and pay your expenses too. There is just one big problem: How do you reduce costs? Wouldn't you have already done that? Not necessarily, and I will explain why.

When you build a new product, let's start with a physical good, you prototype. Prototyping is usually done with off the shelf components and whatever will get the job done. In electronics, this means buying from retail stores like RadioShack, or online component stores like Digi Key. These stores are great for small quantity orders and quick shipping, but miserable at volumes. So, two things are making your product cost more. First, you used the same parts you prototyped with, and those parts, while expedient, may not be optimized for cost. Second, you might be buying from a non optimal (for volume) supplier or the wrong quantities (price breaks at volume). Either way, your prototyping process is very different from the scaling up for production process. You need to now spend some time (and, probably, money) investing in cost reducing your manufacturing process, parts, components, design, and everything for the product you previously only prototyped.

There is a problem. It may take money, time, and resources to invest in those cost reductions of your products. If you are insolvent, this is money that you can't afford. Instead, you should invest in this earlier, when you know the product is selling, but before you have reached solvency issues.

For service businesses, similar issues can arise. Do you know the optimal number of service staff to make the business run smoothly and efficiently? If your service takes supplies (parts, chemicals, etc.), have you found a good supplier that offers you volume and repeat purchase options for your supplies? Remember, optimizing a service business for cost is the same as for a product—you need to optimize the process and eliminate costs where you can. Buying in bulk, reducing steps, getting the optimal staff size, and reducing do overs (unplanned service calls) are all essential to optimizing your service business.

So, what is more important—building and designing for cost or rapid prototyping to find product market fit? Actually, they are both important in the right order. First, you must find product market fit, which means rapid prototyping and service deployment. You should not be optimizing costs when you are still trying to figure out if customers want your product or service and how to sell to them. However, once you start to gain traction, that's when investing in cost reductions is important, because the extra margin can save the day and balance the scales of solvency when you need it most.

Renegotiating

Suppliers don't want you to go out of business. If you've gotten a line of credit from a supplier, but you've extended lines of credit to resellers (a common scenario), you aren't in that bad of shape. Often, you can call your suppliers and renegotiate payment terms. They may want to see your contracts with resellers and look at your books to become a bit more confident in your status, but it is likely they will extend your credit and change the payment terms to help you out (if they can). The bigger the supplier, the more likely they will be able to help you out of your jam. Renegotiating is a great way to get unstuck from your solvency issues.

You can also renegotiate with investors, landlords (rent), employees (deferred salaries), and even banks (unlikely). Each of these parties—in fact, everyone you interact with—has a vested interest in you surviving. Nobody wins in bankruptcy, but a few months' delay in paying back an investor or paying rent could save your company and make you solvent forever after that.

Raising or Lowering Prices and Calling in Receivables

Renegotiating with resellers is a bit more difficult. Calling in a receivable early is pretty uncommon, and most companies wouldn't do it. You might get them to pay early if you offer them a discount or rebate to do so. Odds are, though, you may not be able to get people who owe you money (in a receivable or other instrument) unless you incentivize them or they are just sitting on piles of cash (unlikely). Instead, many banks and investors offer loans on your receivables. These loans (called *factoring receivables*) are great, but just like any small business loan, they will likely require collateral. The collateral for a startup with solvency issues is your house, so don't do that. It's better to go bankrupt with your business than to go bankrupt and lose your house too. Never put your personal assets at risk with your business. It's just not smart. You can always start a new business if this one goes bankrupt.

Another technique to consider is raising prices. While raising prices seems like it would help tip the scales towards solvency, the problem is that customers don't like it. Very few people want to pay more for something that was cheaper last week, and they will find out. Instead of raising prices, offering gold plated versions (or versions that are premium in some way) is a way to raise average prices without changing your core offering. The problem there is that gold plated versions cost money (R&D or increased costs), which you cannot afford to gamble with right now.

What about lowering prices? Wouldn't that hurt margins? Yes, it would. If your costs are the same and you offer discounts or lower prices, you don't make as much per sale. That said, if the discount gets you incremental sales, then it may increase total margins by selling more volume. Moving inventory can also help your cash position in the short term and help you survive another month. The math is actually pretty complex here, but the following table may help you decide if lowering prices makes sense. The core idea is, if lowering prices or offering discounts does not make sense in the long term to drive more sales, it doesn't make sense to do it to solve your solvency issues, either—try something else.

Table 11.1: When to Lower Prices

Question	Formula	Decision
Is there any per unit margin left to raise prices?	Price—Cost > 0	If you can't lower prices very much because of tight margins, then don't lower prices.
Do you have inventory that is moving slowly?	Inventory > 1 month supply	If you don't have a lot of excess inventory, anyway, then don't lower prices.
Would lowering prices cause sales to increase enough to cover the lowered price?	Margin Loss * Total Units Sold < New Total Margin * Increase in Units Sold	If reducing price doesn't cause enough new units to be sold at the new margin to cover the margin lost, then don't lower prices.
Will it hurt your brand to offer lower prices or discounts?	Are you a premium brand?	If no, and if all the above are okay, then offering discounts may help improve both your short and long term cash position.

The Rapid Decline in Price

So, you lowered the price or started offering discounts. This is common, and it feels like the right thing to do according to the matrix above. There are three problems that can now occur that may cause a slippery slope for those increased volumes. All three of these problems can cause a rapid decline in your price and, ultimately, more solvency problems than you had before.

First, the increase in volumes by decreasing price (a very natural thing) can cause you to think that you can go lower in price and get even more volumes. While it is true that price and volumes are related, the relationship is non linear.

Many economics courses in college draw linear relationships between price and volume (the demand curve). However, most real economics are nonlinear, and may even have discontinuities. These discontinuities are market factors that happen in the real world, such as brand erosion and discount dependency. Figure 11.2 below shows the classical demand curve from micro economics as compared to a more realistic one from my own experience. The classic demand curve shows that as price goes down, demand goes up, and more sales can happen. It also shows that there is an optimal point at which to price a product, right where supply and demand optimally intersect with each other. My more realistic example comes from when I sold tablet computers at Key Ingredient. We found that there were certain prices that the market expected, and those caused discontinuities in price (it was non linear). Sure, we could discount a little and get some boost in sales, but discounting more didn't seem to help at all because of the price discontinuity—we were suddenly in a different price band where price changes didn't matter again until we went much lower. We also found that discounting too heavily eventually caused sales to decrease, because people expected that the product would not be very good. We also found that the demand curve was more controlled by the presence of competitors than it was with our own price. How competitors priced their products actually affected our sales more in the long run than our supply or price. All of this is to say, if lowering price worked once for you, do not expect it to work again. Follow the formulas from the prior section each time to ensure that it makes sense to give it a try.

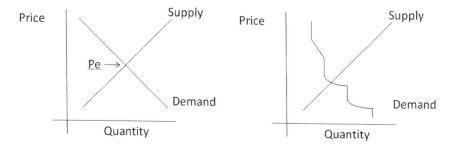

Figure 11.2: Classic Supply and Demand Curve vs. Realistic Supply and Demand Curve

Second, customers can become accustomed to the price declines, your competitors can become accustomed to the price declines, and suddenly, your premium product is a commodity. Once you start to lower prices, you will find that competitors will react. Once they react, you may have to react again. All of this combined with your end customers getting these great deals, and suddenly, a really good Blu ray player costs $50 and gets barely $5 of margin. All these factors can cause your great product to be worth less, simply because you took the first step toward price wars. My advice: don't do it! Instead, consider launching multiple versions of your product at different price points. This can help keep your premium product pricing strong while entering new markets. Pricing adjustments should only accompany new market entrances and goals. The timing should be right, and ideally, margins held strong throughout.

Finally, those increased volumes can become addicting and can make sales expectations from your board of directors go up even higher than before. Just because your pricing discount caused you to move more volume this month does not mean that next month it will be the same. Moving too much product too soon can cannibalize your market, leaving you with too few remaining customers to sustain that growth. If you had grown more slowly, the board pressure for sales would have been kept at the right level, and you could have focused on market expansion techniques from Chapter 9. Instead, by getting those incremental sales, you may be left with unreasonable and incorrect expectations for the future. A better investor (your board of directors) would understand that sticking to a pricing and volume plan is more important than getting those incremental sales too early. In fact, if things are going well, and you have at least three months left before solvency issues, it's a good time to raise those additional funds for market expansion.

Raising Additional Funds

Timing is everything. Knowing when to raise additional money from investors is a particularly important thing to time correctly. The ideal timing is right after you have achieved a major milestone, but well before you actually need the additional funds. Your milestone achievement gives you a step function up in value, while your lack of needing money today gives you plenty of time to negotiate the best terms for the deal. Mess up any of that, and you may end up releasing control of your company to the investors. This happens when investors (not founders) own more than 50% of the company. When that happens, bad things can happen quickly (see Chapter 12).

Milestones are major events that signal something very positive about your company. These are often customer related, such as getting a major customer, a huge order, or hitting some sales milestone. They can also be market related, such as launching in a new market, releasing a new product, or getting some amazing new press. It could even be cost savings related—hitting some new low cost metric of production or bringing that new factory online. Whatever the event, you will know, because it means investors now believe even more in your company and should be willing to pay a higher stock price than before. This is important to you, because it means you will get more capital for the company without giving up quite as much as you otherwise would have. Remember, at the end of the day, when you sell the company, it's how much you own (after the liquidation preferences) that determines how much wealth you create for yourself and your future endeavors.

If you are too close to insolvency, however, despite hitting a major milestone, investors will be able to sense it (by seeing it in your financials) and will get more of your company than you would otherwise have accepted if you had plenty of cash available. They know that you don't want to slow down or lay anyone off, and they are counting on your good nature to make a better deal for themselves. It's not evil, it's just business. Your defense is to say "no," and be willing to make all the cuts described in this chapter. In fact, you need to have either cash, profitability, or both in your back pocket, or else you could end up losing control of your company when solvency issues arise, as they so commonly do. Delaying that funding until you are profitable may be the only way for you to say "no" to a bad investment deal.

Deciding When to Go for Profitability

So, when is the right time to go for profitability? Is it just when you are nearing insolvency? Is it when investors are sensing your weakness? The answer to this is simple: strategy. There are two strategic elements to consider as the right time to go for profitability.

First, it is strategically important to go for *contingent profitability* as soon as possible, but not actually achieve profitability. This is strategically important because it gives you all the ammunition you need to say "no" to investors. What does contingent profitability mean? It means that if you wanted, you have a contingency plan that puts your monthly net income into the black (becoming profitable starting the following month, and staying so). This plan may involve any combination of cuts, pricing adjustments, and credit adjustments, but ultimately, if you wanted to be, you could be profitable. This should be a well documented contingency plan that you can share with investors at any time. You can honestly say, "If we wanted to be profitable next month, we could—here is how." For the power to be effective, you need to be willing to put it into place at least a few months before you would otherwise be insolvent. This gives you time to raise more funds from investors, but be able to decline bad terms. It's power. The power of profitability (even contingent profitability) is incredible.

Second, going for *real profitability* is a strategy question that is related to your industry and goals. If you have a goal of running this business as a lifestyle business, meaning growing it enough to generate your own personal income and wealth, but not necessarily for a big exit, then you should go for real profitability as soon as the company has reached the size that you desire. Once the company is as big as you want it, you can stop re investing your profits into growth, and instead, start paying out dividends to yourself and any investors you may have. You will still retain some of the profits for cash and rainy day funds, and maintain your current level, but any excess can be paid out as dividends. Dividends to investors obviously don't occur until all of your loans are paid out and you have plenty of cash to weather the normal uses and needs of your business. Many companies, however, are not designed to ever reach real profitability. Instead, they are intended to grow as fast as they can (by investing all profits into growth), such that eventually they can be sold or IPO as big as possible. Technology companies are examples of this type, and they may not even achieve profitability after the IPO or sale, as they continue to invest and expand. Continual growth is valued more than mere profits. Strategically, if you are able to invest profits and keep growing and expanding, most investors and public markets will want you to. You will only harvest profits after you have reached a massive size or peaked out your growth. It's all about strategy. However, having the plan for contingent profitability is all about power—your power to control your own destiny!

A Quantitative Contingent Profitability Plan

If you wanted to, could you be profitable right now? It's an important question that is worth calculating and considering at all times. This is your contingent profitability plan. Being profitable doesn't get you out of Chapter 11 bankruptcy, nor does it make you turn from insolvent to solvent, but it does show a path forward. It is important to understand at any time whether you could be profitable if you chose, and what that company would look like. Knowing this and knowing your cash rate can allow you to make different decisions today that might avoid Chapter 11 or insolvency tomorrow. If you can see that you are headed for insolvency and that investors are threatening to delay their investment (to get more of your company), call their bluff and execute on your contingent profitability plan. Sometimes, just having the plan is enough. The following table outlines the steps to create a contingent profitability plan.

Table 11.2: Contingent Profitability Plan

Steps	Quantitative Action
1. Calculate how close you are to profitability now.	Net Income Gap = (Prior Month's Net Income)
2. Determine what marketing and sales efforts are needed to maintain current sales (not incrementally grow more sales).	# of Salespeople, $ Marketing Spend
3. Determine what other key employees/staff are essential to maintaining current sales (not growing or expanding new product lines).	# of Other Employees Necessary
4. Determine how much savings you could get by cutting expenses, without sacrificing any long term relationships or breaking any contracts or leases.	$ Savings in Non lease/Non contract Expenses
5. Create a financial model where you have the salespeople and staff from 2 & 3, marketing spend from 2, and lowered expenses from 4.	Does this model show net income going positive? If so, done!
6. If still not "contingent profitable," calculate if you should break your lease, reduce inventories, and even consider lower prices to move more sales. Now, remodel.	Does this model show net income going positive? If not, you probably cannot get to contingent profitability today. Consider investing in cost reductions, and optimizing marketing and sales efforts for best effectiveness.

This contingent profitability plan is a set of cuts and changes that would make you profitable, as well as a new financial model based on this plan. Growth under the contingent profitability plan will likely be very slow, if at all, and that is okay. You are not growing under this plan. You are saving up to grow later. If you can generate net income every month and save it up, you can then eventually either get an investor, or simply invest that cash excess in growth projects.

Note that this plan does not assume any improvements from cost savings or increasing sales. The reason for this is that cost savings usually require an investment and are not guaranteed to pan out. Also, increasing sales is not as easy as hiring more salespeople or spending more in marketing—it's usually far more involved than that. A contingent profitability plan must be doable at your current sales level, or else it's not possible. If it's not possible, the world is not over, you just need to realize that you probably need to cut costs of production or further expand your sales to be able to cover your expenses. This might mean that you have to give up more of your company to investors than you wanted. If this happens, all is not lost, and Chapter 12 can help you avoid getting fired.

The Story of IngZ, Inc.

"This is going to be so cool."

This was the sentiment of the entire IngZ, Inc. team as we pushed hard to build what we thought would be an amazing game. *Traveller AR* was going to be a role playing game (RPG) like no other. It would be based on the popular pen and paper RPG called *Traveller*, for which we had a license to build the game for mobile (iPhone and Android). It was going to have augmented reality (AR) technology and use your geolocation. It would also overlay the game of a space battle all around you in the air.[1] It was going to be a game of epic scale and grandeur. It was going to be awesome.

My role at IngZ was in marketing. I was tasked with building a website, videos, marketing materials, and attracting a huge pre launch audience. I was given a budget, goals, and free reign. It was super fun to be featured in online articles, discussed in forums, and even showcased at Comic Con (the most intense trade show in the world for games like this). We were quite successful in generating a ton of buzz and excitement around the game. The market was ready.

The CEO of IngZ was Tony Howlett, a very successful entrepreneur in past endeavors. He had been so successful that he was funding the entire company himself and had already launched several successful apps into the marketplace. These apps were getting decent downloads and doing well for their category, but certainly did not generate enough money to fund the company, its prior apps, and the development of the new *Traveller AR* game.

Tony was also a huge fan of *Traveller* pen and paper games, and wanted nothing more than to see this game launch and be a huge success. He had built a great team of programmers and artists to create the game, and development was proceeding along many different paths at the same time. The AR features were coming along nicely, and the back end server systems were going well. The front end graphics were coming together, especially the expensive 3D graphics. Marketing was going well, as we had built up excitement, e mails, preorders, and more through our marketing efforts. So, what went wrong?

---

[1] https://www.youtube.com/watch?v=SwUuCO6CVj4

There were three problems that all came together to put IngZ, Inc. into insolvency. First, IngZ's burn rate was tilted way to the left. Expenses—specifically, art contractors and programmers—were much too high because of the intense development going on with *Traveller AR*. Although the game was shaping up, the scope of the game was so big that it was going to take a lot more resources to finish the game and get something playable into the marketplace. At the same time, development and marketing of IngZ's other apps had diminished, and growth had stalled. The other apps all had good potential, but almost the entire IngZ team and dollars were shifted to *Traveller AR*. As a result, income from the other apps, which was already low, nearly dried up. The prior money invested in those apps was now a sunk cost. Finally, exacerbating all of this was the fact that very few, if any, investors were interested in investing in app and game companies. Tony would have had to shift almost all of his focus to fundraising—and do so for many months, if not years, before he really needed it (in case of insolvency)—in order to raise funds for his app/game company.

In the end, *Traveller AR* took up too many resources and Tony's self funding ran out. He smartly decided not to risk his house or his retirement, and decided to end the project. Bankruptcy was completely avoided because Tony had no debt to pay off. The only casualties were employees (who were given plenty of notice) and *Traveller AR*, which never really got launched out of the early beta version.

What could Tony have done differently?

Although bankruptcy was avoided due to Tony smartly not taking on debts he could not pay, in hindsight, many things could have been done differently with other possible outcomes. First, the scope of *Traveller AR* was so big that it was probably unrealistic to believe that the game would ship or be successful with all the features the team had wanted to include. Things may have been different if *Traveller AR* were a bit less ambitious and if the scope of the project were smaller so that it could have been launched into the market sooner. There was demand for a *Traveller* game, but did it really have to be AR? Augmented reality was perhaps a bit ahead of its time—as of 2017, it's still not commonplace.

Second, the decision to not seek outside funding early on in the IngZ, Inc. history meant that they were dependent on only Tony's personal investment. This dependency created a cliff wall where the company would end. This cliff could have been calculated regularly, and plans could have been put into place at least six months before the end. Those plans could have included seeking outside funding, as well as making cuts and pushing for profitability. Which cuts? Cuts in the scope of *Traveller AR*, for sure, but also cuts in operating expenses, marketing expenses (yes, that would have included me), and even internal headcount. Although it is unlikely that profitability could have been achieved, the runway might have been extended a bit further and given the company more time to seek additional outside funding.

In the end, IngZ, Inc. died too early. Several of its apps had huge potential, and, given time, I believe investors would have seen that potential. The potential for even a much lighter 2D only version of *Traveller AR* was also significant, and I believe the game would have made a big splash in the market. The future of *Traveller AR* with all the features that Tony and the team envisioned would have been grander still, but shooting for the moon all at once was probably the decision that led to insolvency.

Chapter 12
I Got Fired and I'm the Founder—How?

This is what happened as I remember it.

"Listen, if you don't agree to hire Mr. Howse as the new CEO, the other board members are going to overrule you, vote you out, and may even take their investments back out of Bigfoot's bank account," Brian said, as we stood in my small office during a break in the monthly board meeting at Bigfoot Networks. Brian was our first investor in Bigfoot Networks, and he had $4 million dollars invested in us. He had a board seat, but his was not the biggest at the table. Our other investor, Northbridge Ventures, had two seats. They had invested $8 million, and were planning to invest another $8 million very soon.

I just looked at him, dumbfounded at what he was saying. Those were some scary comments, and in truth, I couldn't say exactly what it was that I didn't like about Mr. Howse. On paper, Mr. Howse had some prior experience that could really help us. He had extensive experience marketing gaming hardware products, and he had experience as a startup CEO. The only thing that wasn't perfect about him was his "California ness." He lived, after all, in California, and Bigfoot Networks was based in Austin, Texas. My silence seemed to have provoked Brian to say more.

"Harlan, you have to understand, I'm trying to help you. The other members sent me to talk to you about this. They are serious. They are going to overrule and replace you if you refuse to hire Mr. Howse. You have to step down as CEO and take a role as CTO and VP of Engineering. It's Mr. Howse, or the game is over," Brian said, sounding like he was on my side.

"What do you think?" I asked.

"I think he's the best we're going to find. We've interviewed ten others, and he's the only one who the other board members will accept. It doesn't matter how things are going, they want a new CEO who will light a rocket under Bigfoot Networks. They also want you to focus more on the technical side," Brian explained.

"But he said that he won't move to Austin. He's going to move the headquarters to California," I said, still not convinced.

"That's good for you. You get to keep running the engineering side here," Brian said.

"Brian, this seems like a slippery slope. He's going to cost money, want to hire more people, and spend the money really fast," I started.

"That's the point—the board wants him to spend faster than you are," Brian said, as if he weren't also part of the board. "They want you to focus on tech.

DOI 10.1515/9781501507083-012

Listen, it's kind of irrelevant, anyway. You don't have a choice. If you don't agree to hire Mr. Howse, the board is threatening to take back their investment and close down the doors of Bigfoot forever."

Later that day, I made my biggest mistake while running Bigfoot Networks—I hired my replacement CEO. I was out as CEO of Bigfoot Networks. Within twelve months, I had resigned altogether as an employee of the company that I had started. I was the person with the original idea, the gumption to launch the company, and I had raised $20 million, but I was out. Despite all twelve of Bigfoot's patents being in my name, I was no longer the CEO and guiding force of Bigfoot Networks.

What the hell happened?

How to Get Fired and Lose Your Startup

There are four ways to get separated from the startup that you founded or co founded. First, if you commit a crime and get sentenced to prison, or lose a lawsuit of some kind in which you have to give up your assets, you could get fired and lose your stock. Second, if you personally have less than 50.1% of controlling stock and your co founders (and investors or whomever has enough stock to control 50.1%) all agree that you should be fired, you will get fired. Third, if you and your co founders have less than 50.1% and the other shareholders (usually investors) all agree and have enough stock to vote you out, you are out. Finally, you can quit. Each scenario is possible, but none of them are the end of your life. You can and will go on after being separated from the startup you created. You can always start another.

Most companies in the United States are run by a CEO. The general operation of the company, including hiring and firing of the other employees, is the sole purview of the CEO. There is a distinction between being an employee and being a stockholder. Employees are paid wages and are on the payroll of the company. Stockholders simply hold stock of some kind, and may or may not also be employees. During the early days of a company, there are probably no employees. It is most likely just you and your co founders (if any). You are not employees, per se, because the company isn't paying you yet. More than likely, you have some founder stock, and if you are smart, you and your co founders are still vesting in that stock, in exchange for you all to be working on the company without pay.

Eventually, one or more of the founders may need to go full time and work for the company. This means making them an employee (or even just a contractor), in which case, the company is now paying the founder for work. This is usually in addition to the founder stock they are already vesting in. Usually, the first person to be hired will be the CEO, followed by a technical employee, then marketing, and last, finance. Hiring the CEO is actually one of the sole responsibilities of the company's board of directors. So, who are they?

The board of directors of a company are those shareholders (people who own stock) who have demanded by right of ownership to have a seat on the board. In large, public companies, these seats are elected by the shareholders, and it's not that different for a startup. As founders and co founders, you will agree who is on the board—usually the first founder, and maybe one or two of your co founders. During this phase of your company, management is easy, because you have just each other to deal with. Once you have investors, though, all of that changes. While you are still small, just you (the founder) and your co founders will choose the CEO. This choice may not seem like that big of a deal, but in reality, it is huge. The CEO is the one who will have the power from that point on, and the board of directors will have just one power: to hire or fire the CEO, if they can. If you are the CEO and you have 50.1% of the voting stock, you cannot be fired unless you quit. Being in that position is the only true safety you can ever have in controlling your own destiny within the company.

Managing Boards of Directors

As your company grows, you may end up taking on investors. Investors are non founders who get stock in exchange for putting money into your company. If these investors put in enough stock (50.1% in total), this can force you to give them a board of directors' seat by means of a shareholder vote. These investors could also make a board of directors' seat a requirement for their willingness to invest. This is quite common in investments that get over 10% of your company stock. Regardless of how it happens, eventually, you may find yourself on or reporting to a board of directors. Managing that relationship is vital to the company's continued success.

A board of directors is motivated by two competing forces.[1] First, they have a duty to do what is best for the corporation, ensuring its survival and its ability to grow and thrive. Second, they usually have a personal duty to the stockholders whom they represent, and to look out for the best interests of the stockholders. If these two forces are ever in conflict, the board is supposed to look out for the

---

[1] https://www.forbes.com/sites/hbsworkingknowledge/2015/09/16/the-real-duty-of-the-board-of-directors/#581fcdf9768f

interests of the company above those of the shareholder. In practice, for small private companies, this is very subjective and open to interpretation. The key point here is that board members should never threaten to destroy the company on behalf of their shareholders. If board members threatened to take their investment out of a company they had already invested in, this would be against the company's interests, and would violate the board of directors' role. Nevertheless, as in the case of Bigfoot Networks, threats can and do get made. It's up to you to first try to prevent the threats from ever being made, and second, to know your rights and your power as a founder, CEO, and minority or majority stakeholder.

The power that boards of directors do have is limited to what the company has agreed they will have in their charter and founding documents, such as their articles of incorporation. Most commonly, those powers are the standard powers that all boards of directors in the United States automatically get—the ability to hire and fire the CEO, and the ability to inspect the company's books at any time. Although these powers are the ones they certainly get, most boards are also investors. Remember, your current investors are likely your future investors, so keeping them happy is important, even if they are minority stakeholders (less than 50%). As a result, most boards of directors also function in the following way.

First, boards of directors usually meet, in person or virtually, every month or quarter for a business update. That update is a chance for the CEO to present the financials of the business, as well as any business updates that the board may be interested in hearing. Second, boards of directors usually request—and the CEO provides—a business forecast in the form of a business plan, and the financial forecast for the coming year. This forecast is usually based on a realistic model of what the company expects to happen financially over the year. As each month or quarter progresses, this plan might be changed based on what really happened, and these results may be presented to the board of directors. A simple KPI plan versus reality dashboard, as shown in Table 12.1 below, is all that is required to show how well things are going. Although not every number is met, a good trend is demonstrated, and Q3 was particularly strong. This CEO is doing well, but it would have been better to meet the plan every quarter than to miss two of the three quarters of the year.

Table 12.1: Board of Directors' KPI Plan Versus Reality Dashboard

	Q1	Q2	Q3	Q4
Planned Sales	$250,000	$350,000	$450,000	$550,000
Actual Sales	$210,000	$300,000	$475,000	TBD
% Achieved	84%	85%	106%	
Planned Net Income	$50,000	$40,000	$96,000	$143,000
Actual Net Income	$100,000	$60,000	$44,000	TBD
% Achieved	100%	50%	46%	

The most important thing you can do to maintain good relations with a board of directors is to have a clear plan that you consistently meet or exceed. Failing to meet the plan that you set out for the year or quarter is the first sign to board members that they may need to use their other power and fire the CEO. They probably wouldn't jump right to that, and would instead ask for explanations, reasoning, an action plan, and may even ask you to hire or fire someone from the team. In the end, though, your failure to meet or exceed the expectations that you helped set is what may cause the board of directors to consider a change.

Another way to ensure good relations and manage your board is to also understand their unwritten expectations. This is one area where I personally failed in the past. Although I was setting and meeting expectations quarterly and annually with Bigfoot Networks' board of directors, our growth was simply not as fast as some of our board members wanted. They wanted Bigfoot to grow faster now, not a year from now, which was a reason they wanted a new CEO. I wasn't investing their money into the company fast enough, nor growing as fast as they wanted, despite hitting my plan. Understanding, uncovering, and addressing their hidden motivations, as well as convincing the members that your plan is better, is a step toward keeping the big chair (CEO).

As previously mentioned, the only way to be sure to keep your seat as CEO is to maintain 50.1% ownership of the company. In practice, this would work out as a shareholder vote. The board of directors could decide to fire you (their only power), but if you are also on the board (and with 50.1%, you should be), you can negate their decision. If pressed or voted on by the board, you would simply demand a shareholder vote, and, since you control 50.1%, you would win and stay on as CEO. If it gets there, though, those investors would probably not invest in you again, and you may have bigger troubles in the future. If you can resolve it before it gets to a "We'll fire you" stage, you should try.

Firing and Laying Off Co Founders

It's not just the founding CEO who might get fired. Any employee of the company could be fired at any time for any reason (at least in Texas and most of the USA). Even a non employee who is vesting in stock could be fired. This would happen if you had, say, a co founder who was no longer pulling their weight or stopped working. You would simply say, "I'm sorry, we're going to have to let you go and terminate your vesting." This would end their vesting and, although they weren't technically fired, they would only get to keep the stock they vested into, and the company would keep whatever they didn't vest. Another way of laying off a co-founder is simply not hiring them in the first place, and possibly terminating their vesting. You can do this as long as you and the other co founders not getting fired all collectively agree and control 50.1% of the stock. Once they are an employee though, things get harder.

Deciding to hire a co founder as an employee or even a contractor means that you want them to work more on your startup and commit more time to the startup. If you hire them as the CEO, you now can only fire them with a board of directors' vote (which you may very well control, anyway, if you have 50.1% of the common stock). Nevertheless, firing a CEO can have other dire consequences, as will be discussed later. If you hire them for any other role, then it's the manager or the CEO who can fire them after that. Firing a co founder, though, is not something to be taken lightly. You are essentially firing someone who helped you start the company. They will keep any stock they have vested. They also know a lot about your company. It's not impossible to do it, but it might be better to do it a little carefully.

One approach is to convince them that it's not working out and ask if they'd be willing to step down. This way, they get to resign and save face. They may disagree, though, and think that they are doing fine or will get better. In that case, you could offer them a different role in the company—maybe a lower role, or one in a different department. This, again, allows them to save face, stay involved in the company they helped to co found, and hopefully do a better job. This is actually quite common when you want to grow the team bigger. You might ask the co founder who was, until now, your VP of Sales to step down to Director of Sales as you plan to bring in a seasoned VP to take on the VP role. It might not go well, but if the company needs that seasoned VP, you have to do your best here. Offering a lower role and explaining how it will help everyone's stock is the best you can do. Ultimately, they will agree and stay, or quit—it's on them. As a worst case scenario, simply saying that it's their last day, and terminating them will be painful now, but if it's necessary, it's necessary—that's why you're the CEO.

Avoiding Getting Fired

There are two scenarios to consider for you to avoid getting fired yourself. First, consider the scenario in which you are the founder/CEO and you have less than 50% of voting stock. This means you could be fired at any minute. You avoid getting fired by keeping the board of directors happy with your performance. That means having a clear, executed plan, and hitting your numbers. If things go badly and you miss some numbers, clearly communicating why it happened and your plan to fix it could save your job. There is something else that could also save your job, which will be covered in detail later—threatening to sue if they fire you.

A second scenario is that you are a founder or co founder and you are not the CEO. Whether you control 50% of the voting stock or not, you could be fired by the CEO (it's their prerogative). You might then challenge the CEO as a stockholder, fire them, and take on the role of CEO (if you own enough stock), but for a short while at least, you'll be fired. Most likely, though, if you are not the CEO, you probably also don't own more than 50% of the voting stock. Regardless, avoiding getting fired is what you would do in any job. Perform well and provide good evidence that you are preforming well. It's not enough to be doing well if nobody knows about it. You should prepare regular reports to your boss (probably the CEO) about the performance you and your team. These reports should have quantitative data as to the goals you were given by your manager (or CEO) and your achievement of these goals. Table 12.2 shows an example of a KPI dashboard for a VP of Engineering.

Table 12.2: Example KPI Dashboard

	Q1	Q2	Q3	Q4
Planned New Product/Feature Launches	1	3	5	8
Actual New Product/Feature Launches	1	4	6	TBD
% New Product/Feature Launches Achieved	100%	133%	120%	

In addition to performing well, having a good relationship with your managers, a positive attitude, and generally a healthy company will all help you avoid getting fired. "Fired" is a strong term, and it implies wrongdoing or poor performance. Being "let go" because the company can no longer afford you is similar to being fired—you are still without a job. As a co founder or founder, in particular, you should do your best to try to stay abreast of the company's financial status. How is the company doing? Is money tight? If it is, you should think hard about how you can help extend that runway, even offering cuts for your department to help out. It also goes without saying that staying out of trouble with the law (including civil court) will help keep you from getting fired too. This means no sexual harassment, no embezzlement, no fraud, and generally being a good citizen.

As a founder or co founder, getting fired is unlikely, as long as you are doing your job and not breaking the law. Firing a founder can generate bad press and cause a potentially big lawsuit (see later in this chapter). That said, it doesn't mean your newly hired CEO who doesn't really want you there won't make your life miserable. After all, if you quit, they don't have to fire you.

To Quit or Not to Quit

If you were a founder or co founder, you had power. The power to work on what you want, keep your own hours, and to generally see that what you do matters. You had complete control, or at least a big say in the direction of the company. Life was good. Then, you missed a quarter's performance. Then you missed another. Not by a lot, but just a little. Your board of directors convinced you, bullied you, or outvoted you into hiring a new boss (or CEO). You are now just an employee with some stock. Your life is now miserable. What does this miserable life look like?

As a former CEO or senior leader in what used to be your company, there are a number of things that may now feel like utter pain. First, you no longer have as big a say, if any, in the direction of the company. This means that what you thought was the best possible plan is now shredded, and a new plan has been put into place by the new bosses. All that hard work, all that vision you had, and all those hours are wasted. The new plan may not even seem like a good one to you. In fact, it may seem super conservative and not very visionary at all. That's why they hired this new leader in the first place. They wanted someone who is not like you. They wanted someone more cautious, but willing to spend money to push the ball forward more quickly (usually in sales and marketing efforts), while you probably wanted to continue innovating. To you, the company feels completely different now.

To make matters worse, the new bosses have brought their own culture to the company. Gone now are the *beer Fridays* and the team lunch Wednesdays. Gone is the camaraderie and clowning around that used to make every day fun at work. Now, work is work. In fact, you have to keep somewhat normal hours now. People no longer work until 8 pm or 9 pm every day. Most people leave at—gasp—6 pm. What happened?

If that weren't all, your new role sucks too. The actual job you are asked to do doesn't use your talents one bit. In fact, you are bored out of your mind with your new role. You feel marginalized and that what you do no longer matters to the company. You don't even have much of a team anymore. You are barely in management at all. It's so bad, you are thinking, *Hey, maybe I should just quit*.

I don't want to be just doom and gloom. There are some good sides of your new role (often, VP of Business Development, CTO, or Sales Director). First, you have been seeing more of your family and friends with those 9 am–6 pm hours. You got a pay increase, even though you have lower responsibility (probably because you were underpaying yourself before, as is common and quite correct). You are getting to travel more for business, and even going to conferences just to learn things. Your day to day expectations aren't that high. Maybe you shouldn't quit this sweet gig.

I cannot tell you whether to quit or not. Personally, I quit. When this happened to me, I decided to give up and go start something new. Some days I regret it, because maybe I could have made a difference in the final outcome. I certainly would have made more money staying on, but money is not everything. In most cases, it is financially smarter to stay on than to quit. Start your new business on the side while you are still getting paid. Be sure to only work on the new business at home on your personal gear to avoid IP entanglement. Start something completely non competitive to be safe. I often wish I had taken this path. I didn't, though. I quit. Why? It was just too painful to see my culture die, all the funding I had raised slip away, and the core of the company's vision completely forgotten. For you, decide whether you can you stomach it for a bit longer. If you can possibly stay, and start your new thing on the side, it's probably better for you financially to stay on as long as you can stand it.

Corporate Innovation

Quitting from a corporate innovation project can be slightly different than quitting from a startup. First, it may be possible to simply go back to your old job or transfer to another department. It may take time, but letting management know you are in need of a change back to your old job or something new is totally possible inside a corporation. Moving around to different jobs is quite common in larger organizations.

While quitting a role is something unique to corporate innovation, getting fired (the subject of the rest of this chapter) is not unique at all. If anything, getting fired or pushed out of the corporation altogether, is probably worse than getting fired from a startup. Startups grow and die all the time, so leaving or being let go from one of them is commonplace. Being fired from a big organization usually will require more explanation to people that may want to hire you in the future. Was there downsizing involved? Why were you cut and not someone else? Be ready for the outside world not to understand why you were the one to be asked to leave, if it happens. One good answer: because I wanted to work on faster, more innovative things, and my internal project simply got too big for me.

When to Sue

The power of the founder/co founder is much higher than you might think, regardless of how much stock you have. The power of the CEO founder/co founder is even higher still. That power? It is your ability to sue or threaten to sue. It may sound dirty, devious, and wrong, but it is a power you should not ignore. As with all power, if you threaten to use it, you must follow through as well. So, when should you sue or threaten to sue, and how is this so powerful?

The short answer is that you should only threaten to sue if you intend to follow through. Before you make such a threat, hire a lawyer. Never hire the company lawyer—instead, hire someone who is a trial lawyer and has experience suing. Many of these lawyers will work for a contingency fee (they only get paid if you win or settle). Contingent lawyers are fine, but pay them for this first task in cash. Write a letter to the board of directors that demands what you want or else you will seek legal recourse, and have your lawyer review and edit it for you. If the board refuses you, then you get that contingent lawyer to file suit. Sue their asses. You sue the company, the board of directors, and the shareholders all as a group. You will be instantly fired, and that is fine. Why do you sue them? You sue them to get what you want: to get paid. You won't be able to sue them and get your job back. You can only sue them for cash. The cash value plus a premium of your stock holdings will do to start. Add at least $1 million to that as well (for you and the lawyer to share), and go to court. You will probably win.

How is it that I can predict you will win without even knowing the issue? The answer is simple: minority shareholder rights. You are a minority shareholder. You asked the board for something (like not to fire you, or not to hire that new CEO). They overruled you and did it anyway. As a minority shareholder, they overruled you. Your contingent lawyer will show that they violated your minority shareholder rights—as a board of directors, they did NOT do what was in the best interest of the company, and, as such, are in the wrong. As I said, you will be fired as soon as you file suit. You may be escorted out of the building. It's fine, your payday is coming. *Never* let the board of directors bully you into doing something you don't think is right. Threaten to sue, and if they persist and overrule you as a minority shareholder, you can sue them and get the full value of all your stock, plus at least $1 million in damages for your hurt reputation. If those board members are part of a big venture firm or have any reasonable net worth, they will offer to settle that suit very quickly and it will never go to court. Jury members don't take kindly to rich people abusing their power over an average Joe. That power is so strong that you may only need to threaten it (and thus keep your job, but not get paid). Board members will back off fast if you threaten to sue, or else they won't and then they will lose in court. I've personally seen it happen three times, and every time, the CEO/founder got paid off (in a settlement).

Of course, if you are the majority shareholder you shouldn't have to sue. All you have to do is out vote them. The best part is, they probably can't sue you and win. Why? Because you are not the rich investor, you are the visionary founder. The jury will side with you in most cases. It doesn't matter that they are the minority shareholders—the jury will usually side with the founder on what is best for the company. After all, the founder *is* the company, in many ways.

This power should not be used lightly. It can only be used once or twice, and all your threat letters will be used later if you follow up and sue. The more complaining you did, the less likely you are to win. Nevertheless, don't let them bully you. As you read earlier in this chapter, I did let them bully me. As a result, the company did not go on to be nearly as big a success as it could have been. I made almost nothing from my founder stock. I eventually quit and never sued, and I regret that decision. The board was not right in their bullying tactics with me, but I didn't know about my secret power until it was all done. Founders have huge powers with their minority shareholder rights. Use them.

Negotiating Your Exit

Sometimes, it just makes sense to hire a new CEO. Your company is too large, and you don't really want to work there anymore. For whatever reason, you decided to quit. The right time is just when the new person is coming on board. Let it be known that you support the decision (if, and only if, you think it really is the best decision), and that you would like to negotiate an exit for yourself. Professional investors will understand. Several of my colleagues have done this, and they all say that it was smart. If you are getting replaced or *demoted* to a lesser role and you aren't really that happy about it, go ahead and ask to negotiate an exit for yourself. It's not quitting, it's an exit, and there is a difference.

Quitting is giving a notice that you are leaving. It is a decision. You've already made it, and you can't take it back once you say it. Don't go that route if you don't have to. It's better to negotiate an exit for yourself.

Negotiating an exit is different than quitting. It's having a private conversation with your CEO (first) and the board of directors (second) about how you would like to negotiate an exit for yourself. What does this exit look like? First, you are willing to stay on as long as needed for the transition and to delay announcing your departure until they would like to announce it. Second, you are willing to transfer all knowledge and keys, and even sign an agreement not to sue. Aren't you nice? All that you want in return is a timeline of when you would be able to leave and a very friendly exit package. In that package, you would like some (or all) of your stock to be purchased from you at a fair value (usually the last funding round value, plus a few extra percentage points). You would like at least six months of severance pay in addition to that. It seems fair to me. It's a place to start negotiating your exit. You will be surprised at how happy your board will be to negotiate this with you. Stick to your guns and remember that, until you have this negotiated, you still have your ability to sue as a minority shareholder. You should be able to at least get two months of severance pay and all of your vested stock purchased at the price of the last round. The following table is an outline of the things you should ask for, and what you can expect to eventually get. Be sure to ask for everything initially, so that you have things to give up later in the negotiation.

Table 12.3: Negotiated Exit Ask / Get List

Item	Ask For	Likely Get
Cash for your stock	100% of your stock (both vested and unvested) purchased at last funding price + 10%	100% of only your vested stock at the price of last funding
Severance	6 months	2 months
Accrued unpaid bonus	Your yearly bonus in advance	Pro rated bonus based on end date
Any back pay	All unpaid back pay (if any)	All unpaid back pay
Health insurance coverage	6 months, paid by company	1 month paid, you pay for COBRA after that
Maintain a board seat	Keep your seat	Lose your seat
Unpaid vacation	All unpaid vacation	All unpaid vacation
Legal expenses	All your legal expenses for your exit covered	All your legal expenses for your exit covered, up to $10,000 cap (should be much less than this)
Non compete agreement	None (don't mention it)	A direct non compete agreement limited to companies that make the same product (but not including those that sell to the same customers)
Non disparagement agreement	None (don't mention it)	Both you and the company agree to not disparage one another
Agreement not to sue	None (don't mention it)	Agreement not to sue each other

What to Expect from the Outside

Regardless of how it happened—fired, sued, quit, or negotiated an exit—you are no longer with the company you started. You have some decent money in the bank from your exit package (hopefully). You don't have to work for six months, if you don't want to. What is it like to be outside looking in at the company you started?

First, your friends and colleagues will start to lose touch. They are busy at your work. You might still occasionally get together, but if you are like me, you will miss the people you got used to working with.

Second, as an outsider, you will likely see lots of screw ups by the company now that you are gone. They will make bad deals, launch crappy products, and generally perform poorly, now that you are gone. Whether this is reality or your perception doesn't matter. You will not like what the company does after you are gone.

If you have a board seat, you will lose power very quickly. As a now outside board member, your opinions matter much less and you will be ignored. Everything you say will sound like you are a disgruntled former employee. You want this seat, though, because it gives you visibility into what is happening. It is especially important if you still have some leftover stock that they didn't purchase.

Eventually, if you are lucky, the company will be acquired. You will see all your friends and colleagues get bonuses and new jobs at the acquiring company. Maybe you will see some dollars from any stock you had left over. I did not. Liquidation preferences have to be paid out first before common stockholders (you and your co founders, regardless of whether you are employed or not) get paid. A 1x liquidation preference means that the investors will be paid back all the money they invested before any remainder is paid to you. A 2x liquidation preference means the investors get paid back all their money twice over (200%) of what they invested. It's completely unfair and unreasonable for the investors to get so much if it means the rest of the company (all the minority shareholders) end up with nothing or very little. In fact, you should block the sale of the company (using your shareholder rights and secret power) if this will be the case. Renegotiate to a 1x preference in order to let the exit go through. You are the founder or the co founder, and you need to look out for all the shareholders, not just the ones who stand to make a big profit while you get almost nothing. Sue them if you have to—it is wrong. They should have never insisted on those 2x (or sometimes even higher) liquidation preferences in the first place.

If the company does exit, and you were not an employee, do you benefit at all? If you have some stock and the exit trickles down to you, then yes, you will eventually get a check. There is more, though. You will get to say that you had a successful exit. If pressed (which I have never been asked), no, you weren't employed there when the company was sold. You exited early. Nevertheless, it's still a successful exit under your belt. I claim my company (Bigfoot Networks) as my successful exit. That I wasn't there as an employee doesn't mean I wasn't a part of that exit. I was. I had the idea, I raised the first money, I built the first products, and I was a co founder. So are you and you deserve to claim that for yourself. Why? It can help you raise money later, get a job later, and become part of your history.

If the company doesn't exit, though, and instead, crumbles and falls to nothing, you still get to look like the smart one. Why? You left early. You negotiated an exit for yourself and took money off the table. It sucks that your colleagues and friends were left without an exit, but they won't resent you for yours. In fact, they will probably join you at your next one.

The very best part of being on the outside looking in is that you no longer have to put up with the new management, and you get to do what you want again. If you are like me, one of the driving forces to starting your own company is to be your own boss. You get to be that again, at least for a while. For me, it means starting a new company on the heels of the last. All those friends and employees will eventually be my employees and colleagues once again. Why? Because they know I can get it done. I will almost certainly be able to raise money again (provided that I didn't have to sue anyone), and I know how to grow a company. I've proven it, and investors know it too. They will know you can do the same, and you will then be on your way toward a likely better company that you keep 50.1% of, and one that may have an even bigger payday than your first. It's what happened to me.

The Rest of the Story of Ken Cho, Spredfast, and People Pattern

Spredfast was discussed in Chapter 5 as an example of a pivot that dramatically helped the company succeed. I think it is important to share a bit more of their story here—in particular, the negotiated exit of the co founder and CEO, Ken Cho.

Spredfast had grown a lot since it was first founded as Social Agency in 2008. It had taken on more funding and continued to expand its product portfolio and customer list. As the leader in social network marketing platforms and services, it had established itself as one of the fastest growing companies in Austin.

Spredfast even had recently turned down an exit opportunity for $6 million.[2] Investors, though, as they are wont to do, did not think growth was fast enough. Missing just one or two quarters of a financial plan can cause investors to lose just that much confidence. The board eventually convinced Ken (through tactics not dissimilar to my own) that a new CEO was called for. They said the company needed someone who could "grow the company to the next level," as investors like to say. Ken was convinced and agreed to step down, but not without some very deep thought and a plan.

Ken's plan was simple—first, he knew he had to step down, and that meant he would not stay on with the company after he gave up the CEO role.[3] He knew not being the CEO would not work for him, and so he had a limited window to act. Second, he would negotiate an exit plan for himself. His idea was to ask for a partial liquidity event for himself on the way out. He knew that this would also be a good time to include some of the other co founders and employees in the mini liquidity (exit) event, thus also taking care of his team. Along the way, he had cultivated and kept relationships with key customers. Those personal relationships would be important later, so he made sure to know them all, and for them to know him. His plan was to leverage those relationships in what he did next, but not directly compete with his former company. His plan was to start a new company with the money from this one. His plan worked out.

Ken was able to get not just himself, but also all the common shareholders a chance to sell their stocks back to the company at a fair price. His agreement allowed him to sell half of his shares now and keep the rest for any future exit the company might have. This was a big deal, and Ken was able to take home several million dollars on his way out. It was enough for Ken to take a break, travel, and just be with his family, while also creating a sizable nest egg.

It wasn't long until Ken started getting antsy. He wasn't ready to retire, and that restless feeling got into his bones. After taking just a little time off, he then went to work creating his next company, People Pattern. He put his funds into the company to get it started and, more importantly, to apply all of those customer connections. In less than two years after leaving Spredfast, Ken's new company was up and running with customers. Many of those customers were from relationships he had made while at Spredfast. They were all interested in his newest idea that was non competitive with Spredfast. What was Ken's new idea?

---

[2] https://www.bizjournals.com/austin/blog/techflash/2014/05/spredfast-ceo-co-founders-considered-selling.html

[3] https://venturebeat.com/2015/11/08/founders-what-to-do-when-youre-replaced-as-ceo

Identify the people and their preferences and sentiments using machine learning to understand your customer, speak their language, and market to them better than before.

Ken was able to also leverage his success with Spredfast by raising money from investors. Despite him leaving the company through a negotiated exit, Ken now had a success under his belt with Spredfast. Investors knew that he could successfully grow a company to a certain size. They trusted him. That trust is all that is needed to get investors who are interested in what you are doing over the hump and invest. Some of the very same people who invested in him at Spredfast, invested in his new venture too.

Founders don't just start new companies, though. Ken also put much of his exit money to work as an angel investor after setting aside plenty for his family. As you will see in the next and final chapter, this is not an uncommon story for a post exit. For Ken, though, the future continues to be bright with his newest venture, People Pattern.

Chapter 13
Sold!—Now what?

"That's it, the final document. We're done. We are now part of Groupe SEB," I said to nobody in particular. I was standing in a room with my lawyer and a field of paperwork.

"Yep," Key Ingredient's lawyer, Bob, said. "All done."

But we were not done. It took more than two weeks for all the money to get transferred and for employees' final checks to be written. Nevertheless, Key Ingredient had been fully and finally acquired by Groupe SEB, and it was time to celebrate. Groupe SEB had made an early investment in Key Ingredient and had brought me on as CEO just two years earlier. I was hired to replace the founder/CEO, who had been fired. Yes, I was that guy—the same guy who had taken my own place, although the situation was a little different. Key Ingredient, a recipe website, had no CEO at all when I was hired, because the board had already fired the prior CEO. And yes, that CEO sued the board and got a settlement. That's not really what this story is about, though.

"Ryan, here's your check," I said to Ryan, as I had been saying to folks all day. Everyone with common stock in Key Ingredient was getting a payday that day. Obviously, the check sizes varied based on stock, but everyone was delighted. Personally, my check was the biggest because I was hired as CEO and given a large share of stock to come on board and take over. I had done a good job guiding the company from a decent website to a real business. I had launched the site in three new countries and launched our e commerce site as well. We were making several million per year from just the e commerce site.

As a company, we had a beer and pizza party to celebrate. There were several questions from the team, such as, "Who would be the new boss?" It was a good question. For now, it would still be me and we'd still operate as a separate company. Everyone nodded their heads. The following Monday, though, it was back to work.

Work was still the same. We had our process for deploying cool new technology and launching new and exciting projects. The chairman of the board of directors simply became my manager instead. I still prepared a yearly and quarterly plan (now called a budget), I was still assessed on how well I performed on that budget, and I still had to deliver results. I had several new incentive programs that would allow me to earn even more money from the acquisition if I reached them. At least for a few months, nothing changed, except my bank account. It was big—so big that I moved money into money market accounts, investment

DOI 10.1515/9781501507083-013

accounts, and college funds. My lifestyle didn't change; I just kept working as normal. Why would it? Being CEO of a company is a blast, especially when you are working with great friends (including Ryan) and a great team. We were doing cool things, and I was still getting paid very well with big incentives for success. I didn't even think about quitting.

Six months later, all I could think about was quitting. Somehow, without my really noticing it, Key Ingredient had slowly become more bureaucratic. I spent more time working with our new acquirers (Groupe SEB), and less time working with my team building cool products. We were acquired for our technology and innovative ideas, but suddenly, the expectation was for us to become a profit center. We were by no means profitable when we were acquired, and we were given no instructions to downsize, but suddenly, we were in trouble because we were lacking in profits. Of course we weren't profitable, and we weren't supposed to be yet—we were still innovating. My direct manager was still somewhat supportive of our innovation, but he quickly lost internal political support to keep on funding our crazy ideas. Our goals did not include profitability at all, but we were suddenly under audit for not being profitable. When we started getting monthly visits from the Groupe SEB audit teams, I knew it was time to think about what was next. The politics of being a subsidiary, and an unprofitable one at that, were just not fun at all to me. I like to build things, not count things. In private conversations, I negotiated my exit with my now boss (former chairman). I announced my resignation to my team shortly after that. What would I do with my time now?

Acquisition Exit Analysis

This is the ultimate question: How much money do you stand to earn if the exit happens? If you sold your company today, how much would you get, your investors get, and your team of employees get? This question will determine how much and how hard you will have to work in the future. If the exit is big enough, you may not have to work at all in the future, but you probably will, anyway, because doing startups is so much fun. If your exit is not very big you might just get a nice vacation, then have to go back to work in a day job. Me? I put some money away and paid to go get a PhD. Hey, to each their own. Now I get to show you how to do this fancy calculation, so there.

Corporate Innovation

In Chapter 1, I asked the question: what is your goal? For a startup founder, the goal is usually an exit of some sort, or at least personal wealth and freedom. For the corporate innovator, things are a bit more complex. Your rewards will probably not look like what a startup founder might get. Your rewards for success are likely to be a mix of financial, political, and career based rewards. Rather than an equity payout, you might just get put on a bonus plan. Rather than pay, you might just earn the clout to do another cool project. Rather than a big retention package, you might simply get a promotion to management or other leadership role.

As a corporate innovator, I still believe it's useful to understand the mechanics of an acquisition, however. Read the rest of this chapter with an eye towards how the people from startups you acquire might think, but also with an eye towards your own situation in your big company now. Being unhappy in your role may mean a change is in order, and that change can happen both inside and outside your current company. Corporate innovation is, after all, a way to make changes that need to be made inside corporations. Your frustration with your own company may just be a signal for you to stop procrastinating and just do it already! Whatever "it" is!

Table 13.1 shows an example of the simplest form of exit: cash for common stock. This calculation is if you have nothing but founders in the company. If nobody else gave you money, you had no loans, and you don't owe anybody except co founders and employees, the math is really simple. You simply divide up the acquisition price based on the fully diluted equity of the company, and you are done. Fully diluted equity is the equity of the company as if everyone were 100% vested and fully converted into stock (in the case of stock options). Most likely, founders and co founders are already fully diluted and vested, and have real stock and not stock options. Employees, founders, and co founders, though, almost always get 100% vesting on an exit (it's in their stock agreement). Is it ever really this simple? Maybe a simple exit like this has happened somewhere, but I've never seen it. Often, for example, the *cash* isn't cash at all, it's stock. In that case, you divide the stock based on the percent ownership. Occasionally, it's both cash and stock, and you have to split the cash evenly—first, based on percent of fully diluted stock, and then the stock. From there it only gets more complex as the reality of your cap table, stock options, and investor rights have to all be accounted for.

Table 13.1: Founders Only Exit Example

Person	Common Stock Held	Cash
Exit Price		$1,000,000 Cash Exit (Yippee!)
Formulas	% = Shares / Total	Shares * Price Per Share
Founder	10,000 Shares (47.6%)	$476,190.47
Co Founder 1	5,000 Shares (23.8%)	$238,095.24
Co Founder 2	5,000 Shares (23.8%)	$238,095.24
Employee 1	1,000 Shares (4.76%)	$47,619.05
Totals	21,000 Total Shares	Price Per Share = $1,000,000 / 21,000 Price Per Share = $47.619 / share

Stock options are an example of one of those added complexities. On an exit, you don't ask for a check from advisors, employees, or anyone with a stock option to pay cash to turn their options into stock, and then turn around and pay them for the stock they just bought. Instead, you perform a cashless option conversion. You simply pay them the difference in the option price versus the per share stock price. You calculate the per share stock price based on the exit price and the fully diluted number of shares (including all options as though they were stock). The two formulas for this are below. Table 13.2 below shows how this calculation works if you have some employees with stock options. Advisor 1 does not get as much as Employee 1 because they have options and not shares. Notice, though, that the total amount paid out does not equal $1,000,000. Where does the extra go? It goes into the company cashbox, to be used for the operation of the company. It's essentially investment into the company, albeit a very small one. I should note here that this is not the only way to do this. Another method is that the total number of shares is reduced by the amount of the stock option conversion price, such that the $1,000,000 is then paid out fully across all the shareholders at a slightly higher price (because there is slightly less stock in existence at the payout). This method is even more complex and requires a real spreadsheet formula to calculate the adjusted stock price.

Per Share Stock Price = Total Sale Amount / Fully Diluted Number of Shares of Stock

Cash Payment per Option Share = Per Share Stock Price—Option Price

Table 13.2: Exit Calculation with Founders + Employee + Advisor

Person	Common Stock Held	Cash
Exit Price		$1,000,000 Cash Exit (Yippee!)
Formulas	% = Shares / Total	Shares * Price Per Share
Founder	10,000 Shares (47.6%)	$476,190.47
Co Founder 1	5,000 Shares (23.8%)	$238,095.24
Co Founder 2	5,000 Shares (23.8%)	$238,095.24
Employee 1	500 Shares (2.38%)	$23,809.50
Advisor 1 (with 500 options at $10/share option price)	500 Shares (2.38%)	$23,809.50–$5,000.00 = $18,809.50
Totals	21,000 Total Shares	Price Per Share = $1,000,000 / 21,000 Price Per Share = $47.619 / share Total Cash Paid: $995,000 Cash Left Inside Company: $5,000

Okay, enough simple stuff. Now it's time to see what happens if you owe debt. There are two kinds of debt you might owe: real debt and convertible notes. Real debt is debt that you owe to a bank. In an exit or acquisition of your company, you will almost always have to pay off that debt first. Paying off debt almost always also means paying any fees for early payback (which you should try to negotiate out of your debt deal because of this very issue) and the payment of any accrued unpaid interest. Table 13.3 below shows how this amount simply comes out of the initial proceeds of the sale, and the remainder is then simply split between founders, employees, and advisors (or anyone else with stock options). As before, the remainder is split among shareholders.

Table 13.3: Exit Calculation with Founder + Employee + Advisor + Debt

Person	Common Stock Held	Cash
Exit Price		$1,000,000 Cash Exit (Yippee!)
Debt + Interest + Payback Penalty	$100,000 + $10,000 + $2,500 = $112,500	– $112,500 (Boo)
Remainder to Split		$887,500
Formulas	% = Shares / Total	Shares * Price Per Share
Founder	10,000 Shares (47.6%)	$422,619.05
Co Founder 1	5,000 Shares (23.8%)	$211,309.52

Person	Common Stock Held	Cash
Co Founder 2	5,000 Shares (23.8%)	$211,309.52
Employee 1	500 Shares (2.38%)	$21,130.95
Advisor 1 (with 500 options at $10/share option price)	500 Shares (2.38%)	$21,130.95 $5,000 = $16,130.95
Totals	21,000 Total Shares	Price Per Share = $887,500 / 21,000 Price Per Share = $42.262 / share Total Cash Paid: $882,500 Cash Left Inside Company: $5,000

In the event that the debt is convertible debt, the debt may or may not convert, depending on the terms of the convertible note. Usually, the conversion to stock is automatic on an exit. Sometimes, though, it is converted at the discretion of either the company or the investor/debtor. Depending on whom it benefits, they will decide to be paid back as a debtor (usually with interest, as in Table 13.3), or paid back as an investor as the debt and interest are converted into stock at some price. This price is usually specified in the note as the valuation cap. A *valuation cap* is essentially a pre money valuation of the company if the stock converts. Therefore, debt converts to stock, giving the investor a percent of stock as though they made the investment at that pre money value. So if the debtor provided $300,000 on a $3,000,000 valuation cap, they would get 10% of the shares of stock at exit (however many that may be). They would decide to convert their debt into stock if it makes them more money to do so. For example, if the sale price of the company is less than $3,000,000, it would probably not make sense for them to convert, because they would not get their entire $300,000 back on the conversion. If the company is sold for $6,000,000, though, then they would probably decide to convert to stock to get 10% of the $6,000,000 ($600,000), and thus get a 100% gain. Whether the debtor converts or not actually affects the fully diluted stock of the company, and thus, the stock price, so it is important to be able to guess if it will convert or not. Table 13.4 shows an example of a convertible debt holder who decided to convert to stock and get paid as a stockholder instead of as a debt holder because they got a liquidation cap of $500,000 and the company sold for $1,000,000.

Table 13.4: Exit Calculation with Founder + Employee + Advisor + Converted Debt

Person	Common Stock Held	Cash
Exit Price		$1,000,000 Cash Exit (Yippee!)
Debt + Interest of Convertible Notes	$100,000 + $10,000 = $110,000	*Convertible note holder decides to convert their debt to stock*
Remainder to Split		$1,000,000
Formulas	% = Shares / Total	Shares * Price Per Share
Debt Converted $110,000 @ $500,000 Cap = (22%)	22% * (Others' Shares) / (100%−22%) 5,923 Shares (22%)	$219,997.77
Founder	10,000 Shares (37.14%)	$371,429.63
Co Founder 1	5,000 Shares (18.57%)	$185,714.82
Co Founder 2	5,000 Shares (18.57%)	$185,714.82
Employee 1	500 Shares (1.8571%)	$18,571.48
Advisor 1 (with 500 options at $10/share option price)	500 Shares (1.8571%)	$18,571.48−$5,000.00 = $13,571.48
Totals	26,923 Total Shares	Price Per Share = $1,000,000 / 26,923 Price Per Share = $37.14 / share Total Cash Paid: $995,000 Cash Left Inside Company: $5,000

All of the above is still relatively simple, as crazy as that sounds. Once professional investors (like venture capitalists or angel groups) get involved, things get quite a bit more complex. The complexity comes by means of liquidation preferences, anti dilution clauses, accrued dividends, and more. Also, don't forget, the law firm that handles the exit paperwork has to get paid too. Sometimes, this is handled by the cash already in the company, but occasionally, the legal fees come out of the transaction itself, or are a percent of the exit amount. Additionally, sometimes a broker is involved in the deal. Usually this is a seller's broker who shops the sale around and finds multiple bidders to bump up the sale price of the company. In this case, the broker gets a percentage as well. Table 13.5 below shows this more complex, and, sadly, more common exit scenario. In this scenario, the bank has debt, there are legal fees, brokerage fees, a VC investor (who has a 1x liquidation preference and a 6.67% dividend accrual), a convertible debt holder (who would have converted when the VC invested), and the usual employees and advisors.

To understand all the stock conversions, realize that the convertible debt would convert when the VC invested, giving them their 3.67% just before the VC comes on. The VC then comes on and gets their 20% of the company, diluting founders and the converted debt as well). Finally, at exit, the VC's accrued interest is converted into stock and it actually slightly dilutes the 20% that the VC already has (along with everyone else). Don't worry, the VC ends up with more than 20% once they add in the new 1.33% they get from their accrued interest.

Table 13.5: Exit Calculation with Everything, Including Investors and Liquidation Preferences

Person	Amounts	Cash
Exit Price		$10,000,000 Cash Exit (Yippee!)
Actual Bank Debt + Interest + Early Payback Fees	$1,000,000 + $100,000 + $5,000 = $1,105,000	– $1,105,000 (Boo)
Legal Closing Fees	$50,000	– $50,000 (Boo)
Brokerage Finder's Fee (5%)	5% of $10,000,000 = $500,000	– $500,000 (Mega boo)
VC Investors 1x Liquidation Preference ($1,200,000 Invested)	1 x $1,200,000	– $1,200,000 (Triple boo)
Debt + Interest of Convertible Notes	$100,000 + $10,000 = $110,000	$0 *Convertible note holder decides to convert their debt to stock*
Remainder to Split	Common Stock Held	$7,145,000
Formulas	% = Shares / Total	Shares * Price Per Share
VC Accrued Interest (6.67% over one year) $1,200,000 * 6.67% = $80,000 at a $6,000,000 Valuation (1.33%)	1.33% * (Other Shares + VC's Current Shares) / (100%—1.33%) 367 Shares (1.33%)	$94,952.60
VC Investment $1,200,000 at a $6,000,000 Valuation (20%)	20% * (Other Shares) / (100%—20%) 5450 Shares (19.73%)	$1,410,058.98
Debt Converted $110,000 @ $3,000,000 Cap = (3.67%)	3.67% * (Other Shares Pre VC) / (100%—3.67%) 799 Shares (2.89%)	$206,722.41

Person	Amounts	Cash
Founder	10,000 Shares (36.21%)	$2,587,264.19
Co Founder 1	5,000 Shares (18.11%)	$1,293,632.09
Co Founder 2	5,000 Shares (18.11%)	$1,293,632.09
Employee 1	500 Shares (1.81%)	$129,363.21
Advisor 1 (with 500 options at $10/share option price)	500 Shares (1.81%)	$129,363.21−$5,000 = $124,363.21
Totals	27,616 Total Shares	Price Per Share = $7,145,000 / 27,616 Price Per Share = $258.73 / share Total Cash Paid: $7,140,000 Cash Left Inside Company: $5,000

As you can see, figuring out how much you personally will get is rather complex. Paying off lawyers or brokers is the easy part—like a loan, it comes off the top. Dealing with liquidation preferences is harder because it requires a double dipping. The investor gets their liquidation capital off the top like a loan, and then gets their stock bought as well. The amount paid off at the top is most commonly 1x (e.g. paid back the amount invested). If it is 2x, though, you were unlucky and got a bad deal, and now you have to pay 200% off the top (unless you threaten to sue over it—see Chapter 12), and then still pay them again for their stock.

Handling accrued dividends is similar to converting debt to equity. The accrual converts to equity at the same price that the investor originally paid for their stock. What are these dividends? It's really just interest and is negotiated into some (bad) investment deals. Having to pay 4% or even 8% in accrued dividends to investors who are already going to participate in all the upsides of the deal is just not fair, and accrued dividends should be avoided when you are raising money. If you have to deal with them, you do it like converted debt.

The example in Table 13.5 does not show any anti dilution clause kicking in. The reason is that there was no dilution that occurred in this example. In other words, the price of the stock was higher than the price when the company was sold. If it were not, then the investor might get even more of the company than they would otherwise get. This is more commonly applied during a subsequent funding rather than on an exit. Liquidation preferences are there to protect the investor from losing their investment, and the anti dilution is about raising more money later, not selling the company. In the end, the VC ends up with $1,200,000 from their liquidation preference, $94,952 from their accrued dividends, and $1,410,059 from their participating shares from his original investment. $2,705,011.58 is not too shabby for their measly $1,200,000 investment, giving them a return of 225.4% (cash on cash). Consider that the founder got less than the VC investor with only $2,587,264, and you realize the power of those liquidation preferences. Now, imagine if the company had sold for only $2,000,000. The investor would get their full $1.2 million back off the top and then participate in the sharing of the $800,000, leaving the fonder with less than $290K, despite the investor getting 100% of their money back plus interest, and a bit more. Fair or not, most VC deals come with the liquidation preference of 1x. 2x would be criminal, in my opinion.

There is one final thing worth mentioning. That check you just got for $2,587,264 (or the measly $290K, if the exit was smaller) is not actually all yours. The IRS is going to take a big chunk of that, and how you deal with that is really important. Hopefully, you had a lawyer help you with your incorporation paperwork. Hopefully, you filed taxes properly. With this amount of money coming into your pocket, you might consider getting a tax attorney to help you with the filing. You will have to pay 20%, 30%, or even 50% of this in taxes, depending on how it is handled. At a minimum, you should set aside 20% to pay taxes on this. Your check just got smaller. It's about to get smaller still as you spend it. Lucky for you, the earning is not over.

Earn Outs and New Golden Handcuffs

When a company buys another company for a positive outcome, there is usually a good reason. Usually, there is a product, a team, a technology, and more that are working well enough to make the acquiring company want what you've got. A big part of what you have is in you, the founder, and your team. Companies will therefore want to incentivize you to stay on and help them, at least to get integrated. These incentives might be big salaries, titles, earn outs, bonuses, or other wonderful forms of golden handcuffs. Be wary of what they are, though. Even handcuffs that are golden keep you bound up.

An earn out is where you (and all the shareholders) don't actually get full price for your company all at once. Some conditions are set before you are able to "get the rest" of your money. What this looks like in practice is two (or more) exits, rather than one. The first exit is what you get now (without the earn out). It's a lower number than you might normally accept, but it gets paid out according to the payout tables in the last section. The second exit involves only those people involved in the earn out. It might be all the stockholders, or it might just be a subset (maybe just you). It happens only after the earn out condition has been met. The amount is determined by the acquisition contract.

There are at least three kinds of earn outs. First, a time based earn out is simply like a bonus (or second exit) when you or whoever is involved works at the acquiring company for the specified time. This is usually one or two years of service to get the second payout. A second kind of earn out is metric based. In this kind, a key revenue or profit goal is set for you to achieve after the acquisition, and if it is achieved (usually within a given time period), you and the other shareholders get the second payout. A final kind of earn out involves stock price. You get the extra payout only if the acquiring company's stock gets to a certain point in a window after the acquisition. There are probably other kinds of earn outs too, but this is just a sample. Regardless of the type, earn outs mean handcuffs for you because you will want that money, and unless it is impossible, you will do all you can to succeed at getting it. It can mean two years or more of your life—it had better be worth it.

Bonuses are different than earn outs because they are simply part of your new employment contract or agreement. When you get acquired by a company, they will usually offer you a job too. Without an earn out, you are free to decline—it's a negotiation. Often, a big bonus is offered if you take the job and stay on for a period of time. It's similar to an earn out, except other stockholders don't get it. Only employees get bonus offers. Again, it's a handcuff, because usually that bonus is big enough to make it worth it. This kind of bonus is super important if you got screwed by liquidation preferences. In fact, it's one way to solve the liquidation preference issue. Sure, the investors get most of the acquiring dollars, but you get a $500,000 bonus if you stay on for a year with the acquiring company. That can make a bad deal go well for you.

Stock in the new company is also offered to new employees as part of their new compensation package. That stock is usually stock options with vesting periods. These are golden handcuffs again, because if there is a lot of stock, you will want to stay on to get the vesting of those options.

Lastly, there is another kind of golden handcuff that is more subtle. The fun of having more funds, working on an exciting project, and staying with your team can be intoxicating. The acquiring company probably has many more resources than you are used to. You might get to do those insane projects you always wanted to do, which can be a fun reason to stay on at any company. There are downsides to that money, though, and one of the big ones is called bureaucracy.

Big Company Politics

Welcome back to the world of the big company. Did you earn enough in the exit to be able to say "screw you" if you don't like your new job or boss? Did you earn enough money such that you never have to work again? If you didn't, I advise that you skip this section. You don't have the option to quit, and this section will just frustrate you. My advice is to find a new job in a small company as soon as possible. If you did get "screw you" money, read on for some tips on how not to quit on the second day of your new job.

Big companies suck for entrepreneurs. They have layers of management beyond reckoning. You rarely know how or if your projects and work actually do anything for the company. There is a process for everything. Nobody wants to take a risk. It's a lot of wasted time and effort dealing with the bureaucracy. Hang in there! You want the rewards from your golden handcuffs, right?

The first thing to understand is that most companies operate in budget cycles. This is where you have to learn to pad numbers and be sure you spend it all in the coming year. Seriously, you will create a budget, similar to your P&L for your startup, but you will add a bunch of extra dollars and headcount you are not sure you will need. Why? Because once you have your budget for the year, there is usually no changing it. To account for this, you need a lot of extra money in your budget to account for the things you didn't anticipate.

Speaking of P&L, you may have gotten P&L responsibility as well. This is usually a separate process from the budgeting process. In this process, you will underestimate the expected sales and earnings of your group as much as you can. It's not usually necessary to be profitable, it's more important to just be *right*. The good news is your method of P&L will naturally be better, because you know how to do a bottoms up planning method, while your peers are probably doing a tops down method. Just be sure to pad here too, and underestimate as much as possible. You may be told to go for a higher number, so if you estimate low, that higher number you are *forced* to go after may be attainable, after all. Your ability to achieve the P&L you set is usually directly tied to your bonus.

In some cases, though, the entire purpose of your group changes. Instead of being a center of innovation, you are asked to become a center of profit. This has happened to me, without me even realizing it. A profit center is a group of a company that is supposed to change focus to profits instead of growth. When you are growing, you reinvest profits into the business and you take big gambles to try to grab market share. Once you enter the profit center mode, though, you are expected to grow slower, but to become more operationally efficient. This means cutting expenses, investing in cost savings, stopping investments in crazy projects, and focusing on getting larger net incomes. You'll know you are in this mode when your new bosses are all talking about profits and operating efficiency.

Big companies have many departments that you may not be used to. They may have a legal department, an HR department, a compliance department, an accounting department, and even a "risk management" department. When you hear the term "risk management," you should run and hide as fast as possible. These are the auditors who will look at every policy, every penny you spend, and all those startup things you used to do. Beer Fridays will be gone, as will almost every business lunch or trip you are used to taking. When big companies say "risk management," what they mean is the risk of giving a lowly manager like you too much autonomy that might put their big company at risk. They worry about sexual harassment, inappropriate expense reports, and your collection and payment of taxes. Let your new big company worry about audits and risk management while you try to stay hidden from those arduous meetings and responsibilities. You should be able to hide for a while.

Speaking of audits, your new job will probably audit your department regularly. This means combing through your receipts and checks every year or more, and making sure that every transaction is logged in the accounting system correctly. This also means auditing your equipment, hardware, and even the hours you work. Be prepared to *explain* things to the audit team so they can note it in their little books. Here's the good thing. Nothing bad is going to happen, no matter what they find. They are just preparing a big report. The worst thing that will happen is that you will get a mandate to "fix" something that the auditors find. Fix it, and you will be fine. They will even tell you how to fix it.

Many of these new departments will actually be helpful. The new HR department will manage your healthcare headaches from now on. The new legal department will handle contracts and problems as they come up, without a huge bill in your hand. The new IT team will solve your team's computer problems. The new centralized marketing team will help you create assets and give you access to new marketing tools. Having all these new resources can help you focus more on your core job, and that's not all bad.

What is bad? The worst part of big company life is bureaucracy. Not the layers of management, which is really just a formality, but the layers of paper you need to have to do anything. Instead of just kicking off a new project, you'll need to have it in the budget first, and then get the approval of legal, HR, your manager, and their manager. Nothing is as easy now.

As you navigate this bureaucracy, you will likely find that projects and budgets don't get approved based on rational things such as IRR or sound business modeling. Instead, these decisions get made based on if someone likes you or trusts you or thinks you are the right kind of person. This means making friends and allies. You now have to decide if you will kiss your bosses' behinds or not. If you don't, you will not get that new project funded. If you do, you will hate yourself. Good luck with that. It's about this time that I start thinking, *Maybe those golden handcuffs aren't worth it, after all.*

Remember that awesome power I told you about—minority shareholder rights? Remember how they couldn't fire you and, more often than not, you could use that threat to get what you wanted? That power is gone. If you don't step in line and fill out your timesheets and expense reports correctly, you will get written up. Then, you will lose bureaucratic power. Finally, you will be let go. If your budget isn't approved and gets slashed to pieces, you can't threaten to sue, because you have no minority shareholder power anymore. You are not the CEO— the CEO is. You are the department manager, or the minority CEO of a fully owned subsidiary (which makes you a department manager). Shape up or ship out, because there is no longer an alternative. You are now part of the big company that bought you, and there is no going back, there is only getting out.

Quitting Again

The question will haunt you: Should you quit? If you are used to working in a startup and then have to work in a big company, you will think about this daily. It's so foreign, so slow, and so stale, that you may think about it more than once per day, maybe at every meeting. When should you quit, then?

First of all, if you have strong golden handcuffs, like six or seven figure handcuffs, take a breath. If you have only one or two years to get to that money, it's probably worth playing the corporate game for that long. Remember, some people, most even, play this game their whole lives. You can do it for a few more months.

If the handcuffs are small, or if the time to get them is more than two years, you should quit as soon as you have another option. One option is that you have "screw you" money, and you can quit whenever you want. Another option is that you have another job lined up, and it'll be much more fun. Finally, you may have another startup idea and are ready to take the plunge again. Regardless of the option, be sure to quit correctly.

The right way to quit any job is to first, try to negotiate an exit package (see Chapter 12). This works even for a big company, especially if you were part of an acquisition. You might be able to get severance pay or even partial payment of your golden handcuffs. Just let them know that you are not happy and need to negotiate your exit in a friendly calm manner. You aren't quitting, but you are planning to quit soon and want to discuss your options. If they don't take the hint, ask them how much notice they would like when you do quit. If they still aren't getting it, ask them if they would like to discuss the timing of your last day, which you think will be in the next month. They will get it then. Always give notice, by the way—it's just the right thing to do.

Investing Your Take

Okay, so you had a windfall. This is cash in your pocket that you always hoped for, but never really counted on. This is that big check at exit, that big bonus payout or that stock that you are now permitted to sell. Congratulations! Now, let's be smart with your money.

First things first, you and your family need to be taken care of. This means building up an interest bearing nest egg so that if you were out of work for a year or two, you wouldn't have to worry about much. It's not exactly "screw you" money—it's more like "I don't really have a job yet, but I'm going to quit anyway" money. "Screw you" money is enough that you wouldn't have to ever work again if you didn't want to. That means about 75 years or more of your normal salary. Personally, I've never made that much. If you didn't either, I suggest not saving much more than two or three years of salary in interest bearing accounts as your family nest egg. There are many better ways to invest your money!

What do I mean by a nest egg, interest bearing account? This is money that you can't *play with* or use for your next startup. It is money you will live off of if you have to go without a salary in the future. The interest bearing account should be something very low risk and quick access. The safest option is money market savings accounts (usually 1% or less interest). Less safe, but more interest would be to use a non retirement investment account at a brokerage house (like Fidelity or E*Trade) and put your money into index mutual funds. It needs to be non retirement accounts, though, so that you can sell that stock for cash whenever you might need it. This is now your liquid nest egg that takes care of your family if you need it.

So, what do you do with the rest? Well, this depends on how much you got. If you got more than $1 million, you should probably hire a professional to manage your accounts. Professional money managers will know how to set aside a safe nest egg and put the rest to well balanced investment strategies. If you got less than $1 million, you may be better served just investing it yourself into more mutual funds. At some point, though, you're going to be tempted (wisely so) to invest in another startup—yours, or someone else's. This is where you need to understand risk in a new way.

Investing in startups is the riskiest thing you can do with your money. As a result, you should apportion no more than 5% of your net worth to this, and probably less. If you have more than $1 million and got yourself a professional, ask them for advice on investing in startups. They will tell you to become a limited partner in a VC fund. It's still risky, but the risk is spread over a much larger number of companies. What's more, you, personally, as a limited partner, aren't making the investment decisions. This is good, because you aren't a professional investor and might put your money into things that you *think* are cool or a good deal, where the professionals use other techniques (such as picking people over companies, and picking high growth markets over fun things).

If you decide to take a small portion and do some angel investing on your own (not as an LP), you should do $200,000, and that's it. Don't do it if $200,000 is more than 5% of your net worth. Don't do it if you have less than $200,000. Why that number? With $200,000 you can make 20x $10,000 investments in startups. Statistically, that is enough to have a good chance at actually getting your $200,000 back at some point in the future.[1] Some say that to get a good return on that investment, you'll need to do 50 investments (and thus invest $500,000).[2] The key idea here is that you really do need to invest in more than one company, and you need to put effort into each one and validate that they are as good a company as you hope they are. It's a lot of work, but worth it if you want to give back. Money isn't everything, but you may be better off just putting your hard earned dollars to work in the stock market instead of in these super risky angel investments. There are other ways to give back besides angel investing.

Mentorship and Advisors

One way to give back to the startup community without being an angel investor is to become a mentor or advisor. A mentor is someone who gives their time, ideas, suggestions, and connections to a startup, without receiving any pay or stock in exchange. It's a gift. An advisor is someone who does the same thing as a mentor, but receives some small amount of stock in the company they are helping. This is usually 0.5% to 1% per year that you advise the company. It usually means a minimum hours per month commitment. Regardless of how you do it (as a mentor or an angel), it's a way to give back to the startup world and support budding entrepreneurs without the huge risk of losing your angel investment.

---

[1] http://blog.gust.com/the-reality-of-returns-on-angel-investment
[2] https://techcrunch.com/2012/10/13/angel-investors-make-2-5x-returns-overall

Sometimes, you start out as a mentor, then decide to angel invest. Sometimes, you start out as a mentor, and then decide you want to be an advisor. Sometimes, you start as an advisor, and become an angel investor. All of these relationships are not mutually exclusive, but they do have to be mutual. You can't be an advisor to a company that doesn't agree. It doesn't hurt to ask, though.

In my experience as a startup CEO, the best advisors are ones who have large personal networks in the industry that I want to be in, and are willing to make introductions for me. Good advisors are also good at fundraising and helping me with introductions to investors, and with my pitches. Mentors just have advice for me, usually about something more operational. The worst advisors are operational people (who are good at marketing or good at manufacturing) who don't have big networks in my industry. Those people should probably be just mentors to you, not advisors who are earning stock.

As a mentor and advisor, I try to commit time to the companies I work with. I coordinate mentor time with my local startup incubator (Capital Factory), and limit it to four hours total per month. I set up advisor time separately from mentorship and do a one hour call every other week, or once per month. As an advisor, I try to leave each call with at least one action item I can do between meetings for the startup that I am advising. This way, I am doing real work in exchange for stock, and not just being a mentor who gets stock.

I have found that being a mentor and advisor is very rewarding. Personally, I haven't made a penny from it yet, so I don't mean financially rewarding. However, watching the startups I help succeed, and being a part of that is well worth the time I put into it.

Teaching

If you enjoy mentoring and advising as much as I do, you might consider a new career. Many colleges and universities have positions for adjunct professors. An adjunct professor is someone who has industry experience and teaches a few classes and is paid part time. Let me tell you now that the pay alone is not worth it. You might make $3,000 in a semester as an adjunct professor teaching one or two classes. It's a pittance and barely worth the gas money, let alone your time. On the other hand, you will get to interact with students who are all potential budding entrepreneurs. You don't have to teach entrepreneurship to bring entrepreneurial spirit to the classroom. I taught "Production Planning" at St. Edward's University in Austin, and was able to use all of my startup stories in the classroom, as I also taught students how to plan and execute an idea. It was every bit as rewarding to see students' eyes light up as their professor, as it was to help startups succeed as their mentor or advisor.

If you find this agreeable, there is a way to do it even more. You can get a PhD and become a full time professor at a university or college. There is the traditional PhD route, where you go full time and study for four or five years and teach and work your butt off doing research. That path will probably be more than you can stomach as an entrepreneur. There are some new PhD programs, though, that cater to former executives. These programs cost a lot more money ($100K+), but allow you to do it on the weekends or evenings, or with just a little bit of monthly travel. I decided to do the Executive PhD program at Oklahoma State University and I do not regret it.[3] I learned how to both do PhD level research and also read PhD level research. I learned a lot about statistics and even got a few papers published.[4]

Once you have the PhD, you will be more easily employed by business schools that require a high percentage of their instructors to have PhDs. You will have to choose to become either a lecturer or a tenure track professor. If you decide to go for tenure track, realize that your life will be completely filled with both teaching and doing original research. You will have to publish many papers to survive as a tenure track professor in the academic world. If you decide to become a lecturer, like I did, you don't have to publish. You only have to teach and do normal service as a professor (such as office hours and community involvement). You will also have time as a lecturer to do other things, such as managing your own startup. The downside of being a lecturer is lower pay (higher than an adjunct, but lower than tenure track), and lower respect. In many universities, lecturers are considered a lower cast of professors because they are not researchers. This doesn't mean things will be bad—that all depends on your department chair and how much they like you. I have found teaching as a lecturer and helping to run the Texas Venture Labs at UT Austin to be incredibly rewarding and a great way to give back.

Starting the New One

The itch will come. Eventually, for almost every entrepreneur, the desire to start a new startup will grow. It may start from a frustration with your boring job. It

---

[3] https://business.okstate.edu/phdexec
[4] https://shareok.org/handle/11244/45340

may be an idea you just can't resist. It may even be someone else's idea that you want to be a part of. When that moment strikes, though, you will need to proceed with more caution than you did before. Unlike your first startup experience, you now have things to lose. You have assets that people might want to sue you to get at (like your nest egg). You have money you could possibly put into your own idea. You probably have a much higher standard of living now than you did before. Are you really ready to go back to eating Ramen noodles every day?

The trick to starting the new one is to remember that a single startup, even your own startup, is risky. The risks of failing at your new startup are almost exactly what they were in your first startup, despite your prior success. You will be tempted to fund the entire thing yourself, and if the amount to do that is $10K, or even $20 or $30K, that's probably fine—it's just like one or two small angel investments. However, if you end up putting too much of your net worth into your new startup, you stand to lose it all, and that's just not smart. Don't even think of investing that nest egg you set aside for your family, by the way. Use that only if you absolutely have to, and use it only to live off of, not as investment into your company—which, if you subsequently paid to yourself, you'd have to pay taxes on a second time, by the way.

So, how will you grow and scale your new company, if not with your own money, then? The answer is those relationships you've built with investors in the past. They will be glad to invest in you again because of your excellent exit! New investors will also be interested in you because of your prior successes. Let other people invest their money into your new idea, but this time will be different. This time, you could turn down the investment that comes at a bad time. You can eat from your nest egg for a while, if you have to. You've learned how to downsize and lay people off when you have to. You can command better terms than you did before. This time, you are likely to have more of the company when the sale happens at the end than you did before. Why? You are smarter now. You've failed almost every way possible in this book, and now you know how to navigate them all and ultimately find success. Consider reading this book from the beginning again. The time to start a new startup is as soon as possible, in my opinion. The world needs those fresh new ideas you have. The world needs job and wealth creation. We need more ways for people in our lower and middle classes to make it big in this world. Entrepreneurship is the way, and through your example, your mentorship, and your passion, others can find their way too.

The Story of Phurnace Software

Phurnace Software was founded by Robert Reeves and Daniel Nelson in 2006 with a simple mission. Their mission was to make money solving a fairly common problem in software—specifically, setting up and configuring servers to deploy apps in WebSphere and WebLogic. The idea was to automate a complex and time consuming task that many companies were currently doing by hand, and it worked.

Phurnace had raised money in two rounds of financing. Their seed round was from the Lonestar CAPCO Fund in the amount of $120,000. With these funds, Robert and Daniel were able to start working full time. They opened up a very cheap office inside the University of Texas' Austin Technology Incubator. Bigfoot Networks and Phurnace had offices next to each other back in those days, and we all became friends and colleagues. Phurnace grew and got more customers much faster than they had planned. They had good problems and used the momentum to raise their Series A funding in two traunches totaling $5 million from DFJ Mercury (another VC fund that was based in Texas) and S3 Ventures based in Austin, Texas in 2008.[5]

As happens with so many startups, Phurnace's founders were convinced to bring on a new CEO in 2007 to help the company grow and position it for its next round of funding and its future exit.[6] Larry Warnock joined the team and brought with him great experience in enterprise sales. Larry had also been a part of several prior successful exits in the space. Unlike most companies who take on a new CEO, the relationship between the founders and the CEO—Larry, Daniel, and Robert—was a good one. The founders were more than willing to work with the new CEO, and it was far more congenial than my own experiences with being replaced as CEO. One reason for this is that Larry was from Austin, and kept the company's headquarters in Austin. The other reason is that the founders and new CEO were well aligned in their goal to keep the company growing, but being open to an exit when it shows up. Rather than burning though all their capital, Phurnace focused on hiring slowly and having consistent growth.

In 2010, the timing was right, and BMC made a bid to buy Phurnace.[7] The founders had smartly negotiated the terms of their deal to not have more than a 1x liquidation preference, so anything above $5.2 million would be split fairly

---

[5] https://www.texastechpulse.com/phurnace_takes_3_7m_more/s-0016452.html
[6] http://www.prweb.com/releases/2007/04/prweb520952.htm
[7] http://redmonk.com/cote/2010/01/07/bmcbuysphurnace

based on their stock ownership. The deal finalized, and everybody made money—the investors, the founders, and all the employees. Although the total amount of the sale was never disclosed, based on the house that Robert bought and other personal conversations, I believe that it must have been a very good exit indeed. I believe they made almost enough to have "screw you" money: at least one or two million each. There was a problem, though—some of that money was tied up in earn outs or bonuses for the founders. Robert and Daniel thus became BMC employees overnight.

Neither Robert nor Daniel liked working at a big company very much. They worked hard enough to get as much of the earn out and bonuses as they could stand, but by 2011, about one year after the acquisition, both founders had moved on.

In a Reddit AMA (or "Ask Me Anything," a forum in which commenters can ask the original poster any questions), Robert spoke about life after the exit.[8] His passion for giving back shined through in his offer to mentor any startup that reached out to him. His interests in guest lecturing and getting a PhD to teach were clear evidence of his altruism and passion for encouraging others. Both Daniel and Robert even donated money to help establish the Texas Venture Labs at UT Austin whose mission it is to foster entrepreneurship at the University of Texas and Austin at large.[9] I am part of that legacy too, having completed my PhD and now working at the University of Texas. One of the best things about entrepreneurship is that it has the tendency to create not just a job, but a lasting legacy. Those legacies live on in the mentorship, giving back to the community, and the fostering of the entrepreneurial spirit, as Daniel and Robert have done.

The legacy does not end there, though. As one might predict, eventually Daniel and Robert grew tired of corporate life and became restless. In 2012, they started another company together called Datical. Datical was created to solve a problem that plagues database administrators everywhere.[10] Datical builds software that automates the set up and installation of databases. Unsurprisingly, Datical was able to attract investors faster than Phurnace. Many of those same investors who backed Phurnace, including Mercury Fund (previously DFJ Mercury) and S3 Ventures, also

---

[8] https://www.reddit.com/r/IAmA/comments/gildd/iama_a_founder_of_phurnace_software_hacked_code/#bottom-comments

[9] http://www.today.mccombs.utexas.edu/2010/06/the-enduring-legacy-of-innovation-at-mccombs

[10] https://www.americaninno.com/austin/app-development-austins-datical-speeds-up-database-deployments

decided to invest in Datical. Datical continues to grow today, having attracted more than $13 million in funding and more than 25 employees. That's job creation and real world solutions combining to likely create new wealth, once again.

Daniel and Robert are at it again. What you will *you* build next? I'd be delighted to hear about it. Although I can't make Robert's offer to mentor any startup, I would love to hear from you, nonetheless, and I promise to reply. Find me on Twitter @harlanbeverly, or send me a message on my website at harlanbeverly.com.

Index

A

Accounting 18, 133, 226
Accumulated cash 134, 136, 137, 180
Accumulated cash line 135
Acquisition 105, 109, 122, 257, 259, 261, 267, 270, 277
Acquisition exit analysis 258, 259, 261, 263, 265
Ads 53, 54, 95, 108, 111, 113, 114, 115, 120
Advertisement 46, 94, 108, 195
Advertising 97, 98, 108, 110, 112, 113, 114, 115, 116
Advisors 175, 260, 261, 262, 263, 265, 272, 273, 274
Agreement 156, 173, 251, 252, 255, 267
Amazon 62, 66, 86, 110, 121, 122, 212, 213, 214
Amount of money 75, 107, 138, 266
Analytical Approach 173
Analytical Tools 72, 73, 75, 77, 81, 101
AnandTech 204, 205, 207
Angel groups 145, 146, 263
Angel investments 272
Angel investors 140, 141, 145, 146, 151, 172, 193, 272, 273
Angels 140, 142, 143, 144, 145, 146, 151, 272, 273
Annual plan 183
Apathy 101, 206
Apps 37, 64, 65, 66, 90, 91, 211, 212, 239
AR (augmented reality) 238, 239
Arbitration 157, 158, 173, 175, 176
Aseem 120, 121, 122
Assessment 77, 78, 82, 193
Assets 126, 139, 143, 168, 174, 225, 226, 269, 275
– personal 139, 156, 169, 174, 175, 231
Assumption 10, 126, 132, 137, 138
ATI (Austin Technology Incubator) 49, 79
Audience 21, 51, 70, 88, 107, 112, 113, 120, 147
Audits 258, 269
Augmented reality (AR) 238, 239

Austin 4, 6, 48, 49, 120, 121, 241, 276, 277
Austin area 100, 121
Austin Technology Incubator (ATI) 49, 79
Avid PC gamers 128
Avoiding Lawsuits 158, 159, 160

B

Balance 123, 125, 179, 181, 182, 186, 187, 230
Bank account 1, 5, 7, 10, 13, 28, 57, 125, 169
Bankrupt 223, 224, 225, 226, 228, 230, 232, 234, 236
Bankruptcy 126, 129, 133, 174, 223, 225, 227, 236, 239
Banks 124, 126, 139, 223, 225, 231, 253, 261, 263
BeatBox Beverages 152, 153, 154
Beer, free 35, 36, 87
Beholden 56, 57, 58, 69, 72, 73
Benefits 93, 95, 97, 98, 100, 102, 163, 253, 262
Bids 112, 114, 115, 153, 276
Big company politics 267, 269
Bigfoot 4, 149, 242, 245
Bigfoot Networks 2, 3, 4, 5, 123, 177, 223, 241, 242
Bloggers 98, 206, 218, 219
Bloggers and influencers 218, 219
Board 35, 183, 184, 241, 243, 244, 245, 250, 257
Board members 172, 178, 179, 183, 186, 241, 244, 245, 250
Board seats 150, 153, 241, 252, 253
Bonuses 179, 186, 253, 266, 267, 277
Boss 3, 4, 5, 6, 7, 31, 32, 267, 269
Bottoms 4, 43, 70, 82, 126, 129, 132, 133, 135
Brand 95, 96, 99, 101, 106, 113, 114, 116, 182
Budget 111, 112, 113, 114, 120, 227, 257, 268, 269
Building 37, 41, 58, 59, 61, 63, 64, 66, 69

Bureaucracy 267, 268, 269
Business dealings 169, 171, 172
Business idea, small 29, 32
Business models 18, 19, 29, 129, 130,
    131, 132, 147, 148
Business plan 1, 61, 148, 153, 244
Business updates 224, 244
Buy now button 39, 42, 53, 59, 70, 74, 85
Buyers 74, 99, 118, 130

C
CAC (customer acquisition cost) 75, 76,
    78, 82, 105, 106
Capital 12, 122, 143, 235, 276
Card 4, 63, 177, 182, 203, 204, 207, 212,
    218
– network 3, 4, 119, 128, 181, 197
Cases 120, 121, 160, 161, 169, 170, 172,
    193, 228
Cash 124, 125, 126, 132, 143, 181, 184,
    225, 259
Cash balance 125, 135, 139
Cash burn 124, 125, 138
Cash exit 260, 261, 263, 264
Cash left 261, 262, 263, 265
CEO, 133, 183, 185, 243, 244, 245, 246,
    247, 257
– new 172, 241, 245, 250, 251, 255, 276
Channels 95, 107, 111, 116, 117, 118, 119
Claims 100, 102, 156, 162, 163, 165, 166,
    169, 254
Clicks 42, 53, 75, 78, 111, 112, 113, 114,
    116
Co founder, technical 66
Co founders 242, 243, 246, 247, 248,
    253, 254, 259, 261
Coffee 70, 71, 72, 146
COGS, 75, 76, 78, 82, 105, 106, 110, 120
Collateral 139, 174, 231
College 3, 233, 273, 274
Commodities 87, 129, 233
Company 138, 143, 157, 161, 169, 171,
    179, 242, 253
– acquiring 253, 266, 267
– big 41, 189, 194, 259, 267, 268, 269,
    270, 277
– new 174, 254, 255, 256, 267, 275

– old 174
– start 6, 7, 17, 23
Company and products 80, 195
Company culture 180, 187, 188, 189
Company name 41, 163, 167
Compass 1
Competitors 88, 96, 102, 106, 114, 117,
    198, 208, 233
Consumers 25, 32, 85, 211, 218, 221
Content 113, 147, 156, 162, 163, 200, 218
Contingent lawyers 250
Contingent profitability plan 236, 237
Contract 158, 159, 160, 169, 175, 176,
    228, 229, 231
Control 23, 179, 180, 181, 185, 191, 192,
    206, 246
– span of 181, 190, 191, 192
Control growth 178, 179, 183, 184, 199
Controlling growth 177, 178, 182, 183,
    184, 185, 186, 200, 201
Controversy 204, 205, 220
Conversion 112, 136, 262
Conversion Rate (CVR) 45, 50, 75, 76, 78,
    108, 115, 132, 135
Conversion rates 45, 50, 75, 76, 78, 79,
    108, 115, 135
Copyright 162, 163, 165, 167
Corporate innovation 18, 55, 58, 89, 111,
    124, 227, 249, 259
Corporate veil 168, 169, 171
Corporations 18, 62, 68, 164, 168, 169,
    227, 243, 249
Cost reductions 182, 197, 230, 237
Cost savings 229, 234, 237, 268
Costs 75, 92, 134, 135, 136, 206, 227,
    229, 230
– cutting 227, 229
– high 129
– legal 159, 160, 170
– low 74, 129, 165
– overhead 75, 78
Countries 19, 118, 120, 123, 145, 163,
    164, 168, 174
Court 156, 157, 158, 171, 173, 174, 175,
    250, 251
CPAs 107, 108, 110, 111, 112, 114, 115, 119,
    120

CPC, 108, 119, 120, 135, 136, 219
Credit 227, 231
Creditors 126, 225
Crowdfunding 12, 141
Culture 185, 188, 189, 194, 195, 196, 248, 249
– winning 185, 188, 189
Customer acquisition 106, 107, 110, 116, 119, 136
Customer acquisition flow 106
Customer demographics 78
Customer feedback 48, 77, 86, 147, 190
Customer interviews 49, 50, 83, 148
Customer lists 151, 161, 162, 254
Customer reviews 208, 211, 213, 221
Customer service 57, 118
Customer support 181, 215, 216, 217
Customers
– making 214, 216
– new 96, 112, 120, 121
– prospective 50, 101, 212
– reach 96, 117
– real 37, 48, 51, 57, 58, 60, 73, 96, 215
– reference 211, 212, 213
Cutting Edge Gamer (CEG) 174, 175, 176

D

Damages 156, 157, 159, 170, 173, 176, 250
Datical 277, 278
Day job 30, 72, 258
Dealerships 18, 19
Debts 223, 225, 226, 227, 239, 261, 262, 263, 264
– converted 263, 264, 265
Decisions 17, 18, 72, 158, 188, 189, 191, 192, 251
Defense 162, 215, 235
Demand curve 233
Demographics 39, 78, 90, 113, 114, 116, 120
Departments 18, 111, 124, 133, 246, 248, 249, 268, 269
Design patents 164
Development 59, 61, 62, 64, 75, 78, 100, 238, 239

Directors 168, 171, 183, 243, 244, 245, 246
– board of 179, 183, 186, 187, 234, 243, 244, 245, 250
Discount 32, 54, 64, 108, 138, 151, 231, 232, 233
Disputes 158, 174, 176
Distributors 99, 118, 152
Dividends 135, 236, 265
– accrued 263, 265
Doing Business As (DBA) 163
Dollars 2, 4, 5, 6, 7, 8, 36, 127, 176
Downsize 224, 228, 229, 258, 275
Downsizing 200, 201, 228, 229, 249
Due diligence 151, 152, 153

E

Early adopter market 181
Early adopters 58, 93, 107, 108, 147, 182
Early customers 36, 100
Earn outs 266, 267, 277
Employees 135, 193, 228, 242, 246, 254, 260, 261, 263
– cutting 228
Empowerment 189, 194
Engineers 136, 177, 189, 224
Entrepreneurs 8, 9, 11, 13, 17, 18, 22, 23, 37
– common goals of 6, 7
– successful 6, 12, 22, 33, 193, 238
Entrepreneurship 2, 4, 7, 17, 18, 19, 22, 275, 277
Epic comeback 174
Equity 107, 259, 265
– diluted 259
Estimate 13, 57, 75, 173, 268
Exchange 57, 141, 242, 243, 272, 273
Exit 105, 150, 251, 252, 253, 254, 258, 259, 266
– successful 8, 13, 49, 253, 254
Exit calculation 261, 263, 264
Exit price 260, 261, 263, 264
Expenses 134, 135, 136, 184, 185, 225, 226, 227, 228
– controlling 184, 185
– cutting 227, 229, 237, 268
– legal 181, 252

Experiment 47, 73, 76, 96, 101, 102, 108, 120
Experts 4, 18, 58, 133, 210
Exposure 13, 95, 116, 121, 159

F
Facebook 89, 90, 91, 103, 104, 112, 114, 115, 119
Facebook ads 111, 113, 114
Failure to start 17, 24, 33, 36
Fears 23, 24, 27, 28, 29, 33, 34, 68, 69
Feedback 44, 54, 58, 63, 86, 87, 88, 190, 193
Fees 118, 130, 141, 166, 261, 264
– credit card 118
– legal 157, 160, 170, 173, 176, 263
Filing patents and trademarks 165, 167
Financial model 129, 133, 137, 147, 148, 153, 183, 237
Financial plan 126, 130, 142, 186, 227, 255
Financing 36, 59, 276
Finding profits 223, 224, 226, 228, 230, 232, 234, 236, 238
Fired 241, 242, 244, 246, 247, 248, 250, 252, 254
Firing 174, 193, 211, 242, 246, 248
Firms, venture capital 141, 142, 145
Flame wars 214, 215, 216
Fliers 44, 91, 170
Focus 45, 46, 119, 120, 177, 178, 179, 197, 241
Formulas 7, 8, 9, 75, 88, 105, 161, 260, 261
Forums 44, 54, 194, 203, 214, 215, 216, 221, 238
– public 214, 215, 216
Founder stock 242, 251
Founder/CEO, 187, 188, 192, 196, 197, 198, 247, 257
Founders 152, 171, 242, 243, 248, 251, 261, 276, 277
Freebeer.ai 35, 87, 88
Freelancers 67
Funding 136, 137, 138, 139, 143, 226, 239, 252, 276

Funding and finance 123, 124, 126, 128, 130, 132, 134, 136, 138
Funding based on business model 131
Fundraising 125, 146, 149, 239, 273
Funds 18, 142, 144, 146, 147, 174, 238, 239, 276

G
Gamers 4, 5, 6, 175, 176, 181, 203, 207, 221
Gaming hardware company 79
Gas 15, 76, 104, 107, 110, 201
Goals 2, 7, 8, 9, 10, 11, 21, 36, 207
– common 7, 9, 186, 190
Golden handcuffs 266, 267, 268, 270
Google 95, 108, 110, 111, 113, 114, 115, 120
Google Analytics 63, 91, 111, 208
Google search 90, 114, 115, 121
Google search ads 111, 114, 115, 116
Grants 61, 62, 139, 140, 144
Graphics 97, 162, 163, 200, 238
Groceries 30, 92, 120, 121, 122
Groupe SEB, 55, 257, 258
Growth 133, 138, 178, 179, 181, 182, 183, 196, 199
Growth metrics 179
Growth phase 178, 180
Guarantee 116, 209, 213, 214
– personal 139

H
Habits 1, 2, 8, 144
Hardware 60, 63, 65, 67, 68, 198, 269
Headcount 180, 181, 185, 268
Hiring 122, 158, 194, 196, 209, 242, 243, 246, 248
Hitting 42, 104, 107, 110, 120, 234, 235, 245, 247
Home page 42, 43, 50, 61, 85
Https 62, 63, 127, 163, 165, 205, 221, 274, 277
Hypothesis 9, 10, 47, 49

I
Idea 16, 17, 25, 31, 33, 36, 37, 45, 51

Idea sucks 35, 36, 38, 40, 42, 44, 46, 48, 50
Idea validation 37, 46, 49, 70, 71, 74
Inc 2, 3, 4, 94, 99, 100, 238, 239, 240
Income 30, 67, 86, 239
Indiegogo 52, 54, 57, 59, 141
Indiegogo campaign 52, 53, 57
Industry 3, 127, 197, 236, 273
Infinite upgrades 175, 176
Influencers 218, 219
IngZ, 238, 239, 240
Initial public offering. See IPO
Innovation 19, 69, 89, 111, 164, 229, 258, 268
Innovators, corporate 9, 59, 89, 227, 259
Insolvency 225, 226, 227, 228, 229, 235, 236, 239, 240
Institutions 138, 139, 141
Insurance 156, 170, 171
– liability 170, 171
Intel 3, 4, 18, 155, 189, 203
Interest 113, 114, 226, 261, 262, 264, 265, 266, 271
Interviews 37, 38, 45, 46, 83, 147, 194, 195, 196
Invention 163, 164, 165, 166
Inventor 5, 30, 31, 61
Inventory 29, 49, 120, 121, 122, 124, 125, 183, 232
Investment 109, 124, 138, 141, 142, 143, 180, 265, 272
– professional 28, 30
Investment amount 138, 151
Investment dollars 59, 107, 122, 180
Investor money 105, 107, 109, 143, 169
Investors 126, 143, 144, 146, 149, 150, 171, 172, 179
– big 74, 122
– finding 142, 144, 145
– professional 151, 183, 251, 263, 272
Investors/founders 171
IP (intellectual property) 68, 106, 151, 155, 160, 161, 162, 163, 164
IPO (initial public offering) 105, 122, 138, 142, 143, 150, 236

J
Job 3, 13, 23, 30, 197, 247, 250, 267, 270
– new 253, 267, 268, 269
Judge 19, 48, 49, 73, 156, 157, 158

K
Karmaback 35, 79, 80, 81, 82, 131, 132
Key Ingredient 35, 51, 55, 171, 172, 189, 195, 257, 258
Key Performance Indicators. See KPIs
Keyboard 64, 65
Keywords 114, 115
Kickstarter 12, 52, 57, 59, 74, 141
Killer NIC, 5, 6, 7, 9, 182, 196, 207, 223
KPIs (Key Performance Indicators) 179, 180, 181, 185, 187, 198

L
Lag 4, 119, 128, 203, 207
Landing page 41, 42, 64, 65, 112, 113
Launch 1, 2, 6, 8, 13, 29, 56, 71, 121
Laws 68, 69, 156, 157, 158, 159, 168, 174, 248
Lawsuits 156, 157, 158, 159, 160, 171, 173, 174, 175
– civil 157, 161
– potential 57, 159, 160
Lawyer 27, 28, 29, 150, 151, 156, 158, 165, 250
Leader 179, 186, 187, 189, 193, 227, 254
Leadership 185, 186, 187, 189, 190, 194
– transformational 186, 189
License 68, 71, 153, 158, 161, 162, 169, 238
Light bulb
– compact fluorescent 93
– new compact fluorescent 93
LinkedIn 115, 116, 145, 146
Liquidation preferences 150, 235, 253, 263, 264, 265, 266, 267, 276
Loans 124, 126, 139, 231, 236, 259, 265
Loitering 69, 169, 170
Loss 22, 23, 133, 135, 136, 172, 173, 174, 227
Low margin products 129
LTVs 75, 76, 78, 103, 104, 105, 106, 119, 120

M

Magazines 97, 116, 208
Mail address 86, 95, 96, 146, 208, 212,
    213, 217
Mails 42, 44, 70, 71, 73, 83, 206, 209,
    212
Management 185, 186, 187, 189, 191,
    192, 194, 243, 249
Management span of control 190, 191,
    193
Managers 133, 134, 135, 183, 184, 186,
    193, 247, 269
Manufacturing 68, 197, 273
Margins 10, 117, 118, 225, 232, 234
– gross 134, 136, 184, 225, 226, 227, 229
– high 129, 130, 131
– low 48, 129, 130, 131
Market 29, 50, 106, 107, 119, 127, 156,
    182, 234
– new 69, 76, 96, 105, 118, 120, 181, 182,
    234
Market validation 25, 55, 148, 153
Marketers 80, 111
Marketing 88, 89, 95, 96, 97, 111, 118,
    185, 237
Marketing efforts 91, 95, 97, 178, 185,
    221, 223, 238, 248
Marketplace 61, 108, 114, 115, 238, 239
MBP (minimum buyable product) 59, 60,
    61, 64, 69, 71, 73, 74, 77
MBP experiment 73, 74
Media 98, 209, 210, 218, 219, 220, 221
Meetings 123, 131, 144, 145, 146, 147,
    193, 194, 269
Mentor 36, 193, 272, 273, 274, 277, 278
Mentorship 272, 273, 275, 277
Messaging 46, 91, 97, 100, 102, 107, 119
Metrics 2, 60, 73, 179, 180, 207, 225, 267
Minimum order quantity (MOQ) 12
Minimum viable product 55
Mission 111, 125, 194, 276, 277
Modeling 129, 132, 133, 135
Models 6, 19, 67, 126, 132, 135, 137, 237,
    244
Money 29, 30, 107, 124, 138, 142, 157,
    172, 271
– accepting 55, 56

– earn 28
– making 4, 7, 45, 51, 124, 132
– screw you 268, 270, 271, 277
Money valuation, pre 150, 151, 262
MOQ (minimum order quantity) 12
MVP experiment 73, 75, 76

N

Navigate 1, 13, 18, 33, 45, 46, 69, 269,
    275
NDA (non disclosure agreement) 140,
    147, 151, 158, 159, 165
Nest egg 271, 275
Net income 134, 136, 142, 180, 181, 185,
    199, 237, 268
Net present value (NPV) 18
Networks 145, 146, 152
New investors 151, 275
New product 16, 18, 44, 55, 96, 221, 229,
    230, 234
New product idea 45, 99
Non disclosure agreement. See NDA
NPV (net present value) 18

O

Objections 83, 84, 85, 96
Offline 48, 115, 116
Online 28, 30, 67, 68, 75, 115, 116, 212,
    221
Online retailers 48, 117, 212
Options 86, 215, 216, 217, 260, 261, 262,
    263, 270
Organization 9, 18, 89, 111, 124, 186,
    187, 249
Ownership 150, 151, 177, 178, 189, 190,
    199, 243, 245

P

Page website 21, 39, 41, 43, 53, 61
Paperwork 28, 163, 167, 225, 257
Parents 3, 4, 15, 16, 114, 124
Parties 21, 27, 150, 152, 157, 159, 160,
    173, 176
Partner 11, 99, 102, 123, 146, 159
Partnership 117, 118, 123
Passion 23, 25, 26, 27, 36, 38, 44, 190,
    277

Patent 29, 30, 161, 162, 163, 164, 165, 166, 167
– provisional 164, 165, 166, 167
Patent Cooperation Treaty (PCT) 164
Payment 59, 60, 62, 64, 77, 226, 228, 261, 269
– partial 65, 74, 270
PayPal button 62, 64, 71, 72
PC, identical 204
PCT (Patent Cooperation Treaty) 164
People pattern 100, 254, 255, 256
Performance 133, 193, 194, 195, 247
Personas 90
Phurnace 276, 277
Phurnace Software 276, 277
Pitch, verbal sales 59
Pivot 45, 46, 47, 49, 50, 73, 83, 100, 105
– big 46, 47, 50, 74, 76, 98, 99, 101
Pivoting 36, 46, 47, 49, 50, 55, 77, 88, 97
P&L projection 133, 134, 135
P&L responsibility 133, 268
Place pivots 99
Plan 149, 183, 184, 208, 225, 236, 237, 245, 255
Planning 24, 71, 126, 133, 138, 187, 197, 198, 199
Platform 48, 49, 57, 59, 74, 81, 82, 211
Players 103, 104, 120, 200
Pocket Legends 200
Post money valuation 150, 151
Potential customers 37, 38, 43, 44, 45, 48, 75, 86, 101
Power 235, 236, 243, 244, 245, 248, 250, 251, 270
Power of profitability 199, 235
PR, 54, 98, 203, 206, 208, 211
PR agencies 53, 206, 209, 210, 211
Preorders 56, 57, 58, 60, 65, 73, 74, 147, 149
Press 42, 45, 203, 204, 205, 206, 207, 208, 220
– bad 206, 248
Press plan 206, 207
Press release 207, 210
Price 39, 40, 45, 74, 93, 232, 233, 262, 265
– average 93, 231

– lower 102, 232, 233, 237
– lowering 231, 232, 233
– option 260, 261, 262, 263, 265
– raising 76, 231
Price and volumes 232, 233
Price of hamburgers 89
Pricing 40, 48, 95, 96, 106, 134, 147, 148, 234
Pro rata rights 150, 151
Problem
– big 38, 155, 230
– real 38, 49, 57, 221
Problem question 85, 86
Product 42, 58, 68, 88, 90, 96, 182, 212, 217
– finished 130
– free 218, 219
– shippable 63, 67
Product development 177, 184
Product launches 64, 210
Product market fit 230
Product pivot 98
Product price 50
Product reboot 214, 216, 217, 218, 221, 229
Product sales 51, 121
Production 60, 63, 73, 75, 134, 227, 228, 229, 234
Production costs 61, 229, 237
Product/service 8, 39, 86, 96, 227
Profitability 136, 138, 142, 199, 224, 235, 236, 237, 239
– contingent 235, 236
– real 236
Profits 133, 135, 136, 138, 185, 225, 227, 236, 268
Projections 126, 134, 135, 136
– down financial 126
Projects 18, 55, 57, 177, 178, 239, 267, 268, 269
Promotion 88, 89, 98, 99, 114, 117, 259
Property, intellectual 68, 106, 160, 161, 162, 163, 164
Prototypes 29, 37, 52, 53, 54, 59, 74, 139, 153
Provisions 150, 151
Psychographics 39, 90, 113, 120

Psyko 221
Purchase 45, 75, 78, 95, 112, 253
Purchase intent 39, 49, 50

Q
Quarter 179, 185, 244, 245, 255
Quit 30, 242, 243, 248, 249, 251, 268, 270, 271
Quitting 1, 249, 251, 258, 270

R
Refund 56, 58, 72, 213, 215, 217, 221
Register 162, 163, 208, 212
Rent 21, 30, 57, 134, 135, 195, 228, 229, 231
Resellers 85, 86, 99, 226, 231
Restaurants 19, 20, 21, 99
Retailers 110, 117, 118, 212
Return 57, 65, 105, 109, 140, 143, 150, 266, 272
Revenue 117, 118, 134, 136, 179, 181, 184, 196, 200
– potential 127, 128
Revenue growth 181, 183, 184
Reviewers 204, 214, 219, 220
Reviews 204, 205, 206, 208, 210, 211, 213, 214, 219
– bad 203, 204, 205, 206, 212, 213, 214, 218, 220
– negative 214, 216, 221
Reviews and press 205, 206
Rewards 30, 33, 101, 106, 131, 132, 186, 188, 259
Rights, voting 150, 153
Risk management 269
Risks 22, 23, 33, 41, 58, 156, 171, 269, 272
Roadblocks 119, 120
RocketLawyer.com 165, 167, 169
ROI, 143
Role 185, 186, 190, 193, 194, 195, 238, 244, 246
RPG (role playing game) 238

S
Salary 5, 30, 75, 133, 172, 228, 271

Sales 82, 83, 91, 110, 111, 112, 131, 132, 237
– complex 118, 130
– direct 75, 117, 118, 131, 148
– early 20, 153
– five 106
– increasing 237
– incremental 232, 234
– indirect 75
– profitable 106
Sales call 80, 83
Sales channels 48, 117, 119, 120, 147
Sales director 246, 249
Sales efforts 110, 111, 178, 237
Sales funnel 74, 83, 84, 95, 111
Sales managers 90
Sales process 83, 112
Sales representatives 117, 118
Sales scale 110
Sales team 135
Salesforce 111
Salespeople 135, 140, 148, 162, 237
Salesperson 118, 136
SAM (serviceable addressable market) 75, 76, 78, 126, 127, 128, 129, 148
Scale 19, 105, 106, 107, 108, 110, 117, 119, 121
Scale phase 105
Scale sales 118
Scaling 105, 106, 107, 108, 109, 110, 114, 115, 229
Scandal 216, 217, 218, 220
Self confidence 21, 22, 41
Series 138, 139, 140, 141, 142, 143, 149, 276
Service 9, 19, 20, 42, 44, 65, 90, 96, 182
Service businesses 39, 118, 184, 198, 212, 230
Settle 157, 158, 159, 172, 173, 174, 175, 176, 250
Settling 156, 160, 173
Share stock price 260
Shareholder rights, minority 250, 251, 270
Shareholder vote 144, 150, 243, 245
Shareholders 168, 169, 242, 243, 244, 250, 251, 260, 261

– minority 250, 251, 252, 253
Shares 28, 38, 255, 260, 261, 262, 263, 264, 265
Shark Tank 16, 152, 153
Ship 51, 56, 57, 58, 60, 63, 64, 66, 72
Shipping 29, 51, 52, 56, 57, 72, 73, 197, 198
Shipping labels 48
Shotgun 144, 145, 146
Sign 39, 42, 135, 138, 140, 143, 152, 158, 159
Sinking 177, 178, 180, 182, 184, 186, 188, 190, 192
Site 42, 43, 45, 74, 115, 205, 207, 208, 215
Small business 17, 18, 19, 20, 21, 212
Small pivots 45, 46, 47, 58, 74, 76, 98
Snake oil 203, 204
Social agency 99, 100, 254
Social media 79, 80, 98, 100, 206, 215, 216, 218, 220
Software 49, 63, 65, 68, 176, 198, 212, 276, 277
Solvency 225, 226, 231
– scales of 225, 226, 230
Solvency issues 230, 231, 232, 234, 235
Spacetime Studios 199, 200, 201
Spending 43, 46, 106, 112, 120, 237
Spreadsheet 111, 116, 125, 223
Spredfast 99, 100, 254, 255, 256
Start Reason Number 21, 23, 24, 25, 27
Startup CEO, 241, 273
Startup community 145, 272
Startup founders 40, 259
Startup idea 11, 270
– new 29, 79
Startup journey 104, 105
Startup journey roller coaster 104, 105
Startup success 1, 2, 7, 9, 10, 13, 33, 45, 46
Startups 1, 2, 8, 17, 18, 19, 30, 126, 141
– new 106, 107, 131, 274, 275
– normal 227
– small 140
– successful 1, 31
State 28, 145, 157, 158, 159, 161, 163, 225, 226

Statements 90, 183, 187, 188, 189
– product positioning 90, 91
Step 25, 26, 29, 39, 62, 89, 93, 95, 96
– final 26, 43, 208
– next 25, 33, 42, 50, 71, 83, 176
Stock 138, 143, 242, 243, 246, 259, 260, 262, 265
– acquiring company's 267
– common 149, 153, 246, 257, 259, 261, 262, 263
– preferred 150, 151, 153
– vested 252
– voting 149, 183, 243, 247
Stock options 259, 260, 261, 267
Stock price 138, 139, 260, 262, 267
Stockholders 143, 242, 243, 247, 262, 266, 267
Story 61, 186, 206, 207, 208, 209, 210, 220, 254
Strategies 107, 119, 203, 214, 229, 235, 236
Street 16, 17, 86, 98, 100, 106, 161
Students 7, 22, 61, 62, 70, 71, 72, 273, 274
Success 1, 2, 13, 22, 23, 45, 46, 50, 69
Sued 155, 156, 158, 160, 162, 164, 166, 168, 170
Suing 27, 157, 172, 173, 175
Suppliers 124, 126, 159, 172, 223, 224, 229, 230, 231
Supplies 134, 159, 230, 233
Support 10, 21, 49, 110, 134, 148, 181, 187, 215
Surveys/Interviews 88, 102
Sustaining Growth 181
Sweepstakes 79, 81, 82

T
TAM (total available market) 126, 127, 128, 129, 148
Target audience 21, 39, 87, 88, 112, 113
Target customers 21, 43, 87, 106, 114, 127, 147
TBI (traumatic brain injury) 61, 64
TBI drug company 61
Team 100, 110, 153, 186, 187, 188, 189, 229, 258

Teamwork 187, 189, 190
Technology 16, 19, 59, 61, 175, 196, 197, 200, 221
Technology companies 155, 236
Temperature 52, 53, 54
Term sheets 123, 149, 150, 151
Test 25, 26, 40, 41, 45, 76, 108, 111, 115
– idea validation 73
Testimonials 96, 102, 107, 211, 213
Texas 4, 6, 48, 49, 120, 122, 149, 276, 277
Tools 62, 63, 73, 100, 101, 186, 187, 192, 193
Total cash 261, 262, 263, 265
Total shares 260, 261, 262, 263, 264
Total shares price 260, 261, 263, 265
Track 43, 49, 77, 111, 116, 124, 125, 135, 207
Traction 30, 68, 88, 101, 105, 106, 107, 141, 230
Trade 69, 79, 83, 91, 98, 116, 185, 188, 195
Trademark 155, 156, 157, 160, 161, 163, 164, 165, 167
Traveller AR, 238, 239, 240
Trolls 214, 215, 216
Trust 23, 74, 76, 96, 102, 107, 142, 146, 147

U
UI (user interface) 58, 60, 65
Understanding customer 93
Unit sales 127, 136
United States 28, 127, 153, 156, 159, 163, 168, 242, 244
Units 53, 54, 75, 78, 125, 127, 134, 136, 229
University of Texas 4, 6, 11, 48, 120, 149, 152, 277
Users 51, 63, 65, 86, 88, 90, 119, 120, 181

V
Validate 29, 36, 37, 38, 49, 51, 53, 76, 77
Validating 21, 29, 36, 37, 38, 39, 40, 51, 132
Validation 20, 21, 36, 48, 54, 105, 106, 121
– next level of 37, 38
Value 92, 93, 98, 101, 102, 160, 161, 163, 164
Value definition 190
Value statements 187, 188, 189
Variables 129, 132, 135, 136, 229
VCs 142, 144, 145, 146
Vesting 242, 246, 259, 267
Viability 60, 73, 74, 75, 76, 82
Vision 120, 164, 185, 186, 187, 189, 193, 248
Volumes 131, 230, 232, 233, 234

W, X
Website 32, 43, 44, 50, 62, 114, 115, 195, 218
– new 43
Winning 156, 165, 172, 173
Wix Editor 41, 42
WordPress 41
Writer 163, 206, 208, 209, 210, 220

Y
YouTube 23, 96, 113, 218

Z
ZBB (zero based budgeting) 18
Zero based budgeting. *See* ZBB

Made in the USA
Lexington, KY
09 April 2018